Bildner Center Series on Religion

Volume I
AN ENDURING FLAME:
Studies on Latino Popular Religiosity
Editors: Anthony M. Stevens-Arroyo
& Ana María Díaz-Stevens

Volume II
OLD MASKS, NEW FACES:
Religion and Latino Identities
Editors: Anthony M. Stevens-Arroyo
& Gilbert Cadena

Volume III
ENIGMATIC POWERS:
Syncretism with African
and Indigenous Peoples' Religions
Among Latinos
Editors: Anthony M. Stevens-Arroyo
& Andres I. Pérez y Mena

Volume IV
DISCOVERING LATINO RELIGION
A Comprehensive Social Science Bibliography
Editors: Anthony M. Stevens-Arroyo
with Segundo Pantoja
Foreword: Robert Wuthnow

An Enduring Flame:
Studies on Latino Popular Religiosity

Edited by
Anthony M. Stevens-Arroyo
and
Ana María Díaz-Stevens

Program for the Analysis
of Religion Among Latinos
PARAL Studies Series
Volume One

This publication is made possible by grants from The Lilly Endowment and The Pew Charitable Trusts

Copyright © 1994 by Anthony M. Stevens-Arroyo and Ana María Díaz-Stevens

All rights reserved under International and Pan-American Copyright Conventions. Published in the United States by the Bildner Center for Western Hemisphere Studies, New York.

Library of Congress Catalog-in-Publication Data

An Enduring Flame: Studies on Latino popular religiosity / edited by Anthony M. Stevens-Arroyo and Ana María Díaz-Stevens.
     p.   cm. — (PARAL series: v. 1)
  Includes bibliographical references and index.
  ISBN 0-929972-07-4 (hbk.). — ISBN 0-929972-08-2 (pbk.)
  1. Hispanic Americans—Religious life and customs. 2. Hispanic Americans—Religion. 3. Hispanic Americans—Ethnic identity. 4. Christianity and culture—United States. 5. Religion and sociology—United States I. Stevens Arroyo, Anthony M., 1941- II. Díaz-Stevens, Ana María, 1942- III. Series.
BR563.H57E64 1994
306.6'089'68073—dc20   94-33702
                                                                                                 CIP

Cover, book design and layout by André Boucher
Manufactured in the United States of America
First edition

CONTENTS

	Acknowledgements	7
	Contributors	8
	Introduction Anthony M. Stevens-Arroyo	9
1	**Analyzing Popular Religiosity for Socio-Religious Meaning** Ana María Díaz-Stevens	17
2	**Resistance and Accommodation in Latin American Popular Religiosity** Gustavo Benavides	37
3	**Towards an Understanding of Synthesis in Iberian and Hispanic American Popular Religiosity** Jaime R. Vidal	69
4	**The Penitential Doctrine of Restitution: Its Use by Bartolomé de Las Casas to Liberate Popular Religiosity During the Conquest of America** Luis N. Rivera Pagán	97
5	**Popular Religion As the Core of Cultural Identity in the Mexican American Experience** Virgilio Elizondo	113
6	**The Ideological Dimensions of Popular Religiosity and Cultural Identity in Puerto Rico** Samuel Silva-Gotay	133
7	**Para El Niño Dios: Sociability and Commemorative Sentiment in Popular Religious Practice** Richard R. Flores	171
8	**Linking Theory and Methodology for the Study of Latino Religiosity in the United States Context** Meredith McGuire	191
9	**Brevia from the Hispanic Shift: Continuity rather than Conversion?** Kenneth Davis, OFM Conv.	205
	Glossary	211
	Index	215

Preface

The Bildner Center for Western Hemisphere Studies sponsors research, forums, seminars and publications that address the practical resolution of public policy problems facing the nations of the hemisphere. It is part of The Graduate School and University Center of The City University of New York (CUNY). The Center serves as a link between CUNY's intellectual community and other experts and policymakers working on contemporary issues in Latin America, North America and the Caribbean, and provides a window on New York for scholars and public officials throughout the Americas. The Center was established in 1982 by the President of CUNY's Graduate School and University Center, the University's board of Trustees, and Albert Bildner, a philanthropist with extensive experience in hemispheric affairs.

The Program for the Analysis of Religion Among Latinos (PARAL) coordinates a national effort at systematic study of religion in the experience of people of Latin American descent living within the 50 states and Puerto Rico. With its office located at the Bildner Center for Western Hemisphere Studies in New York City, PARAL promotes regional and comparative research among academics, provides information to churches and co-sponsors an annual competition for the Olga Scarpetta Award to the best student paper on Latino religion.

The PARAL Studies Series on Latino religion is published by Bildner Center Books in New York, under the general editorship of Anthony M. Stevens-Arroyo. With grants from the Inter-University Project for Latino Research, the Lilly Endowment and the Pew Charitable Trusts, PARAL invited the leading scholars of Latino religion into a process that included a three-day conference at Princeton University in April of 1993. The four volumes of the series are the result of continued dialogue and research on key topics of scholarly inquiry.

Bildner Center Publications
General Editor: Ronald G. Hellman
Coordinating Editor: Peter Robertson

Acknowledgements

Many thanks to Segundo Pantoja, the graduate research assistant of PARAL, whose careful attention to detail and insightful appreciation of the scholarly impact of the project made the collection of manuscripts an easier task. At Bildner Center Books, Peter Robertson was a calm and efficient manager of the complex process of manuscript preparation and publication, while Gene Miller diplomatically provided an overseer's skills to the financial details. Our thanks to Luann Dragone and Carol de Ortiz who edited the manuscripts at various stages. André Boucher contributed a stunning design for the cover, which is always a seldom considered but extremely important contribution to any book publication. Most of all, our thanks to our Latino people whose faith and vital sense of religion inspired us every step of the way.

    A.M. D-S. and A. M. S-A.
    August 16, 1994

CONTRIBUTORS

Anthony M. Stevens-Arroyo — Bildner Center,
Graduate School
and University Center
of the City University of New York

Ana María Díaz-Stevens — Union Theological Seminary

Gustavo Benavides — Villanova University

Jaime R. Vidal — Cushwa Center,
University of Notre Dame

Luis N. Rivera Pagán — University of Puerto Rico

Virgilio Elizondo — Cathedral of San Fernando,
San Antonio, Texas

Samuel Silva-Gotay — University of Puerto Rico

Richard R. Flores — University of Wisconsin

Meredith McGuire — Trinity University

Kenneth Davis, OFM Conv. — Oblate School of Theology,
San Antonio, Texas

INTRODUCTION

Anthony M. Stevens-Arroyo

Popular religiosity has become an important focus of scholarly research today on religion among Latinos. In many conceptions, including ones found in this volume, popular religiosity is in religious expressions that fall outside of ecclesiastical control. Freed from the constrictions of clerical interference, popular religiosity creates its own space at the frontiers of social identity. For many scholars, popular religiosity incubates the unique difference in the United States between the religion of people of Latin American heritage and that of all groups. Moreover, popular religiosity is often projected as more influential in the daily lives of Latinos than the doctrines and dictates of institutionalized religion. More than a few scholars consider it a form of Latino resistance to assimilation, not only in matters of religion, but in much else as well.

Popular religiosity is important to social science because many Latino cultural attitudes towards family, gender, tradition and political society derive from religious sources, even if not every Latino believes or practices a religion. One reverences the elders, for instance, not only because of peer pressures to conform to this aspect of social behavior, but also because one has to fulfill a duty that lies heavy on the conscience. Thus popular religiosity does more than cast the long shadows of quaint rituals or family traditions. It also burns as a normative guide for feelings and behavior. It is "an enduring flame" that glows constantly within the Latino consciousness of a distinctive social and cultural identity.

Yet, despite the frequency of its appearance in guises such as "folk practices," "locus theologicus," "family values," and the like, popular religiosity remains a term freighted with ambiguities. This volume, by a distinguished array of experts, focuses on the essential issues for continued debate on Latino popular religiosity. The Program for the Analysis of Religion Among Latinos (PARAL) anticipates that this publication will make popular religiosity a more manageable topic for further exploration by social scientists and students, as well as theologians and pastoral ministers.

The 1993 PARAL Symposium at Princeton asked the participants to adopt a common departure point in their treatments of this topic. Hence, rather than "popular religion," which is found in English and North European scholarship, we have used instead, "popular religiosity" which is a translation of religiosidad popular, a term generally used in Iberian and Latin American studies. We think that key aspects of religion among Latinos have more in common with Spain and Latin America than with the Euro- American experience. Nonetheless, as Gustavo Benavides stresses in his contribution to this volume, one should not impose the contours of popular religiosity in Latin America indiscriminately upon the Latino experience in this country. The key issue of ecclesiastical control varies from place to place, dependent upon a host of subtle variables. In particular, since the role of majority religion is inverted in the United States and Latin America, many aspects of Latino popular religion which appear similar to Latin American expressions are considerably altered in the U.S. context. Knowing how to draw distinctions between Iberian or Latin American roots and contemporary Latino expressions in the United States remains one of the challenges in the study of popular religiosity.

The terms "popular religion" and "popular religiosity" have slightly different meanings. "Religiosity" refers to a disposition or inclination to popularize faith expressions, while "popular religion" is most often used as a description for the material aspects of a people's traditions or practices. PARAL decided that in order to analyze Latino religion systematically, its material aspects would be better treated as elements of syncretism. This theme is explored extensively in separate volume within this series.

Admittedly, the distinction between the material elements of religion and the inclination to be religious is somewhat artificial. It might be asked, "How can one analyze a tendency to incorporate disparate religious expressions of a popular culture without analyzing the content of these disparate expressions?" In fact, several articles included in this issue offer extensive consideration of the process of religious syncretism in their treatment of popular religiosity. However, religiosity as "disposition" is the focus maintained throughout the chapters.

Consideration of popular religiosity as a disposition makes it possible to understand how this religious expression is created outside of ecclesiastical control. But even if the clergy does not control such religious expression, that does not mean that popular religiosity necessarily falls outside theological orthodoxy. A procession to Our Lady of Guadalupe is theologically acceptable within Catholicism as a demonstration of devotion, comparable to European devotions to Our Lady of Lourdes and of Fatima. Such Marian devotions are distinguishable from other religious traditions, such as eating a meal at the cemetery grave site of a deceased relative on All Souls Day, for instance, which derives from Meso-American religion. But in the perspectives of all the authors in this volume, the historical connection to European or Meso-American religion is not what makes a tradition "popular religiosity." Despite its theologically correct roots in Mediterranean Catholicism, a Marian procession may acquire the characteristics of popular religiosity according to our definition when control of the event slips from the grasp of clerics and passes over to the people. Given the vulnerability of clergy to patterns of prejudice in U.S. society, in one particular parish, a pastor may oppose the procession to Our Lady of Guadalupe as vehemently as the cemetery visitation, lumping both together as the same sort of questionable practice. Thus, the tendency of the people to rescue banned traditions from clerical censure may manifest itself in maintaining both the theologically correct procession and the Aztec influenced commemoration of the dead. Indeed, over time popular religiosity can bestow orthodoxy upon traditions with non-Christian origins.

It appears that the major differences between Latin American religion outside the United States, and Latino religion within the U.S., concern the nature and context of clerical control over devotions. Thus, for instance, the class and ethnic identity of the clergy will often influence whether they accept or reject a particular devotion. The significant contribution of the article by Ana María Díaz-Stevens is to draw attention to the issue of social distance between clergy and people as a measurable aspect in popular religiosity. Based on her own award-winning study of the Puerto Rican experience, she provides an insightful sociological analysis of categories and processes internal to the religious experience. Her article gives us an insider's view of how ecclesiastically controlled faith expressions in one context can become popular religiosity in another.

Meredith McGuire, on the other hand, provides an equally perceptive analysis of contextual factors outside of religion that color the same process. With no loss of clarity or insight into popular religiosity, she offers here a focus upon the public and secular forces that shape popular religiosity. McGuire's writing draws from the richness of her acclaimed book on the social context of religion, and her experience as president of two leading scholarly organizations in the social science study of religion. Her contribution in this volume demonstrates the same lucid analysis of Latino experience that she has already brought to other themes.

These two articles ought to be read together for their complementarity. The forces in the public sphere that weaken or strengthen popular religiosity usually have parallels within religion, because the social and the religious are interactive categories. Moreover, while Díaz-Stevens describes elements of Latino popular religiosity most familiar to Latinos themselves, McGuire addresses issues that frame general appraisals by an ever-widening company of non-Latino scholars interested in the connections of Latino religion to the churches of the United States. The juxtaposition of both perspectives in the same volume contributes to the strength of the analysis provided by this book.

The insider-outsider perspectives are echoed in those articles that supply a theological context of popular religiosity. Jaime Vidal stresses the normalcy for Catholicism in incorporating religious symbols and practices from other religions into its own system. He aggressively defines such incorporation here, not as a surrender of Christianity to the power of non-Christian belief, but rather as two-thousand year old evidence of a transcendent "catholic" nature that can universalize particular religious expression by subsuming it under some aspect of Christianity. In an academy self-conscious about a multi-culturalism in which every belief is equally valid, it is too easy to forget that ordinary people, who are more interested in survival than intellectual refinement, often make winners and losers out of different traditions. Vidal's article forces us to consider that Christianity's deep roots in the Americas are a result of genuine acceptance of the faith and should not be hastily dismissed as merely Spanish imposition of an alien religion upon the conquered. As the foremost expert in the U.S. on the medieval origins of Hispanic spirituality, Vidal's examples are provocative and well researched.

Luis Rivera Pagán focuses upon this issue of Spanish imposition of Christianity in the Americas by 16th century Spaniards. His treatment here reflects themes from his important study of violence and evangelization that has now been published both in Spanish and English. He shows how the theological and juridical notion of justification discloses the dialectical relation between ecclesiastical interests and popular religiosity. While condemning the condemnable in the Spanish conquest, Rivera Pagán describes how Christianity nonetheless allows for self-critique. He offers here a succinct assessment of the work of Bartolomé de Las Casas in appraising popular religiosity in the Americas. Rivera Pagán, who is an important figure in the Protestant expression of the Theology of Liberation, suggests that Las Casas' ideas link the sixteenth century experiences to Liberation Theology in the twentieth century.

Gustavo Benavides, a distinguished contributor to theoretic studies of religious interactions, discusses recent social science commentary on some of the Latin American experiences described theologically and historically by Vidal and Rivera Pagán. Benavides focuses on popular religiosity in Latin America as a form of resistance and accommodation by the indigenous peoples. Like Vidal, he compares religious symbols to language, emphasizing that the same symbols may have different meanings for different publics. Benavides' impressive knowledge of the European and Latin American literature on popular religiosity provides some direction for future research on Latinos in the United States.

Samuel Silva Gotay, director of the Caribbean phase of an international study of the history of Christianity in Latin America (CEHILA), links these theoretical considerations with a specific historical process. In a few pages, he compacts a penetrating study of nearly five centuries of the history of religion in Puerto Rico. His chapter provides for a comparison between the imperial aspects of Spanish Catholicism and the invasion of Puerto Rico by a Protestant United States. Although focused upon the island colony, Silva's description of institutions and processes should sound familiar to scholars of the U.S. invasion of Texas, California, and the Southwest during the nineteenth century. As a Protestant scholar, his reflections on past antagonisms and present collaborations among Catholics and Protestants is noteworthy.

From a theological and pastoral perspective that dovetails with the concerns for national identity described by Silva Gotay, Virgilio Elizondo enriches this volume with a Mexican American experience. Father Elizondo, presently pastor of the historic Cathedral of San Fernando in San Antonio, Texas, is generally considered the most eminent and original theologian of Mexican American Catholicism today. His article describes how the clerical role vis à vis popular religiosity need not always be an antagonistic one. In fact, through the Mass at San Fernando that is viewed by a national television audience weekly, Elizondo not only writes about popular religiosity, but promotes its vitality and development.

Richard Flores, noted author of a work on San Antonio's pastorela published by the distinguished Smithsonian Institution in Washington, D.C., contributes an article on one specific example of Mexican American experience. Flores adds an anthropological consideration of space to the various contexts for popular religiosity described by the other authors. His detailed analysis of a San Antonio tradition offers insight into the polyvalent nature of such religious expression. He suggests a refinement in thinking about popular religiosity among Latinos that pays attention to the audience as the determining factor in an expression's popular character.

The volume concludes with insightful comments from Father Kenneth Davis, who writes for the journal, Review for Religious, and is now teaching at the Oblate School of Theology in San Antonio. Drawing from pastoral concerns, he suggests a theoretical framework in which popular religiosity can be considered one of the factors in the popularity of Pentecostalism among Latinos today. Because of its timeliness, this issue has been included as brevia; however, space considerations made it impossible to include as a full length article in this volume.

An Enduring Flame situates the state of research on popular religiosity, but there is a need for further studies of popular religion among Latinos. For one thing, we need to develop a comparative framework for understanding the historical introduction of North American Protestantism and Catholicism as a result of war and invasion. What Silva Gotay has done here for Puerto Rico, should be compared to the former Mexican territories, for analysis of the interplay between governmental policy decisions directed against national consciousness and concomitant effects upon religious expression. Secondly, we need to continue to explain the conditions for the manifestation of popular religiosity so that differences that arise from local conditions do not obfuscate larger similarities nationwide. Lastly, we have to further refine notions such as that of "place," "social distance," and terms referring to the merging of religious symbols and traditions. These are new and fresh terms in analysis and deserve a larger role in shaping scholarly discourse on Latino religion. Further development along these lines will encounter the issues of class, race and colonialism which form the backdrop for Latino popular religiosity.

It is the hope of PARAL that the issues raised here about the "enduring flame" of religious awareness, that is common among Latino peoples, will help illuminate the way for all of us on our life's journey.

Analyzing Popular Religiosity for Socio-Religious Meaning

1

ANA MARÍA DÍAZ-STEVENS

There is a tug-of-war underway about popular religiosity. And it is not only in the social sciences, but also in theology and history where scholars vie to pull others towards their own definitions of this elusive term. For some, "popular religiosity" is "folk religion," lacking in doctrinal rigor, clustered about antiquated rural customs and bordering on superstition. This once pervasive opinion on popular religiosity is happily on the wane, as a higher level of tolerance for popular expression of religion has become generalized in many fields, even in formal theology. Thus, there is no need here to rebut an understanding of popular religiosity as superstitions that are merely "unorthodox or false beliefs."

Once the notion of superstition is dispelled, however, it becomes ever more difficult to find common ground among the disciplines analyzing religion. As example of this difficulty, I would like to mention a recent conference in Europe with purposes similar to the PARAL Symposium of 1993. That gathering of diverse scholars produced three large volumes of collected papers with the title "La religiosidad popular." Yet despite the acumen of the scholars, this elemental confusion about definition is found throughout the works. Luis Maldonado, for example, in analyzing the nature of diverse mixtures of Christian beliefs and other religions, ends by coining new terminology and making a distinction between "syncretism" and "syncretization."

Identifying such religious phenomena as Santería with syncretism, he suggests that a better term for defining the nature of popular religiosity is syncretization. Syncretism, he seems to be saying, occurs when one belief system continues to exist almost intact but borrows from another various trappings in order to camouflage itself. As I understand it, because the intent is not so much harmony as a type of underground activity, this submergence protects the belief system from eradication or domination, but by its very nature impedes the possibility of a new religious reality from emerging. Only when a true syncretization has occurred is this new reality possible. It is this new reality that he wants to call popular religiosity. This understanding of popular religiosity and syncretization, I believe, rests on the assumption that the Christian core must prevail at all cost while the other belief systems can lend Christianity elements which in no way threaten its essential nature. In other words, in the end Christianity must come out winning.

Whether or not this is what Maldonado intended in his dichotomization of these two terms (syncretism and syncretization) is not altogether clear. To further complicate matters, other authors such as Jaime Vidal use the term "syncretization" approximating what Maldonado defines as "syncretism," and "synthetization" for what Maldonado defines as "syncretization" (see Vidal's essay in this volume).

We can likewise fall into dispute about the meaning of "popular." From one perspective, "popular" is contrasted with "literate" adapting Redfield's dichotomy between the philosophies, traditions and practices of the urban elite against those of the rural masses. In this notion, institutional religion belongs to the "high" tradition, while popular religiosity is the property of the "low" tradition. An integralist/universalist approach claims that all religious expression is "popular," at least with some groups, or the expression simply would not exist. In other words, the religion of the upper classes and the erudite is no less popular than those of the lower classes. What is behind the distinction between "popular" (as belonging to the populace) and "official" (as related to the institution and the elite) is a power relationship that the religious expression of the upper classes possesses and is lacking to that of the poor.

Yet, there are those who see in popular religiosity the power to subvert meaning and to constitute an act of defiance or at least a modicum of liberation from oppressive institutional structures. The class related notions in popular religiosity open the door to a deconstructionist approach to popular religiosity. The search for meaning then becomes a matter of symbolic interactions, most of which have meanings far removed from religion.

Undeniably, Latinos have appropriated the notion and expression of "popular religiosity" as a defining characteristic of our religious experience in this country. We have invested considerable energies from different disciplines in justifying this popular religiosity as our mode of faith beyond the official rubrics and pronouncements of an institutionalized church. Because it is so tied to our identity as a people in diaspora, I think it is important that we continue to stake out a special claim to popular religiosity, even with all the difficulties that this term brings. Indeed, the often enigmatic (some would say, ambiguous) nature of the diaspora experience fits exceedingly well with that of popular religiosity.

Our cultural condition of Latinos removed from Latin America and our political situation as citizens of the U.S.A., yet outsiders to the prevalent values and structures of this society, parallel our religious experience where our spirituality and religious production is seen as belonging to, but not sufficiently "orthodox" to officially constitutes an integral part of Christianity. Yet, as Latinos, as Christians and as scholars, we simply cannot return to a circumstance in which "better-than-thou" official religious personnel and scholars dismiss Latino religiosity as not very religious, or characterize the study of our faith experiences as a futile exercise that romanticizes but demands little or no intellectual acumen. At the same time, popular religiosity ought not become merely a slogan to rally ethnic pride or nostalgic self-abandonment. Nor should it be allowed to be commercialized by media events and unscrupulous economic entrepreneurship eager to generalize its popularity among the wider society in return for quick profit.

It is doubtful that we should ever come to perfect agreement as to what really constitute popular religiosity. The phenomenon itself is complex and multifaceted, just as it is ever changing. And while some among us may be inclined to argue ad infinitum as to the proper label given to these diverse religious expressions and to the phenomena that gives rise to them, as a first step, all must consider that each discipline brings with its preference for terminology appearances of intellectual arrogance towards other considerations. Deep down we know that arguing about the advisability of one term over another or the superiority of this approach versus that one, while providing a legitimate outlet for professional discourse, in the long run will not exhaust the fascinating mystery of popular religiosity. Yet, argue we will as we seek to continue our exploration into the nature and function of popular religiosity as a reality worthy of our genuine scholarly consideration. Hopefully, through our patient and honest efforts we will gain deeper insights which will enable the various fields to better approximate its meaning.

In the meanwhile, we must learn to live with certain uncertainty and ambiguity, allowing for differing opinions. It is to be expected, that as popular religiosity continues to take root among the people and as we seek to sharpen our understanding of it as a subject of study, there will be times of confusion and frustration. The differences of opinion, indeed the controversy, regarding popular religiosity will not be put to rest in this essay, this volume or volumes yet to come. And perhaps that is just as well. For as long as a phenomenon exists (even if in the mind alone), it should register change; and, as long as change is registered, exploration and debate ought to take place.

Semantics aside, what I believe has to be recognized is that various peoples give expression to belief according to their own particularities: geography, social class status, level of education and so on. These particularities affect popular religiosity in matters great and small: the place and the occasions for celebration, the preparations for the occasions, the prayers that are said, the manner in which they are prayed, the bodily movements accompanying the prayers, those leading the rituals and prayers, the kind of people gathered, the type of music employed, the religious articles (paraphernalia) used, the expectations that are brought, the emotions that are experienced, the testimony that is given, and the mood that is created through the use of all of the above. Unlike academic theology, which rationally explores and explains belief and practice, popular religiosity leaves these subtexts hidden underneath a plethora of disguises. I believe that the social sciences, especially sociology and anthropology, are more practiced in analyzing these aspects of behavior than theology. However, I also recognize that the context is a religious one and that the social sciences need to form a partnership with theological meaning to fully decipher popular religiosity.

One must understand that historical development also affects meaning, and that the accumulation of experiences through time is what makes an occasional ceremony into a tradition. As a result, neither the sociologist nor historian can live without each other. That is, we must not fail to see that the notion of popular religiosity must be couched in the acceptance of a historical process where the introduction of new religious, cultural, scientific and technological elements bring about clashes, erosion, adaptations and transformations. To echo biblical language, in order for popular religiosity to exist it must be allowed to suffer, to even die in part, as long as the core remains; that is, as long as a re-emergence is possible.

The only definition of popular religiosity with which I am comfortable at the moment, then, is that it is a moving target: it possesses a certain core cohesion which gives it its essence and gives evidence of particular characteristics, but it is also always expanding, contracting, adding on and subtracting, living and dying to resurrect anew. In other words, for me, popular religiosity is transformative. I would suspect that Marxist terminology would rather use the word "dialectic" although "multi-lectic" would perhaps better express it. And there lies the problem: how to define something that is always becoming, how to make sense of what is being articulated by so many, if confusion is almost certain when more than two competing voices are heard at the same time.

As one of the organizers of the PARAL 1993 Symposium, I felt that we should use the term "religiosity," which is more common in the literature written in Spanish than "religion." This limits the discussion to a subjective disposition towards use of certain religious practices, rather than to the content of the practices. It is with the various meanings of syncretic phenomena that PARAL addresses the content and beliefs and traditions. A much harder term to define is "popular." Some notion of class is involved, of course. But since the majority of Latinos in the US are no longer resident in the rural countryside, but are now urban residents, the Latin American sense of "popular" as "campesino" can not be applied to Latinos indiscriminately. We can adopt, at least as a point of departure, the notion of "popular" as contrasted with "clerical."

I know that I am trespassing on theological ground, so allow me to succinctly suggest where I think we stand in relationship to popular religiosity in terms of the Puerto Rican experience. In my earlier work,[1] I talk about a dual (or multi-layered) reality in Puerto Rico and have introduced the notion of social distance in the analysis of the religious expressions of the Puerto Rican people. Tracing the history of the church during Spanish colonization, I claimed that the implantation of Catholicism in Puerto Rico more or less paralleled the estab lishment of other Spanish institutions on the island. Lack of money and settlers meant that only the urban society in the Puerto Rican colony was under direct Spanish influence. Therefore, an urban—rural separation took place which allowed the people of the hinterland to develop different social norms. In economics, for instance, smuggling and illegal trade were the principal activities of the common people even though the urban establishment was ostensibly employed in preventing such enterprises. In similar fashion, cultural expressions as diverse as music, dance, clothing, and linguistic dialect all demonstrated a similar bifurcation between the urban and the rural. Catholicism did not escape this process and the *jíbaros* of hinterlands developed a faith consonant with their environment and needs.

This basic urban-rural difference spun off variations which can be explained here. Thus, for instance, in the rural setting, the rural bourgeois often took on the trappings of their urban counterparts in order to distance themselves from the masses of peasants. To such variations must be added a host of variables including region, race, gender and age.

The question of race will not be dealt with in this essay except to say that it is closely linked to that of region or geographic setting of Puerto Rico. Therefore, in certain regions, consonant with the population, African elements will be more pronounced, while those areas with a whiter population or exhibiting greater mixtures of Indian and Spanish will likewise exhibit in their religious expressions closer affinity to the type of Christianity brought by the Spanish colonizers, be they Castellanos, Andaluces, Canarios, Mallorquines or others. The issues of gender and age are also somewhat connected to that of race. In an article prepared for the Latinos Studies Journal on the matriarchal core of popular religiosity, I have outlined how the role of *rezadora,* for example, fell to faith healers, comadronas, and others, who most of the time were elderly women known for their service to the community, their unselfishness, their wisdom and their personal faith.

Basically then, even within popular religiosity, what we have is a multitude of spheres which may or may not be at the same level of social distance from the institutional church. One way of expressing this is to compare it with a billiard table where, for each billiard ball, there are a number of relational distances from all others as well as from the cue ball. But when one is set in motion either by direct contact with the cue ball or by a chain reaction, some, if not all of these distances are subject to change. The problem with this analogy is that in billiards, the movement always originates from the cue ball, which we may think of as established or institutionalized religion. It is important to understand that the distance between the spheres in popular religiosity is in continuous flux; each new positioning also means a new relationship or social distance from each existing religious expression and from official religion as well. If we were to look closely at institutional Catholicism, however, we should not be surprised to find that the elites and those who are in closer contact with the hierarchical institutional church also form a part of particular spheres, each struggling for a position of legitimacy and for the control of resources and religious production.

When the U.S. took over Puerto Rico in 1898, religion and religious practices were divided along lines of an urban vs. rural dichotomy. Immediately after the military invasion, U.S. Protestant and Catholic missionaries descended upon the island to "convert," "evangelize," "save," "redeem," "restore," "inform," "educate," "set free from obscurantism," and/or "enlighten," the inhabitants of Puerto Rico. That is, their expressed purpose was to Christianize a people who had been practicing Christianity for the last four hundred years. The Protestants pointed an accusing finger at Spanish culture and the Catholic church as accomplices in a harsh colonization process where atrocities were committed against the indigenous population and to enslaved Africans. They were aided by Puerto Rican political and intellectual leaders such as Eugenio María de Hostos, who at least initially, saw the U.S. as the paragon of justice and equality as well as a promise to their life-long dream of complete political emancipation from foreign domination.

The Catholic missionaries on the island, for their part, emphasized their loyalty and nationalism to the United States and their zeal to give orthodox Catholicism an opportunity to grow and develop in Puerto Rico. Meanwhile, Puerto Rican Catholics, such as poet and writer José de Diego, and later political activist and Harvard-trained lawyer Pedro Albizu Campos, emphasized the difference between North American culture based on Protestant ethics, and Puerto Rican culture based on a Spanish Catholic ethos. Their accusation was to highlight the materialistic, belligerent, expansionism of the United States and to remind the U.S. Protestants in Puerto Rico that the U.S. had not been any more benign with the indigenous populations they encountered in the northern lands than Spain had been with those in Central and South America and the Caribbean. Dr. Samuel Silva Gotay has produced an insightful chapter with an historical interpretation on these events. As he shows, for all the mutual accusations and all the pronouncements, the Protestant missionaries responded by making an effort to penetrate the hinterland, the bastion of popular religiosity identified as Catholicism. Protestant control of the public school system on the island until the 1950s insured the transmission of values that were inimical to popular religiosity. But although they had some influence in the hinterland, Protestant missionaries generally preferred to form a new Protestant Puerto Rican urban elite that would carry their message of evangelization and Americanization. Thus, with few exceptions, the urban areas had the greatest concentrations of church resources and personnel under U.S. Protestant rule as they did under Catholic Spain.

I would like to add my own analysis to Silva Gotay's insights, emphasizing certain points. Because Puerto Rico continued to be generally a rural people well into the mid-century, the dichotomy that existed during Spanish colonial times did not evaporate over night with new political impositions from el Norte. The people, for the most part, continued their centuries-old religious traditions centered upon the family and immediate community. While Protestant and Catholic missionaries from the United States battled to rescue Puerto Rican "souls" from each other, it was business as usual for the local *rezadora* and *curandera*.

The Catholic priests did not abandon their yearly rural visitations as a means of continuity. But whereas under Spain, there was a shared cultural context for the urban-rural differences within Catholicism, most of the Catholic priests were now North Americans, lacking not only a common culture but also a common language with the people of the hinterland.

Few missionaries were inclined to view Puerto Rican popular religiosity in the Latin sense of "superstitio" which was "clairvoyance or clarity of vision." Rather than see the rural Catholicism before them as faith with the propensity to invest all occurrences with supernatural meaning, they, no less than their Protestant counterparts tended to view what was specifically Puerto Rican in the countryside as impure or unorthodox or just plain false religion. For instance, there was a propensity to view as mere "bargaining" the Puerto Rican common practice of *promesas* whereby a person seeks a special blessing or gives thanks for mercies already received. This practice which involves such sacrifices as wearing special garments called *hábitos,* reciting certain prayers, fasting, taking care of the sick or performing any other corporal or spiritual works of mercy, were accepted and practiced by the people as part of their deep faith in God's bountiful goodness, and as recognition of their need to be humble and dependent upon God's providence. Moreover, the works of mercy attached to these "promises" were just another way of expressing their commitment to Christian charity and their belief in the communion of saints. *"Hoy por tí, y mañana por mí"* was an often repeated phrase which denoted an acceptance of obligation towards others' needs, recognition of one's own needs and the interdependence always present in the human condition. Therefore, selfishness, individualism or manipulation were seldom the marks of popular religiosity despite what "the more enlightened" would have us believe. And while not everything in popular religiosity should be held up as the paragon of virtue, self-denial and rightousness in its practices and its language, a wealth of orthodox spirituality is to be found.

Furthermore, rather than fatalism or naive self-abandonment common phrases such as, *"Si Dios quiere," "Dios mediante," "Con el favor de Dios,"* or *"Si está de menester, sino sea por las Benditas Almas del Pulgatorio,"* denote that at the core of all petitions was the notion of one's responsibility towards the other, the family, the community, and ultimately of God's saving grace. There was also that sense of spiritual "economy" where nothing should be wasted and where any act (such as not cutting your hair for years, or cutting it because it was beautiful) could be done in praise of the Lord. Inherent was a sense that God *"está al alance de la mano,"* always within one's reach ready to hear and answer one's prayers. That the answer may often be *"no"* or that things did not always go the way one expected them to go did not negate his presence. *"Gracias te doy Divino Señor,"* therefore, was as often heard as *"no hay mal que por bien no venga."*

Perhaps this "economy" of popular religiosity is tied to the women's role in it. In my own spirituality I have been often reminded of how women, especially lower-class and peasant women, construct and make use of our world. Long before the craze of recycling, the humble households of these women have been monuments to their ingenuity in the art of inventing, restoring and finding innovative utility in things which others may discard as useless. It never ceases to amaze me how my mother would often say *"I have nothing to prepare for dinner today,"* and then within an hour serve us a nutritious and delicious meal from all the *"scraps"* she found in the back of the refrigerator. When as a young school girl I needed a new dress for a special event, first came the familiar, *"Mi amor, we can't afford a new dress at this time,"* and then as the event was nearing I would see my mother or my older sister concoct from bits and pieces of cloth left over from previous sewing projects the prettiest dress I had ever owned.

I have thought sometimes that popular religiosity is somewhat like this. What the elites look down upon, what they deem unserviceable, oftentimes becomes central to the religious practices of the ordinary people. Furthermore, it is precisely in the home before a make-shift altar where this transformation most often takes place. It is there, in the kitchen,[2] where the women of the household and other women from the extended family and community, often gather and, over a cup of café con leche, reminisce about the past, give each other counsel and consolation, discuss the events of the community, and plan for family and community celebrations which most often are also religious celebrations.[3]

Both Catholics and Protestants were quick to recognize the importance of popular religiosity, yet each group for its own particular reasons. Because they considered it mere fetishism and superstition, Protestants deemed popular religiosity a target for destruction. The Catholics, while not as superstitious, saw it as a religious deposit where they could to pick and chose elements that could give clear evidence of the differences between Catholics and Protestants. What the Protestants did, including the eradication of such Feast days as Los Santos Reyes and the burning of centuries-old *santos de palos,* may be labeled desacralization and destruction. What the Catholics did, can be labeled cooptation as they sought to institutionalize many of the centuries-old devotions and traditions that the people had managed to keep in their communities and families far from clerical control. In this process, some of the practices lost their popular appeal and character while others were enhanced. In the last analysis, the popular religiosity that survived was not so much a religion of resistance, as a parallel or complementary religiosity.

It was not so much that the people in the hinterland, rejected official institutionalized Christianity. In Puerto Rico neither anarchism nor anti-clericalism was ever as marked as in Spain and other Latin American countries. The common people simply continued to affirm what they had been believing and practicing for centuries. Most were unconcerned with urban expressions and traditions. In the long run these had proven ineffective. Furthermore, the people accustomed to centuries of neglect by urban-based colonial institutions, depended on their own ingenuity and creativity. In terms of religious needs as in most other cases, they knew what they, their families and their neighbors needed and they knew how to supply it without the mediation of competing outsiders, each one claiming to represent the true Christ. The *jíbaros* viewed both sides with a large dose of distrust and sometimes even with disdain for "commercializing" and fragmenting what was most sacred to them, their Christian faith. What was so Christ-like about name-calling and all those condemnations against each other?

This is not to say that there were no conversions or shifting from one church to another. But, in many instances Protestant conversions were no more than another way of being "religious" and the Protestant church, another "temple" or house of worship to visit. The Protestant minister was an alternative to the Catholic priest, especially when marriages and other religious services, which were not easily attainable at the Catholic church could be gotten there. Thus, in Puerto Rico it is not uncommon even today to find people going to Mass on Sunday morning, to a Pentecostal prayer meeting in the afternoon and to consult a *curandera* or *espiritista* in the evening. At night, before going to bed, the same person may kneel before his or her home altar, before the icons or statues or his or her favorite saints amidst lighted candles and holy water. That the official churches fail to recognize or admit that these practices indeed exist among the members of their congregation do not negate their existence. In fact, such negations go a long way towards perpetuating them or at least help create an atmosphere where people feel free to continue these practices unimpeded.

Just as the new missionaries had learned to de-emphasize certain things, and emphasize and co-opt others, the mountain *jíbaro* had learned to appropriate certain religious roles deemed appropriate for the ordained clergy by officialdom, as well as other religious paraphernalia and practices introduced by the newcomers. In fact, they proved more adept at this game of "picking and choosing" and integrating than the missionaries, precisely because they were not constrained by institutional concerns.

As Silva Gotay describes, Catholic popular religiosity of the hinterland was allowed to continue almost unimpeded by Protestant zeal, Pentecostal conversion or Catholic institutionalization, at least until the 1950s when the island was thrust into an industrialization and urbanization mode which would bring about rapid social change. This industrialization program set in motion a series of population shifts from rural to urban, from urban to mainland metropolis. In the process, new marginal urban pockets (ghettos or barriadas) developed, and greater contact (and therefore, conflict) between rural and urban expressions of Catholicism were made possible.

In the new setting in the urban barriadas in Puerto Rico and the ghettos of the U.S., the direct contact between Puerto Rican *jíbaros* (generally rural Catholics) and Protestantism was accelerated. This is the story told to Sidney Mintz by Taso, the worker in the cane, who became a Pentecostal. The fit between a traditional religious expression and the rural environment was destroyed. Many of these Catholics proved a fertile mission land for the Protestant and Pentecostal effort which, among other things, promised upward mobility through education and personal enterprise.

The industrialization effort that began full-swing in Puerto Rico in the 1950s with Operation Bootstrap did more to Protestantize the Puerto Rican rural people than any religious effort on the island. This was done first by destroying the rural environment which had couched a rural Catholic religious expression for more than four centuries. The rapid rural to urban movement that was set in motion caught the *jíbaros* unaware of the circumstances leading to their migration to the city and totally unprepared for urban life. With a wealth of resources at their disposal, the Protestant churches were quick to set up a client relationship with these peasants- turned-urban dwellers. Sanctioned by the U.S. government officials, Protestant missionary personnel literally took over the educational system. Thus, the social distance between a newly-urbanized class of peasant origin and the urban middle-class Protestants was eroded. In the process, the basis of a rural popular religiosity that had taken nearly three hundred years to evolve, was eroded, as well.

Mass migration to the northeastern United States, and New York City in particular, seemed to set Puerto Ricans on the same path to assimilation as hyphenated Americans as had happened with Irish-Americans, Italian-Americans and other Catholic ethnic groups. That was the expectation of Father Joseph P. Fitzpatrick, S.J. of Fordham, who became a pioneer in sociological analysis of this Puerto Rican migration. It was an idea that was repeated in the general literature from authors as varied as C. Wright Mills, Clarence Senior, Patrick Moynihan and Nathan Glazer.

None of these authors advocated the disappearance of Puerto Rican culture, of course, but they all anticipated a gradual Americanization along the lines of the other groups. Fitzpatrick was able to influence policy of the Archdiocese of New York in order to utilize religion as a stabilizing and integrating social force. But as I suggested in my book, *Oxcart Catholicism on Fifth Avenue,* the Puerto Rican sense of religion is larger than the Catholic Church.

As a little girl, who came to Washington Heights in 1953 directly from Barrio Cerro Gordo in Moca, Puerto Rico, I had first-hand experience of how my family's practice of popular religiosity changed St. Rose of Lima parish. The traditions of the hinterland had prepared us to practice our Catholicism without the attentions of the clergy. We knew how to organize with lay persons, assuming much of the responsibility. We had confraternities and kinship systems to prepare for the rites of passage, providing cathectical instruction, peer pressure as motivation (which in Catholic circles is referred to as "good examples") and a community with which to celebrate. These activities led—I am tempted to say, "forced"—a very reluctant pastor to provide first space, then a monthly Mass, later a Spanish-speaking "extern" priest in residence, and finally a "basement" church. I explain in my book, *Oxcart Catholicism on Fifth Avenue,* how the social distance between the upper and basement church helped to give space and time for Puerto Rican popular religiosity to take root in the U.S. urban setting. The experiences of St. Rose of Lima have been verified time and time again as the normal procedure in which New York area urban parishes gradually became Puerto Ricanized.

There were various sociological factors at work, each requiring more analysis than can be provided here. It must be emphasized that the principal cause of a reinvigorated popular religiosity in a most unlikely urban, North American setting was social distance. The basement church symbolized that we were not considered as important to the Catholic parishes as the aging Euro-American population. Until the late 1950s, and in some places even until today, it was not the diocesan clergy, but missionaries who ministered to us. Many of the circumstances of our colonial Catholicism and the urban—rural dichotomy were reproduced. The distance was no longer horizontal, measuring the miles from pueblo to countryside; the social distance was now vertical, upper vs. basement church. Still, it was social distance and it allowed us to transplant our traditional popular religiosity. Even more remarkable was the policy of the New York Archdiocese which in 1953 began to use the patron feast- day of the island, the San Juan Fiesta, to provide institutional legitimacy for the basement churches. It is important to note that the fiesta had begun in 1950 by lay leaders with minimal church support. But priests like Ivan Illich and Joseph Fitzpatrick quickly recognized the opportunity it provided for Catholicism in New York.

The introduction of the Cursillo de Cristiandad to New York in the early 1960s strengthened the role of popular religiosity of Puerto Ricans. Because the Cursillo was based on an Hispanic Catholicism familiar to Puerto Ricans, its education and leadership formation of Puerto Rican lay persons affirmed the role of popular religiosity. But at the same time, it equipped them with skills and created Puerto Rican run organizations that fostered a special brand of Catholicism. In a sense, the Cursillo movement among Latinos in New York was the forerunner of the Hispanic Church.

Whatever the fate of popular religiosity on the island of Puerto Rico, it can be argued that Puerto Rican popular religiosity was alive and well in the northeast U.S., albeit transformed and constantly undergoing changes. It can also be argued that since the greatest portion of the population that brought this religious expression to New York were from a rural setting, the Puerto Rican-U.S. popular religiosity has its seeds in rural Puerto Rico of the decades 1940 to mid 1960. In socio-economic terms the institutions of this mighty empire have proven incapable of assimilating the Puerto Ricans. Puerto Ricans, historically, have been able to differentiate between faith and institution. Therefore, they have been able to remain faithful to the general teachings of the church even when it has neglected them. Rather than abandoning Catholicism, forced into isolation by institutional neglect, they have responded by creating and transforming roles within the community to fulfill their religious needs and to express their faith.

In fact, the readiness of the Puerto Ricans to assume roles beyond the ordinary expectations for a lay person prepared them well for the ordained ministry in the Protestant churches and for the changes introduced by the Second Vatican Council in the Catholic church. In the Catholic church, those ministering to the Puerto Ricans were likewise in an advantageous position after the Council. If nothing else, they were more ready to accept the leadership roles of the Puerto Ricans because in fact they had already experienced the Puerto Ricans' capacity for lay leadership. When considerable numbers of other Caribbean and Central Americans migrated to New York as a result of the change in immigration laws, which coincided with the Second Vatican Council, the urgency in addressing Latino Catholicism was enhanced. The Puerto Rican presence was now viewed as a guide of how to treat the urban poor. But popular religiosity is not easily lumped together with a political agenda. For example, when in the late 60s, Msgr. Robert Fox tried to first hispanicize and later render the San Juan Fiesta a celebration of the urban poor, it failed because the unique Puerto Rican character that had previously given it legitimacy and viability, was eroded.

Ironically, from the standpoint of institutional religion at least, at the same time that the San Juan Fiesta was losing credibility and popularity, La Fiesta Folkórica Puertorriqueña, a celebration containing aspects of popular religiosity but originating and having as its base of support in the secular community, was gaining acceptance and visibility. One may even suggest that it was precisely this lack of clerical control that was responsible for its success. On the other hand, with the National Hispanic Encounters beginning in 1972, the preeminence of Puerto Rican lay leadership was recognized and reinforced as a host of pastoral movements, theological interpretation and institutional efforts provided support and legitimation to the Puerto Ricans' position in the church and to their unique expression of Catholicism.

The test now is whether, the religious practices, traditions and spirituality they brought with them can continue to withstand the test of time in a society reeked with materialism and other social evils and where the institu tional church is undergoing shortages of priests and resources and much internal conflict. Which practices will remain and which will be lost? Of those that remain, what transformations are necessary for their maintenance? This question can also be asked of Pentecostalism and Protestantism among Latinos which also face similar questions about spirituality and culture. This is an area for future research which needs considerable time and careful analysis.

In terms of Catholicism, we are faced with a dilemma. The Puerto Ricans and Latinos in migration no longer live in environments that support their traditional religious beliefs and practices. They are in the process of "creating a new niche" in a situation which besides being urban is alien to their culture, language and mode of religious expression. But there is rising interest in the traditions of popular religiosity among some elements of an urban born and raised generation of Latinos. They tend to look upon these traditions as much for cultural and social identity as for a strictly religious function. But can popular religiosity remain popular religiosity if it is acquired in an urban setting and for cultural, rather than religious purpose? I propose this is an area for greater attention.

On the other hand, Latino Protestants more and more are questioning whether, in converting and adhering to Protestantism, they are not casting aside vital elements of their cultural foundation which, as Justo González clearly acknowledges, is Catholic-based. Many are reassessing the values of traditional Puerto Rican religiosity and spirituality. What elements can be shared with a Catholic-based popular religiosity while still remaining faithful to a particular Protestant denomination and its underlying theology?

As a Latina Catholic, I am pleased to see theology adopt popular religiosity as a central theme. This is my reading of the work of Father Virgilio Elizondo, who has made "religious *mestizaje*" an indispensable concept in the definition of Mexican American Catholicism. But as a social scientist, the acceptance of Latino popular religiosity raises new issues. I would suggest here that beyond the racial and cultural integration implicitly in the concept of *"mestizaje"* and *"mulataje,"* there is another type of religious experience. The migration and diaspora phenomena must be considered, especially as concerns Puerto Ricans and other Caribbean Hispanic people. The concepts of uprootedness, sojourning, constant change, social, environmental and economic unpredictability have to be introduced. We must also consider that in the acquisition of support systems to keep traditions going, popular religiosity runs the risk of being "institutionalized" and thus losing autonomy over cultural and religious creations. Will then the core be lost and these traditions, practices and expressions cease to be Puerto Rican (or Latino) popular religiosity? Or can there be a process of inculturation (or transculturation) where some elements can be borrowed and re-defined while others are cast aside, where there is space for growth and development but always keeping a continuity with all that was positive in the past? Will we be permitted to find new spheres from which to relate and distance ourselves in an ongoing identification and differentiation process, or are we to be subsumed in "the business as usual" of an institutional church which proposes that there is only one true, orthodox way of being Catholic?

As I understand it, the religion of the people is not mono-dimensional any more than religion as a whole is mono-dimensional. It is the conversation, conflict, confusion and resolution that takes place when two or more of these spheres meet (whether horizontally, that is in terms of other spheres; or vertically, in terms of institutionalized Catholicism) that we must look to define the emergence of new modes of popular religiosity for a particular segment of the population at a particular time in a particular place. Something less than this would box in popular religiosity and render all of religion a poor expression of peoples' quest to experience their God.

Endnotes

1. Ana María Díaz-Stevens. *Oxcart Catholicism on Fifth Avenue: The Impact of the Puerto Rican Migration Upon the Archdiocese of New York,* Notre Dame: Notre Dame University Press, 1993; Also see Díaz-Stevens, "Social Distance and Religious Conflict in the Pre-Vatican Catholicism of Puerto Rico," in *MACLAS Latin American Essays,* Vol. IV (1990) pp. 291-301; and "From Puerto Rican to Hispanic: The Politics of the Fiestas Patronales in New York," in *Latino Studies Journal,* Vol. 1, No.1 (Jan. 1990) pp. 28-47; and "The Saving Grace: The Matriarchal Core of Puerto Rican Catholicism" in *Latino Studies Journal* Vol. 4, No. 3 (Sept. 1993) pp. 60-78.

2. Another memory from my childhood was my mother's reference to the church as a kitchen. *"Los hombres ni usan faldas ni cocinan,"* she used to say, *"con la excepción del cura. Ese usa una sotana y todos los domingos nos prepara un banquete."* (Men do no wear skirt nor cook, with the exception of the priest. In fact, the priest does wear a cassock and prepares a banquet for us every Sunday.) Or *"ésta es comida de pobre, sólo el cura cocina un banquete divino y a ese estamos todos invitados."* (This, or what I cook, is food for poor people, only the priest can cook a divine banquet and to that one we are all invited.) The priest does assume a role most often reserved for women

by preparing a banquet (the Eucharist), setting the table (the altar), feeding the family (giving communion to the faithful), clearing the table and cleaning the utensils and putting them and the "leftovers" away until the next meal (wiping clean the vessels and putting the hosts that have been left over in the tabernacle). As irreverent as it may seem, the final "go in peace to love and serve each other" and the last blessing of the Mass by the priest to this day remind me of a remark my mother would often make at the end of our family meals, *"Y con esto y un bizcocho hasta mañana a las ocho. Ahora váyanse a su tarea escolar y luego pueden jugar."* (And with this and a cake it will do until tomorrow at eight. Now, go and do your homework and then you can play.)

3. An excellent example of the role of the kitchen as a place for gathering the family and story-telling can found in Esmeralda Santiago's recent publication, *When I was Puerto Rican.* New York: Addison-Wesley Publishing Co., 1993, pp. 234-36.

Select bibliography

La religiosidad popular. Edited by María Jesús Buxó. 3 vols. (Barcelona: Editorial Anthropos, 1989). These three volumes compiled from the presentations made at the *Primer Encuentro sobre Religiosidad Popular,* sponsored by the Machado Foundation of Seville. Impressive in its scope and treatment, this series is an excellent example of the many ways popular religiosity can be viewed. Although virtually limited to Spain, the presentations give an interdisciplinary cast to the analysis that includes historical analysis and very important sociological parameters that are applicable to the Latino experience.

An example of the folk-literate dichotomy is in Robert Redfield's 1926-27 study of the Mexican village of Tepolztlán published in 1930 as *Tepoztlán—A Mexican Village.* Oscar Lewis adopted a more favorable interpretation of the folk culture in his own 1951 study of the same village, *Life in a Mexican Village: Tepoztlán Restudied.* (Urbana, Ill.; University of Illinois Press).

The writings of Father Joseph P. Fitzpatrick, S.J., particularly his *Puerto Rican Americans: The Meaning of Migration to the Mainland,* (Englewood Cliffs, N.J.: Prentice-Hall, 1972), adopt the notion that folk customs must be understood in order to aid eventual assimilation. Father Fitzpatrick has recently adopted the concept of "inculturation" to soften the assimilation he predicted and to make it more pluralistic within the context of urbanized society. See his *One Church, Many Cultures: The Challenge of Diversity.* (Kansas City, Mo.: Sheed & Ward, 1987).

Gustavo Gutiérrez, *Theology of Liberation: History, Politics and Salvation,* (Maryknoll: Orbis Books, 1973), and Juan Luis Segundo *The Liberation of Theology,* (Maryknoll: Orbis Books, 1976), are now classic texts of this Latin American theological movement. Father Virgilio Elizondo has popularized for Mexican-Americans an interpretation of this theology in his writings, *Christianity and Culture: An Introduction to Pastoral Theology and Ministry for the Bicultural Community,* (Huntington, Indiana: OurSunday Visitor, 1975), *Mestizaje: The Dialectic of Cultural Birth and the Gospel,* (San Antonio: Mexican American Cultural Center, 1978) and subsequent books, like *Galilean Journey* (Maryknoll: Orbis Books, 1990), . Two works by the late Orlando E. Costas may be helpful in adapting Liberation Theology to the Latino Protestant experience; *Christ Outside the Gate: Mission Beyond Christendom,* (Maryknoll: Orbis Books, 1982) and *Liberating News: A Theology of Contextual Evangelization,* (Grand Rapids, Michigan: William B. Eerdmans Publishing Co., 1989). Recent works like Allan Figueroa Deck's *The Second Wave* and Justo P. Gonzalez's *Mañana: Christian Theology from a Hispanic Perspective,* (Nashville: Abingdon Press, 1990), both take as point of departure the premise that religious customs are faith expressions. A third book that looks closely at the Hispanic experience is Eldin Villafañe's *The Liberating Spirit: Toward an Hispanic American Pentecostal Social Ethic,* (Grand Rapids, Michigan: William B. Eerdmans Publishing Co., 1993).

The bibliography on studies of Puerto Rican culture is extensive, but not much is dedicated exclusively to religion as such. Thus, for instance, Sidney Mintz' *Worker in the Cane,* (New York: W. W. Norton and Co., 19974), describes in great detail the conversion experience of a rural couple he had studied while participating in Steward's project, but this remains an individualized case of Pentecostal converts rather than an analysis of conversion to Pentecostalism.

Dan Wakefield's *Island in the Sun,* (Boston: Houghton Mifflin, 1959), is a valuable contribution to the functions of Protestant religion among Puerto Ricans in New York during the 1950s and 1960s, as well as personal testimonies from Piri Thomas in *Savior, Savior, Hold my Hand,* (Garden City, N.Y.: Doubleday and Co., 1972), and Nicky Cruz in *Cross and Switchblade,* but the utility of such studies is limited. More rewarding is Alex Huxley, Westfield's *Three Puerto Rican Families,* (Salem, Wisconsin: Sheffield Publishing Co., 1981), which analyzes the Pentecostalism of Puerto Ricans in a Connecticut town.

Two major surveys by the Archdioceses of New York, *Hispanics in New York: Religious, Cultural and Social Experiences,* (Office of Pastoral Research, Catholic Archdiocese of New York, 1982), and that of Newark, *Nueva Presencia: Knowledge for Service and Hope—A Study of Hispanics in the Archdiocese of Newark.* (Newark, N. J.: Office of Research and Planning, Archdiocese of Newark, 1988), provide data on the frequency of certain practices. Occasional materials published and distributed by the Northeast Pastoral Center are also somewhat useful. Unfortunately, however, these materials are often disconnected from their social context, and, therefore, liable to interpretive error. A national survey by Roberto O. González and Michael La Velle, *The Hispanic Catholic in the U.S.: A Socio-Cultural and Religious Profile,* (New York: Northeast Hispanic Pastoral Center, 1985), only surveyed Hispanics adults who were English speaking. Interesting but dated is *A Gallup Study of Religious and Social Attitudes of Hispanic-Americans,* published by the Gallup Organization, Inc.,(Princeton, N. J.: August 1978). Barry A. Kosmin's and Seymour P. Lachman's *One Nation Under God: Religion in Contemporary American Society,* (New York: Harmony Books, 1993) while presenting overall an excellent statistical basis for the analysis of religion nationwide, undercounts the Hispanic Catholic presence by approximately half.

Ana María Díaz-Stevens, *Oxcart Catholicism on Fifth Avenue: The Impact of the Puerto Rican Migration Upon the Archdiocese of New York,* (Notre Dame: University of Notre Dame Press, 1993), contributes an institutional perspective on religious change by Puerto Ricans. I believe that this approach connects to studies of Latin American Catholicism, such as those by Vallier and Levine. Together with John Coleman's work on *The Evolution of Dutch Catholicism, 1958-1974.* (Berkeley: University of California Press, 1978), this lends a comprehensive dimension, so that one gains insight upon universal Catholicism and not merely a specific parish or diocese.

Resistance and Accomodation in Latin American Popular Religiosity

2

GUSTAVO BENAVIDES

I

In this article we will explore the continuities and the tensions between the culture, religion and interests of the elites and those of the subordinate groups. We will study the way in which social differentiation and hierarchy are articulated in religious terms, mainly through the opposition between popular religiosity and its official counterpart.

Social differentiation gives rise to religious formations that both validate and challenge a given social organization.[1] In small-scale societies in which hierarchy has to do mainly with gender and age, ritual practices help to maintain the boundaries between man and woman, adult and child, ordinary person and chief or religious specialist, while at the same time regulating, through rites of passage, the movement of individuals through the life-cycle. In large-scale societies, position in an increasingly complex and religiously legitimized hierarchy determines the type of labor demanded from individuals, as well as the individual's access to the goods produced by that labor.[2] Increased complexity is also to be found in the religious systems, which can include hierarchically organized priestly groups with access to privileged knowledge and special powers, frequently exercised employing liturgical languages which are incomprehensible to the ordinary population (Schmitt, 1976: 946-947). As a consequence of hierarchical arrangements, then, access to goods, physical and symbolic, becomes restricted, while at the same time there takes place a division of labor occurs, which results in physical and non-physical forms of work being sharply distinguished.

Any attempt to rearrange a group's access to material or symbolic goods requires either the rejection or the rearrangement of hierarchical structures; more importantly, both rejection and rearrangement require access to the legitimizing systems that regulate the contested hierarchy. Rejection or rearrangement, therefore, involve the mobilization of a group's physical and symbolic resources. In many cases, however, when physical—which ultimately means military— mobilization is impossible, rejection or resistance assume a purely symbolic form.[3] It is this form of symbolic or discursive resistance that we will explore in this essay. Our focus will be those symbolic practices, common in Latin America, which although religious, and certainly Christian, seem to want to escape the control of the Catholic Church. Although we will not deal directly with practices among Latinos in the United States, it should be emphasized that the relational and confrontational character of popular religion is also at work in the beliefs and ritual practices of Latinos. In terms of the relationship between Catholicism and Protestantism, the Latino situation in the U.S. is the reverse of the one prevalent in Latin America, where the Catholic Church, as the religion of the majority, and frequently also of the state, enjoys a privileged position. Similarly, the tension between Latinos and "Anglos" replaces the multiple ethnic conflicts found in the Latin American context. A study of Latino popular religion would have to consider a larger variety of religions, the Protestant nature of North American Christianity, as well as the relationship between "Anglo" and "Hispanic" ethnicity. It should be pointed out also that although we will make reference to the role played by popular religion in the management of the physical world—and, conversely, to the ever increasing spiritualization of official religious forms—we will be concerned primarily with Latin American popular Christianity as a form of resistance. Hence, the material aspects of popular religion and dematerialization of official religion, important as these issues are, will be discussed only insofar as these have to do with the issues of resistance.

How to define "popular religion"? In the first place, it is important to avoid hypostatizing this concept, as if popular religion were an atemporal entity recognizable through centuries and continents.[4] It should be kept in mind also that besides "popular," terms such as "folk," "peasant," "local," "non-official" and "subaltern" have been used as modifiers of "religion." There are advantages and disadvantages with each of these terms. "Folk" or "peasant religion," for example, rather like "folk art," may remind one of colorful and wholesome objects and practices which can be safely enjoyed, at a distance, by urban dwellers. The term may be misleading to the extent that folk religion is not always colorful or unthreatening, nor to be found only in rural contexts, and its use may be the result of the desire to romanticize the past. On the other hand, to the extent that "folk" is associated with objects and material concerns, users of this term may be emphasizing a crucial aspect of this form of religion. "Local religion" stresses also the link between the life and the needs of a specific group in a specific territory and its religious representations—as exemplified in William Christian"s splendid work on sixteenth and twentieth century Spain (Christian, 1981a: 1972/1989). "Non-official" is a useful denomination, insofar as it stresses the relational nature of religious formations. The same is even more true of "subaltern religion," a term employed mainly by Italian scholars influenced by Gramsci"s work on ideology and hegemony.[5] It should be remembered, however, that in some cases a subaltern position could refer not to that of a peasant in relation to a priest or bishop, but to that of a grand seigneur who, insofar as he is not a cleric, depends on priests for access to the supernatural.[6]

In any event, whether popular, folk, local, peasant or subaltern, the form of religion with which we are concerned is not to be understood as being constituted merely by the "survivals" studied in the nineteenth and early twentieth centuries.[7] On the contrary, the term "popular religion" must be understood as a perhaps all-too convenient way of referring to a multitude of symbolic and ritual formations, constituted by the interaction of two processes. First, popular religion refers to the practices and beliefs of groups which, being in a relation of opposition, and often of protest against elites, articulate their opposition in symbolic terms.[8] On the other hand, popular religion, and popular culture in general, can be seen as the result of a process of exclusion initiated by elites.[9] This oppositional, or in any case relational, character of popular cultural forms forces us to consider both popular and official formations as eminently contemporary, that is to say, as systems devoted to the mastering of the present and the future, even if, while attempting to do this, these systems tend to make use of archaic liturgical forms. Employing a linguistic analogy, it could be said that a popular religion, far from being constituted by "survivals," is one of the dialects of a conflictive and unstable symbolic configuration, just as the official religion is one of the elite dialects, or rather—if the expression elite dialect appears to us a contradiction in terms—as one of the sociolects used by those who because of their economic and political power serve as cultural models. As a dialect, therefore, popular religion cannot be understood apart from that which it opposes, namely, apart from the official forms of the official imaginary.

A discussion of *religiosidad popular* as a form of resistance must recognize that at the core of the concept of popular religion one finds a situation of ambivalence, since in order to express opposition one has to make use, although against the grain, of the symbolic resources of the cultures and institutions that are being opposed.[10] In the case of popular religion, this ambivalence is particularly pronounced, as the symbols used and reinterpreted by the participants in popular ritual activity tend to be those that play a central role in official religion (Bock, 1965). In this sense, popular religion is constituted by multiple contradictions: in the first place, the external contradiction between popular and elite; in the second, the internal contradiction between the privileged forms that must be assimilated to a certain extent—because otherwise parody would be impossible—and the new forms, including the parodies and distortions. But it should not be forgotten that this is a two-way road, because from the point of view of elites, the realm of the popular is an inexhaustible source of forms which, suitably idealized and spiritualized, can be transformed and neutralized through music, dance, fashion, cuisine, and, not least, religion (see Vrijhof, 1979b: 238-241).

The interaction between the official and the non-official should remind us that, despite the oppositional character of popular religion, one should not think in terms of the dichotomies popularized by Bakhtin in his celebrated book on Rabelais. Rather than participating in the infatuation with purely symbolic transgression current among many practitioners of cultural studies, it may be more productive to consider critiques of Bakhtin's position, such as Aaron Gurjewitsch's.[11] One must also pay attention to the process that led to the increased spiritualization of religion and to the marginalization of certain kinds of material practices which were then labelled as popular.[12] This long-term historical process constitutes the background for the scholarly marginalization and idealization of popular practices, the product of combined efforts of romanticism and industrialization, reflected in eighteenth and nineteenth century scholarship.[13]

Popular religion, then, is part and parcel of a complex system of assimilation and rejection through which subordinate groups sometimes negotiate and at other times struggle over access to cultural and, in the last instance, material goods. In this sense, beliefs and ritual practices function as languages: just as speakers of Quechua and other indigenous languages began to learn Spanish or to incorporate Spanish words into their vocabulary shortly after the Spanish conquest, elements of the Christian pantheon were incorporated into the Andean, Mesoamerican and other pantheons (this is what is generally known under the misleading term "syncretism").[14] In certain cases, having learned Spanish would lead to the abandonment of the mother tongue, but in others, a certain degree of bilingualism has been maintained to this day, a fact that makes possible the switching of codes as circumstances require. The religious realm functioned in an analogous manner after the conquest: more extreme than the incorporation of Christian elements into the indigenous pantheon was the abandonment of the pantheon and the first conversion to Christianity, a religion that was certainly transformed in the process. Subsequent conversions, like the current ones to Protestantism, constitute new attempts to maintain a certain identity and to increase social prestige through the alliance with powerful correligionaries, in this case North Americans.[15]

The colonial assimilation of popular and potentially disruptive religious practices, as well as the use of the symbolic resources of colonial powers by conquered groups, can be found at work in various periods of Christian history, long before the European conquest and settlement of America. Examples include the Christianization of the Roman world and later that of Germanic Europe. As in the Andean, Aztec or Mayan worlds, this process involved, first, the repression of pagan cults (Le Goff, 1967/1977: 230), and then the assimilation of non-Christian practices and their eventual integration into the sanctioned official practices (Huisman, 1979: 60-61; van den Broek, 1979: 40; Flint, 1991). The popular response comprised resistance (Huisman, 1979: 64-65), and then the use of the symbolic resources that had proved their superiority as part of the arsenal of the conquerors. The incorporation of popular groups lead also to the rematerialization of religion, as it happened in North Africa during the fourth century, when Christian funeral rituals became real banquets, with abundant drink, music and dance, or in the Andes, more than a millennium later. These practices were condemned by officials of the Church such as Augustine (van den Broek, 1979: 16-17, 28-29, 31-32), and later by the *extirpadores de idolatrías* in the Andes. Despite the repression, however, the attitude of pre-modern Christians, clerical and lay, to what we call religion was infinitely more physical than that of most modern believers, to whom it would be almost incomprehensible.[16] The attempts to dematerialize and rationalize religion, linked first with the expansion of official Christianity (Le Goff, 1967/1977: 231), and later with the consolidation of modern states, along with the process of industrialization and the rationalization of work, have continued to the present.[17]

II

What has been said about the concept of popular religiosity is valid in general terms for Latin America and for Latinos in the United States. In fact, during the last four-and-a-half centuries of what was Spanish Latin America, from San Francisco Bay in California to the tip of the continent in Tierra del Fuego, we find, in a condensed manner as it were, the repetition of the processes that took place in Europe for more than a millennium.[18] The conquest of some parts of this Latin America by the United States during the nineteenth century placed those lands and the people who have come to be known as Latinos in a very different context. On that account, Latino popular religiosity, while preserving its essential powers of resistance and accommodation, has developed differently. The relationship of Latino popular religiosity to Protestantism, to the culture, technology, and political values of the United States, and to bilingualism are considerably different from such experiences in Latin America. Therefore, the descriptions provided below about popular religiosity must be understood as proper to Latin America.

Throughout Latin America we encounter a situation in which multiple symbolic systems are in competition, multiple dialects which do not, however, coincide with the distinction between laity and clergy, or between upper and lower classes. If we consider the Catholic Church, we find it divided in many ways. Traditionally, the official Church was allied with the landowners who controlled the state (Benavides, 1987). More recently, during and after the Second

Vatican Council, many members of the hierarchy were engaged in the modernization of the liturgy and in the general process of aggiornamento. Politically, some highly placed prelates supported reformist governments, condemned social injustice, and defended the Theology of Liberation. Currently, however, as part of the general abandonment of the changes instituted by the Council, an important segment of the Latin American hierarchy is linked with the Opus Dei, a politically conservative but economically modern religious-lay organization identified with industrial groups and supported by the Vatican. Finally, we have the representatives of Liberation Theology, who after exercising a great deal of influence, have now abandoned Marxist terminology and, like Gustavo Gutiérrez for example, have taken refuge in spiritual pursuits and traditional theological language.

The clerical segments that could be considered to be involved in practices related in some way to the manifestations of popular religion are those that represent political interests opposed to those of the popular classes. In effect, the official Church, which transmits its teachings through sermons, but above all through liturgical means, has otherwise little in common with the needs of low status groups. Nevertheless, as an example of the ambiguous relationship between official and popular forms of religion, it is necessary to keep in mind that it is precisely the liturgical language which provides the vocabulary and the syntax which will be transformed and parodied by popular religion (Le Goff 1967/1977: 229). It can be said, therefore, that it is the official Church, and especially its most reactionary wing which is linked in an almost symbiotic manner with the popular classes, as it was earlier to the old elites, who made use of symbolic language to legitimize their privileged position.

At the other extreme of the political spectrum, we have what would seem to be the natural alliance between marginal urban groups and the Theology of Liberation. When liberation theologians establish a relationship with marginal groups, this is based not upon ritual, nor upon passively accepted doctrine: in principle, the relationship is grounded in the active interpretation of God's liberating Word, present in Scripture. Nevertheless, this relationship remains ambiguous. We have, on the one hand, the liberation theologians' distrust of popular piety, which they share with other reformist or heretical groups.[19] On the other hand, however revolutionary the exegetical attitude towards the Word may be, this is still one based upon a quasi-sacramental system of analogies, in which one of the terms is grounded in the mythology of Christianity. Likewise, the context in which this liberating exegesis takes place has certain undeniable ritual characteristics which may lend themselves to authoritarian practices.[20]

III

In order to deal with symbolic resistance as exercised through the rituals of popular religion, let us consider processions and pilgrimages. Although processions constitute one of the privileged forms of popular religiosity, it should not be forgotten that to parade images of Jesus, Mary and the saints through the streets is an activity blessed by the Church. The same is true of pilgrimages, although in this case the fact that pilgrimages are in fact journeys, contributes in certain measure to the weakening of ecclesiastical control.[21] In America as much as in Europe, the relative fluidity of pilgrimages has prompted clerical and civil authorities to attempt to exercise symbolic control by seeking to provide the ultimate interpretation and sacramental validation of these events. Since such clerical attempts are resisted by popular groups interested in creating their own interpretations, civil and religious authorities have discouraged or prohibited these exercises which, especially since the Counter-Reformation, have become relegated to the realm of popular religion.[22] What is important, then, from the point of view of the study of popular religiosity, is the tension between ecclesiastical and popular interpretations of these events, as well as what happens at the margins of the processions: the gestures, costumes and masks which imitate and parody the appearance and gestures of the priest and other official participants.

One of the liturgical events studied in detail recently is the procession of Santo Domingo, the patron saint of Managua. According to Roger Lancaster, who studied popular religious practices during the Sandinista period, the invocation to the saint, *"¡Viva Santo Domingo!" "¡Viva el doctor de los pobres!,"* can be understood both as an appropriation of the saint by the populace and as a rejection of the pretensions of elites (1988: 39). Ritually more significant than the invocations are certain performances involving the participation of grotesque characters: young men wearing costumes that give them the appearance of cows, albeit androgynous ones, who attack the faithful, using mock violence and sexuality. There are others as well, the *Toros* or *Diablos* (Bulls or Devils), and finally women known as *Gigantonas* (Ibid.: 39-43). All these characters participate in a carnivalesque game, a game that is at once a central and a marginal component of the procession. The ritual attacks carried out by the young men, the costumes, the large dimensions of the *Gigantonas* and the apparition of a black devil seem to constitute a reversal and, therefore, a rejection, if only a momentary one, of everyday reality. In effect, a world in which domestic animals attack their masters, in which women are larger than men, and in which a black devil plays a central role, is in fact a world turned upside down.

Blackness and reversal are also relevant in the case of the procession of the *Señor de los Milagros,* a massive event that takes place in Lima during the month of October. The Christ paraded through the streets is a dark Christ, *El Señor moreno,* and is in a certain sense, the Peruvian counterpart to the Mexican Virgin of Guadalupe. Since in Peru, as in the rest of Latin America, dark skin is generally an indication of low social status, it could be argued that the procession constitutes an attempt on the part of subordinate groups to achieve, if only ritually, a non-subordinate position. In fact, the trajectory of the procession and the organization of space around the image of the dark Christ (Arnold, 1985), provide an indication of the tension between high and subaltern social groups. First, there is the difference in the popular attitude when the image is carried through different parts of the city. More important symbolically, however, is the hierarchical arrangement of groups around the image—one in which spatial closeness to the Christ is inversely related to the social position of the group in Peruvian society.

Since the image of a world turned upside down is indeed a common place in revolutionary situations, we must examine whether in fact the rituals we have referred to have concrete political results, or whether they exhaust themselves in purely symbolic inversions. We must also consider the relationship between these political, or para-political activities and religious movements, such as Liberation Theology, which are explicitly concerned with political action. In his study of Nicaraguan popular religion, Lancaster maintains that despite the common political interests of the liberation theologians and the participants in rituals such as the procession of Santo Domingo, there is a fundamental difference between the methods followed by these two groups (1988: 48-51). Indeed, it seems to be the case that the need to express an attitude of resistance in a symbolic, but above all, ritual manner, could not coexist with the attempts to articulate resistance to political oppression in the discursive and openly political manner employed by the Theology of Liberation (even if, as we saw earlier, the mechanisms at work are ultimately symbolic and ritual). Therefore, it would seem that instead of distinguishing between official or elite religion and popular religion—the first favoring the right, and the second representing the left—it would be necessary to insist on what was said earlier and think rather in terms of a much more fluid situation. Rather than a clear cut opposition between popular and official, we would have the official high Church, fundamentally right-wing, represented in the Nicaraguan case by the Archbishop of Managua, Obando y Bravo, then, the clerics and laity of the left—some of them members of the Sandinista government—and finally the participants in certain ritual activities, such as the processions mentioned earlier.

The political role of the first group would seem to be clear enough: the discourses of resistance appear to be directed against them and against what they represent. But at the same time, it seems clear that the dialect used by Obando y Bravo and the one employed by the young men appearing as sexually aggressive cows, are dialects of the same language. And how does one understand the relation between the liberation theologians and the participation in rituals of resistance? As we have already argued, one cannot assume an absolute opposition between the methods employed by Liberation Theology and by popular religion, because despite the difference between rituals such as processions and pilgrimages, and the expository procedures necessary to write and study theological works and to organize and maintain ecclesial base communities, Liberation Theology is essentially a way of understanding and seeking to remedy the situation of the poor in Latin America through the rhetorical use of analogies in which one of the terms is rooted in the mythology of Christianity: the chosen people/the poor, flight from Egypt/abandonment of poverty and political oppression, and so on. There are, nevertheless, differences and frictions between those who should otherwise be allies, and this is due to the kind of signification at work. In one case there is verbal symbolism in which the verbal analogies that validate resistance are created and conserved in written form, even if they are transmitted and circulated orally; in the other, resistance is exercised orally, but above all physically, through the body, through its movements and its often grotesque transformations.

The discourses of resistance, therefore, cross and touch each other, but they do not merge. In fact, the discourses of resistance represented by the procession of Santo Domingo in Managua, the *Señor de los Milagros* in Lima, and rural ones to be discussed below, have as interlocutors the military parades and other political displays organized by the political authorities, but especially the grand liturgical functions choreographed by the official Church— for example the occasion when the pope, visiting Managua, celebrated a mass, in which he refused to pray for the victims of the contras. In this sense, it is true that popular religion and the traditional Church are adversaries, as Lancaster maintains, but, on the other hand, it must be said that these adversaries speak the same language: the language of ritual and the language of the body, even if one of the partners speaks the measured language of those in power, while the other is forced to use the language of exaggeration and the grotesque.[23] The opposition between the Theology of Liberation and the official Church is no less clear from the political point of view, but at the same time both select from a symbolic textual corpus as the situation requires, appropriate texts— for example, the Epistles of Paul against Exodus—or perhaps even opposite interpretations of the same texts.

The same tensions reappear when we examine rural examples of carnivalesque rituals of resistance. An example of such subversive, or merely pseudo-subversive, rituals can be found in the Ecuadorean Andes during the festivity of San Juan Bautista, celebrated in an *hacienda* in the province of Pichincha. Through the complex ritual transactions of the fiesta, studied by Muriel Crespi (1981), hierarchical social relations between Indians and non-Indians "are symbolically affirmed and renewed each year through alternating duplication and inversion of the traditional hierarchy" (Crespi, 1981: 495, cf. 499-500). Equally complex is the situation dramatized in the carnival of Yura, in Bolivia, studied by Rasnake (1986; 1988). Through ritual performance, the Yura attempt to come to terms with the relationship between the indigenous community, the *ayllu*, and the Bolivian state. What has to be made visible, while maintaining the fiction of the organic oneness of the Bolivian nature, is the subordinate position of the *ayllu*. Ambiguous accommodation in a hierarchical structure is similarly expressed through myth. In Yura mythology, Tyusninchis, who was both Sun and Christ, destroyed the Chullpas, beings who originally inhabited the world, and created the Jach`a Tatas. This means that the Yura, grandchildren of the grandchildren of the Jach`a Tatas, were created as Christians. Such a belief implies that the identity assumed by the Yura is indeed an Andean identity, but at the same time one that recognizes and assimilates, mythically and ritually, the tragedy of the conquest. In this case, the ambiguous character of ritual resistance reaches its climax, because now it becomes necessary to ask whether it is justified to talk of resistance when one does not know who resists whom, and when furthermore, as Rasnake acknowledges (1988: 153), the myths and rituals do not resolve the paradoxes created by social reality.[24]

In the Peruvian Andes the contradiction that cuts through the national identity is dramatized through the confrontations between groups dressed as sixteenth century Spaniards and Indians, groups that represent the confrontation that took place in 1532 in Cajamarca between Pizarro and Atahualpa's unarmed escort. These cases of ritual resistance have been studied both historically and ethnographically. Manuel Burga, for example, has documented the existence of parodic processions in the Andes in the eighteenth century. In *Pilgrims of the Andes* (1987), Michael Sallnow has studied the historical origins and the contemporary functions of a number of shrines and pilgrimages in the Cuzco region. The birth of one of these cults, that of the Lord of Qoyllur R'iti, was contemporary with the rebellion of Tupac Amaru, the great Indian rebellion against Spanish power that took place at the end of the eighteenth century. The details of the apparition of the Christ of Qoyllur R'iti are extremely valuable because we find that Christ appeared in the Sinakara mountain, halfway between those who supported and those who opposed Tupac Amaru's rebellion. In other words, the Lord of Qoyllur R'iti functioned in a manner analogous to that of the Igurramen of the Atlas, studied by Gellner (1969): namely, as an attempt to mediate disputes and to maintain peace during a particularly uncertain period for the inhabitants of the valleys in the Cuzco region. The conflicts between the Arabs and the Berbers in Gellner's study involved issues of a national and religious Islamic identity when contrasted with a local and cultural consciousness as Berber.

For our purposes, however, the origins of these forms of popular religion are less important than the contemporary functions of the sanctuaries and the pilgrimages in articulating space, time and resistance in a world that is understood as Christian. Currently in the

Andes, the sanctuaries form a net that attempts to maintain its independence from the ecclesiastical authorities; so, if it is true that at the local level the sanctuaries have a subordinate position compared to the official religious centers, regionally, the centers of pilgrimage become spatial and temporal points of reference that at once imitate and challenge the ecclesiastic geographical divisions and the liturgical calendars. Likewise the celebrations serve to mark ethnic differences. In effect, whereas the celebration of the Lord of Qoyllur R'iti is considered to be an Indian festivity in which the cross-like receptacle that serves to transport the Christ is adorned with feathers and is, therefore, associated with the *chunchos,* inhabitants of the eastern lowlands, there are other celebrations—the cult of the Christ of Wank'a, for example—that are regarded as *mestizo* celebrations (Sallnow, 1987: 226). As a dramatization of ethnic identity, therefore, the cult of the Lord of Qoyllur R'iti functions again in a manner analogous to that of the Saints of the Atlas studied by Gellner in the 1950s. In the Andes, it is the Indian identity that is being defended against the hispanizing pretensions of the urban groups in Cuzco, whereas in the mountains of Morocco it is a Berber identity, the identity also of a conquered people, that is being preserved against the pretensions of Arab urban groups.

It is precisely during pilgrimages such as the one to the sanctuary of the Lord of Qoyllur R'iti that the essential ambiguity of Andean rituals manifests itself. As in the Bolivian case discussed earlier, despite the fact that these rituals function as indicators of resistance to Christian Hispanic culture, the same rituals also represent through the use of Christian symbols, the tension between the dominating national culture and the Andean culture that attempts to defend itself. During the pilgrimage to the sanctuary of Qoyllur R'iti, we encounter also the tension between ecclesiastic attempts to manage the cult, and the pilgrims' desire for independence. The pilgrims, in effect, try to visit the sacred places before the official festival date, when the ecclesiastic authorities and the members of the official religious fraternities exercise control over the ceremonies.

The tension between ecclesiastic and Andean interpretations manifests itself also in the opposition between the cult of Wank'a, controlled by the order of the Mercedarios, and that of the Lord Just Judge, *Señor Justo Juez.* Whereas the first is a tortured and bloody Christ, common in the entire Hispanic world, the Just Judge, a Christ who would not be out of place in the pantheon of Liberation Theology, represents an iconographic and ritual challenge to the official cults (Sallnow, 1987: 262-264). The incompatibility, mentioned more than once, between popular religious practices and the ritual and iconographic puritanism of Liberation Theology can be observed clearly in the attitude of the Archbishop of Cuzco, Luis Vallejo Santoni, a sympathizer of Liberation Theology, who during the 1970s forbade the worship of two popular forms of Jesus, the Lord of Wimpillay and the *Niño Compadrito*. It is not surprising, therefore, that the archbishop's death in a car accident in 1982 was regarded by devotees of those cults as divine punishment (Sallnow, 1987: 87, cf. 215).

Is this semiotic resistance effective? Was it effective, for instance, in the Nicaragua of the Sandinistas or in the Andes? Despite the rationalization and instrumentalization of the sacred, and the reenchantment of the revolution so passionately described by Lancaster (1988: 59-60), the revolution did not survive. At the end, terrorized by the contras and impoverished in great measure as the result of the embargo organized by the United States, the people voted for the right. It would be instructive to study the transformations of popular religion and its functions as a vehicle of a leftist ideology now that the Sandinistas are out of power, and when the miracles that the free market was supposed to bring about have not materialized. However, it is difficult to believe that the rituals of popular religion, or Liberation Theology will be able to maintain reformist groups in power, no matter what degree of enchantment popular religion may provide.

In fact, if one compares the type of carnivalesque rituals so popular today among anthropologists and literary theorists, with the Corpus Christi processions and the play cycles organized by guilds that took place in English towns such as York and Chester into the sixteenth and even the seventeenth century, one finds that social negotiation of a non-symbolic nature was carried out by means of the processions and the play cycle. According to Mervyn James, the Corpus Christi play "provided a mechanism by means of which status, and the honour that went with status, could be distributed and redistributed with a minimum of conflict resulting" (James, 1983: 18). Such distribution does not seem to take place as a result of the rituals of protest romanticized by Lancaster,[25] or the symbolic forms of resistance glorified by Scott. It would seem, in effect, that the function of these discourses is essentially reactive, of defense, or resistance—

as Marx wrote in that famous phrase about religion as the expression of real misery, of which only the second part, about opium, is generally cited.[26] The same is true of Liberation Theology: in a way that seems to validate Mannheim's theories about the spiritualization of utopia (Mannheim, 1929/1936: 237), gagged or tamed, theologians such as Gutiérrez have abandoned references to the economy and have sought refuge in spirituality.

IV

We will explore briefly the similarities and differences between the conceptions of signification that underlie the ritual approaches employed by popular religion, and the verbal— one is tempted to say "Protestant"—procedures used by the Theology of Liberation. Merely as a hypothesis, it could be said that in the ideological spaces created by the disappearance of the old agrarian order dominated by the *haciendas,* the mode of signification represented by ritual dialects and official liturgies, has been replaced by a type of signification in which arbitrary connections replace apparently natural ones. In other words, whereas ritual activity rests on the assumption—not necessarily explicit or verbalized—that there is a non-arbitrary connection between rites and the very structure of reality, the market economy, whose point of reference and common denominator is money, destroys the assumption of a necessary connection between signifier and signified and allows, or forces, one to regard all elements of reality as essentially interchangeable. As a consequence, the social order, which in the case of Andean and Mesoamerican cultures was based upon analogies of the macrocosm-microcosm type, and in the case of Catholicism was based likewise on symbolic connections that make possible a sacramental activity *ex opere operato,* is replaced by a vision of the world based on arbitrariness and contingency. This arbitrariness renders sacramental activity impossible and hence causes one to perceive communal rituals as useless and wasteful. The rejection of the old ritual order is therefore a rejection of its two main dialects: the official liturgical one and the popular, a situation that may lead to conversion to the evangelical churches.

In this sense there is a strong affinity between the Theology of Liberation, which could be considered as a Protestant Catholicism, centered upon the Word, and the evangelical Churches. In both cases, we find an austere and puritan faith centered upon the Word, a Word that is accessible to believers in their own language. It is, therefore, not surprising that the emergence of the Theology of Liberation in the late sixties was contemporary with the beginnings of a significant number of conversions to Protestantism in Latin America (Martin, 1990: 49-50). It is as if both movements away from a sacramental vision of the world had to develop at the same time, both as a result of movements of agrarian reform, such as the Peruvian and Ecuadorean ones (Muratorio, 1980: 45; 1981: 515), and increased presence of the market economy in the rural areas, but also as a response to those developments. Indeed, it is as if the *Entzauberung,* the "disenchantment" of the world, to use Weber"s unavoidable term, had to give way to two religiously ambiguous, half-enchanted formations. In both cases, the Protestant and the Catholic, there is still the attempt to preserve, if only through the Word, the presence of the transcendent, while at the same time de-ritualizing everyday activities.

The causes and consequences of this de-ritualization have been explained in terms of a rationalization of economic activities, involving, for instance, the rejection of the burden represented by ritual expenditures.[27] We cannot go into the details of these debates, although it should be pointed out that the current rationalization of everyday life, conducive to economic growth, parallels the developments that have taken place in Europe since the early modern period. Taking a broad historical perspective, one could say that the confrontation between the traditional Catholic popular religion, and the new Protestant kind, can be approached in terms of the different attitudes towards the material world and to its modification through work. One finds, in fact, the tension between a religion involved in the management of an agrarian world (concerned with matters of life and death, fertility and disease) and a religion, appropriate for a world undergoing industrialization and open to market relations. The latter is one that, claiming to be concerned with spiritual issues, leaves the material world to be administered in a more rational manner.[28]

The situation of converts to Protestantism is highly ambiguous: as ambiguous, in fact, as that of the groups that engage in traditional ritual resistance. As an example of this situation, we may consider the results of research undertaken by Blanca Muratorio among the Quichua of Chimborazo, Ecuador. Muratorio maintains that the Quichua[29] converted to a politically conservative Protestantism, which created the docile and efficient workers required by capitalism;

moreover, this is a Protestantism that postulated an equality which would only be realized in the afterlife. On the positive side, the new ideology, according to Muratorio, helps the Quichua to maintain their ethnic identity. This is accomplished through the "family service," *culto familiar,* a ritual, which unlike the rituals of official Catholicism, is ruled by reciprocity. The culto involves the extended family and take place once a week. It consists of singing, praying and studying the Bible.[30] Identity and a sense of inclusiveness are also achieved through the much larger *conferencias,* which may involve from 200 to 3,000 Quichuas. The largest *conferencias* contribute to the creation of an ethnico-religious identity by being scheduled, oppositionally one might say, at the same time as Corpus Christi, Christmas and Holy Week (Muratorio, 1981: 527; cf. Santana, 1987: 105). Yet, as Muratorio observes, "this conference only removes the peasant from social situations where they are exploited as peasants and as Indians, and by clouding class solidarity into a religious experience, it conceals the oppressive nature of the larger system of social relations" (Ibid.: 528).

This pessimistic assessment of the situation of Protestant Quichua is not shared by all researchers; thus, in an article published several years after Muratorio's studies, Roberto Santana (1987) presents a much more positive view of the economic and social of the Quichua in the region of San Antonio de Colta, although even in this case, the intra-Quichua process of stratification, necessary as a result of the market economy, could be considered as negative.

As we can see from the previous examples, conversion is related in complex ways to the problem of popular religion. To be sure, in the twentieth century, conversion is no longer that of indigenous groups to an imperial Catholicism, but both of rural and urban groups to a Protestantism that is not infrequently identified with another imperial power, the United States. Conversion to various forms of Protestantism is one of the ways in which ideological resistance can be exercised, and it may indeed be the case that this form of ideological switching is more efficacious than the purely symbolic practices—processions, carnival, etc.— referred to above.

What remains constant, however, is the ambiguity of the situation. For, if converts come primarily from subordinate groups—from the *clases populares, del pueblo,* to use the Spanish expressions—it would follow that their religion, is popular. To be sure, since most Protestant groups reject the pageantry found in most forms of Catholicism, the term 'popular' does not refer in this case to the ritual activity generally studied by anthropologists, and is no longer to be identified with 'folk' religion. Nevertheless, insofar as official forms of religion, perceived now as obsolete, are abandoned by non-elite groups, one is forced to confront again the fact that if the term is to be employed in a non-reified manner, 'popular religion' applies to some extent to forms of evangelical Christianity.

If one considers the rituals of legitimation employed by the state, it can be said that insofar as there remains a connection between most Latin American states and the legitimizing functions of Catholicism, conversion to Protestantism has to appear, to some extent at least, as a symbolic challenge. Concretely, this means that as long as, for example, the independence day of a Latin American country involves a military parade, and a *Te Deum* at the national cathedral, rather than an ecumenical ceremony, or some form of ritual activity in one of the new Protestant temples, Catholicism is still the official ritual system. Although the Catholic Church may have lost its constitutionally guaranteed situation of privilege, as long as legitimization is exercised through Catholic rituals, the official status remains in place. Conversion, therefore, involves creating and securing personal and social spaces in a manner parallel to the spaces created by the rituals we have discussed earlier. This time, however, the protagonists are less concerned with the ritual management of the material and the social world, or with the ritual unmaking of a world perceived as alien or oppressive. Now the concern is to create the spaces in which the relationship between the believer and the divine can be established and maintained. That space need not—indeed, could not—be purely personal, involving rather a community of like-minded believers within which the convert can find support probably similar to that sought by converts to early Christianity and to the most radical among the original Protestant churches. What seems to have emerged with the wave of conversions to Protestant churches is the desire to create a new identity that may replace the old and apparently bankrupt one. Like the *populus,* the popular urban classes provided the majority of Christian converts, creating an ecumene parallel to the Roman one. Networks of new Evangelicals may provide an alternative to the still hierarchical Catholic view.[31]

The resulting religion is one that is spiritual: a modern religion that leaves the world open for less ritual and more instrumental forms of management. This does not mean to say that ritual activity is not instrumental;[32] it means that whereas the instrumentality of ritual tends to encompass in principle all of reality, seeking to relate, for example, human, animal and cosmic fertility, modern instrumentality is less universalizing, focusing on achieving specific results. The apparently paradoxical result of this development is that modern Christianity, having extricated religion from materiality, has created not only a religion that is almost purely spiritual and centered upon experience, but has at the same time, helped to constitute a material world to be administered in a purely rational manner. The new Christians, then, can seek on the one hand the self-validating certainty of a religious experience, while at the same time being free to approach the world as economic entrepreneurs. Economic and spiritual entrepreneurship, combined with puritanical morality, move the converts away from the frequently onerous and morally suspect rituals identified with folk religion, but also from the hegemonic culture—that common language, one of whose dialects is popular culture.

As we saw above, one could maintain that, to the extent that Protestantism does not have an official status, its position is, by definition, popular. Indeed, David Martin regards Pentecostals "the under-proletariat from the country,"[33] as the first popular manifestation of Protestantism (Martin, 1990: 53). It may, nevertheless, be possible to identify more specific points of contact between the old Catholic popular religion and its modern Protestant counterpart. The most important one has to do with communal activity, particularly with the way in which people behave, verbally and bodily, in their ritual gatherings. Despite the parsimonious character of Protestant ritual activity, insofar as people regularly gather in specific places at regular times in order to engage in predetermined non-instrumental activities, it can be said that rituals do take place. What certain Protestant, especially Pentecostal, gatherings have in common with folk Catholicism is the absence of the restraint, the gravitas, that generally characterizes the gatherings of those who exercise power. Even though the lack of restraint is itself ritualized, so that, for example, speaking in tongues takes place at expected times, what is ritualized appears to involve the rejection of the dominant ideology, and the establishment of links with realities whose very existence questions the social order. Thus, to speak in tongues, to transgress sexual norms, or to participate in the inebriation that characterizes certain Andean rituals—ritualized and domesticated as these activities might be—constitutes a symbolic clash with the measured liturgies of the official world.

It would take us too far afield to consider the parallels between some elements of popular religion, including Protestant ones, and the possession cults studied by I.M. Lewis in *Ecstatic Religion* (1989). It will suffice to point out that in both cases we are dealing with oppressed groups, some of which have emerged as a result of social dislocations, brought about by proletarianization (Martin, 1990: 82). Members of these marginal groups articulate their protest by seeking to establish contact with supernatural realities, using what may be the only thing left to them, their language and their bodies. Thus, despite differences between the cults studied by Lewis and the Pentecostals who have consciously distanced themselves in Latin America from the rituals of popular Catholicism, the popular element resurfaces as contestation, one which is exercised through bodily practices. But lest we engage in the romanticization of popular religiosity, we should also emphasize that these movements are successful insofar as their members manage to recreate social networks.

At the conclusion of our inquiry we find, then, that 'popular religiosity' involves realities that are as elusive as they are omnipresent. Ultimately, these have to do with the sometimes purely symbolic confrontations among groups whose position in a hierarchical order is not taken for granted by their members. We can, therefore, assume that as long as hierarchical arrangements remain in place, and as long as people continue to think and act in ways that involve supernatural agents and transcendental sources of legitimation, it is not only official religion that will be found at work, but also popular religiosity.

Endnotes

1. On religion as a system of difference and power, see Benavides 1989a.

2. On the connection between religion, ritual and labor, see Benavides 1993b.

3. On symbolic resistance see the works of James Scott listed in the bibliography. It is not possible to discuss here the romanticization of symbolic resistance found in Scott's work; this idealization is most apparent in Scott, 1990.

4. The relational aspect is emphasized in Rei, 1974, 277-278; Boglioni, 1979, 31; Rousseau, 1979; Bouritius, 1979, 156; Isambert, 1982, 73-74; Dinzelbacher, 1987, 4, 6.

5. On "subaltern religion," and in general on the relationship between religion and class, see Rei, 1974: 275; Rousseau, 1979: 359; Ginzburg, 1979, 399 (and the exchange between Ginzburg and Gabriele De Rosa in *La religion populaire,* 1979: 401-402); Prandi, 1980: 36; Bolgiani, 1981: 33-34; Isambert, 1982: 71; Prat, 1983a: 53.

6. The subordinate position of the religiously *illiteratus* is emphasized by Le Goff; see 1967/1977: 226, and *La religion populaire,* 1979: 403.

7. On "survivals" see Schmitt, 1976: 946; Bolgiani, 1981: 18fff. On *Kontinuitäten* and *Überresten,* see Dinzelbacher, 1990: 20. For a discussion of these issues in the context of economic change, see Muratorio, 1980: 39-40.

8. The oppositional aspect is emphasized in Ginzburg, 1979, and in Le Goff's intervention to the *La religion populaire,* 1979, Table ronde, 402-404 (see also Schmitt's and Ginzburg's interventions on p. 410).

9. On this process of exclusion see Rei, 1974: 265-266, and especially Jaritz, 1987: 22.

10. Although it deals with developments in nineteenth century France, and remains at the purely discursive level, the discussion found in Terdiman, 1985, esp. ch. 1, is relevant in this context.

11. See Bakhtin 1965/1984 and Gurjewitsch 1972/1978, esp. "Beilage: Probleme der Volkskultur und der Religiosität im Mittelalter," 352- 400. See also Boglioni, 1979: 18-24; Prandi, 1980: 37. On the situation in the eighteenth century see Frijhoff, 1979: 78.

12. See Frijhoff, 1979: 80, 83ff; Bouritius, 1979: 128ff.; van Dülmen, 1987: 24ff. (on the separation of religion and work see 25); Dipper, 1987: 82.

13. On popular religion as a field of studies see especially Isambert, 1982, ch. 2, "Constitution d'un objet d'études." On the non-existence of 'Volksreligiosität' before the late Enlightenment, see Dipper, 1987: 75. See also Vrijhof, 1979b: 227; Prandi, 1980: 37; Bolgiani, 1981: 13-18; Prat 1983a: 50.

14. For a discussion of the concept of syncretism in a Latin America, as well as a bibliography, see Benavides, "Syncretism and Legitimacy in Latin American Christianity," in Anthony Stevens-Arroyo and Andrés Pérez y Mena, eds. *Enigmatic Powers.* Bildner Center Books, NY 1994.

15. On conversion to Protestantism see the recent surveys by Martin, 1990, and Stoll, 1990, both of which include substantial bibliographies.

16. See, for example, Dinzelbacher, 1987: 6; or the *Hurenumzug,* referred to in Scribner, 1984b: 18. On the role of Christianity in the management of the physical world see Bolgiani, 1981, 46: 55; Christian, 1981a; Scribner, 1984a; van DÅlmen, 1987: 20-21; Devlin, 1987. It is impossible to refer here to religions other than Christianity; for some references to agricultural rituals in Southeast Asia, see Benavides, 1993b.

17. On the parallels between the emergence of the modern state in the early fourteenth century and demonology, see Schmitt, 1990: 39; for eighteenth century developments, see Dipper, 1987.

18. See Bolgiani, 1981: 29, and Manselli's intervention to the Table ronde, *La religion populaire,* 1979: 400.

19. A Christian parallel would be the Waldensians; see Schmitt, 1976: 949. See also Martin, 1990: 290.

20. See Levine, 1990: 739. On ritual as an extreme form of control see Bloch, 1974.

21. See Levine, 1990: 739. On ritual as an extreme form of control see Bloch, 1974.

22. On the control and prohibition of processions and pilgrimages during the eighteenth century, as part of the rationalization of religion and the creation of a new work ethos, see Dipper, 1986: 84-87; on priestly complaints and attempts at suppression see Devlin, 1987: 51-53.

23. The opposition between official and popular liturgies is explored in Gash, 1986.

24. For an equally complex and ambivalent ritual attempt to deal with "a tense and divided world," see Salomon, 1981.

25. Advocates of Bakhtinian excesss are not always consistent; Lancaster quotes, apparently with sympathy, an informant who complains about the sexual components of religious festivities: "The holy days, like Santo Domingo and Holy Week, had become perverted

an corrupt. They were little more than bacchanalia of public drunkeness, open prostitution and delinquency. The prostitutes used to set up little portable houses along the side of the road, and the celebrants would stop in and visit them along the route" (1988: 74-75). This description would apply in fact to many religious activities in pre-Reformation Europe.

26. See Marx's "Kritik der Hegelschen Rechtsphilosophie," p. 488 (italics in the original): "Das *religiöse* Elend ist in einem der *Ausdruck* des wirklichen Elendes und in einem die *Protestation* gegen das wirkliche Elend. Die Religion ist der Seufzer der bedrängten Kreatur, das Gemüt einer herzlosen Welt, wie sie der Geist geistloser Zustände ist. Sie ist das Opium des Volks."

27. See Wolf, 1966: 15-16; Lewellen, 1979: 247; Muratorio, 1980: 54-55; Greenberg, 1981: 148-159; Annis, 1987: 66, 73, 80, 167-168; Brandes, 1988, ch. 3; Lancaster, 1988: 102.

28. For an insightful discussion of conversion to Adventism among Peruvian Aymara, see Levellen, 1979.

29. Quichua is the term used in Ecuador; Quechua is the form used in Peru.

30. See Muratorio, 1981: 523-524; cf. id. 1980: 53-54. See also Santana, 1987: 105.

31. For early Christian parallels see Mann, 1986: ch. 10. That whole discussion should be compared with Martin, 1990: ch. 10, esp. 202-204.

32. Benavides, 1993b.

33. Martin, 1990: 79, quoting Christian Lalive d'Epinay, "Régimes politiques et millénarisme dans une société dépendante," *Acts of the 15th Conference of the CISR,* Venice, 1979.

Bibliography

Abercrombie, N., S. Hill, B. S. Turner, eds. 1980. *The Dominant Ideology Thesis.* London.

Aers, David, ed. 1986. *Medieval Literature. Criticism, Ideology & History.* New York.

Annis, Sheldon. 1987. *God and Production in a Guatemalan Town.* Austin.

Appadurai, Arjun, ed. 1986. *The Social Life of Things. Commodities in Cultural Perspective.* Cambridge.

Arnold, Pierre, 1985. "Pèlerinages et processions comme formes de pouvoir symbolique des classes subalternes: deux cas péruviens." *Social Compass* 32: 45-56.

Badone, Ellen. 1990. "Introduction," in Badone, ed. 1990: 3-23.

―――, ed. 1990. Religious Orthodoxy and Popular Faith in European Society. Princeton.

Bakhtin, Mikhail. 1965/1984. *Rabelais and his World.* Bloomington, 1984; originally published in Moscow, 1965.

Bauer, Dieter R. 1990. "Heiligkeit des Landes: ein Beispiel für die Prägekraft der Volksreligiosität," in Dinzelbacher and Bauer, eds. 1990: 41-55.

Belmont, Nicole. 1979. "Superstition et religion populaire dans les sociétés occidentales," in Izard and Smith, eds. 1979: 53-70.

Benavides, Gustavo. 1987. "Religion and Politics in Latin America," in Fu and Spiegler, eds. 1987: 107-142.

―――. 1989a. "Religious Articulations of Power," in Benavides and Daly, eds. 1989. 1-12: 197-202.

―――. 1989b. "Millennial Politics in Contemporary Peru," in Benavides and Daly, eds. 1989: 173-196, 219-232.

―――. 1991. "¿Sincretismo religioso o resistencia política en los Andes?" *Humanitas* 20, 5-19.

―――. 1992a. "The Invention of Magic." *Excursus* 5: 10-15.

―――. 1992b. "Spatial Hierarchies and Sacred Order." Paper Presented at the Annual Meeting of the Society for the Scientific Study of Religion, Washington, D.C., 17 November 1992.

―――. 1993a. "A Critique of Purely Discursive Approaches to Religion." Paper presented at the annual meeting of the Society for the Scientific Study of Religion, Raleigh, 29 October 1993.

―――. 1993b. "The Materiality of Ritual." Paper presented at the annual meeting of the American Academy of Religion, Washington, D.C., 21 November 1993.

Benavides, G. and M. W. Daly, eds. 1989. *Religion and Political Power.* Albany.

Bianchi, Ugo. 1981. "Religiosità popolare cristiana e pagana." *Augustinianum* 21: 77-90.

Bloch, Maurice. 1974. "Symbols, Song, Dance, and Features of Articulation. Is religion an extreme form of traditional authority?" *Archives européennes de sociologie* 15: 55-81.

Bock, E. Wilbur. 1965. "Symbols in Conflict: Official versus Folk Religion." *Journal for the Scientific Study of Religion* 5: 204-212.

Boglioni, Pierre. 1979. "La culture populaire au moyen âge: thèmes et problèmes," in Boglioni, ed. 1979: 11-37.

⎯⎯⎯., ed. 1979. *La culture populaire au moyen âge*. Québec.

Bolgiani, Franco. 1981. "Religione popolare." *Augustinianum* 21: 7-75.

Bossy, John. 1987. *Christianity in the West 1400-1700*. Oxford-New York.

Bouritius, G.J.F. 1979. "Popular and Official Religion in Christianity: Three Cases in 19th Century Europe," in Vrijhof and Waardenburg, eds. 1979, 117-165.

Brandes, Stanley. 1988. *Power and Persuasion. Fiestas and Social Control in Mexico*. Philadelphia.

⎯⎯⎯. 1990. "Conclusion: Reflections on the Study of Religious Orthodoxy and Popular Faith in European Society," in Badone, ed. 1990, 185-200.

Broek, R. van den. 1979. "Popular Religious Practices and Ecclesiastical Policies in the early Church," in Vrijhof and Waardenburg, eds. 1979, 11-54.

Christian, Jr., William A. 1972/1989. *Person and God in a Spanish Valley*. Princeton [new revised edition].

⎯⎯⎯. 1981a. *Local Religion in Sixteenth-Century Spain*. Princeton.

⎯⎯⎯. 1981b. *Apparitions in Late Medieval and Renaissance Spain*. Princeton.

Clawson, David L. 1984. "Religious Allegiance and Economic Development in Rural Latin America." *Journal of Interamerican Studies and World Affairs* 26: 499-524.

Connerton, Paul. 1989. *How societies remember*. Cambridge.

Davis, Natalie Zemon. 1974. "Some tasks and Themes in the Study of Popular Religion," in Trinkaus and Oberman, ed. 1974, 307-336.

Deiros, Pablo A. 1991. "Protestant Fundamentalism in Latin America," in Marty and Appleby, eds. 1991, 142-196.

Devlin, Judith. 1987. *The Superstitious Mind. French Peasants and the Supernatural in the Nineteenth Century*. New Haven.

Dinzelbacher, Peter. 1987. "Volkskultur und Hochkultur im Spätmittelalter," in Dinzelbacher and Mück, eds. 1987, 1-14.

---. 1990. "Zur Erforschung der Geschichte der Volksreligion. Einführung und Bibliographie," in Dinzelbacher and Bauer, eds. 1990, 9-27.

Dinzelbacher, P. and Hans-Dieter Mück, eds. 1987. *Volkskultur des europäischen Spätmittelalters* [*Böblinger Forum* 1], Stuttgart.

Dinzelbacher, P. and Dieter R. Bauer, eds. 1990. "Volksreligion im hohen und späten Mittelalte" *Quellen und Forschungen aus dem Gebiet der Geschichte,* N.F. Heft 13. Paderborn-München-Wien-Zürich.

Dipper, Christof. 1986. "Volksreligiosität und Obrigkeit im 18. Jahrhundert," in Schieder, ed. 1986, 73-96.

Dülmen, Richard van. 1986. "Volksfrömmigkeit und konfessionelles Christentum im 16. und 17. Jahrhundert," in Schieder, ed. 1986, 14-30.

Dupront, Alphonse. 1979. "De la religion populaire." *La religion populaire,* 411-419.

Flint, Valerie I.J. 1991. *The Rise of Magic in Early Medieval Europe.* Princeton.

Foster, Robert and Orest Ranum, eds. 1982. *Ritual, Religion, and the Sacred.* Baltimore.

Freeman, Susan Tax. 1978. "Faith and Passion in Spanish Religion: Notes on the Observation of Observance." *Peasant Studies* 7, 101-123.

Frijhoff, W.Th.M. 1979. "Official and Popular Religion in Christianity. The Late Middle-Ages and and early Modern Times (13th-18th Centuries)," in Vrijhof and Waardenburg, eds., 1979, 71-116.

Fu, Charles Wei-hsun and Gerhard F. Spiegler, eds. 1987. *Movements and Issues in World Religions. A Sourcebook and Analysis of Developments since 1945.* New York-Westport-London.

Fuller, C.J. 1992. *The Camphor Flame. Popular Hinduism and Society in India.* Princeton.

Gash, Anthony. 1986. "Carnival against Lent: the Ambivalence of Medieval Drama," in Aers, ed., 74-98.

Geary, Patrick J. 1979. "La coercition des saints dans la pratique religieuse médiévale," in Boglioni, ed., 145-161.

---. 1986. "Sacred Commodities: the Circulation of Medieval Relics," in *Appadurai,* ed., 169-191.

---. 1978/1990. *Furta Sacra. Thefts of Relics in the Central Middle Ages.* Princeton.

Gellner, Ernest. 1969. *Saints of the Atlas.* Chicago.
Ginzburg, Carlo. 1979. "Existe-t-il une autonomie du populaire en face des représentations et manifestations de la religion officielle?" in *La religion populaire.* 398-399.
Greenberg, James B. 1981. *Santiago's Sword. Chatino Peasant and Economics.* Berkeley.
Greyerz, Kaspar von. 1984. "Introduction," in Greyerz, ed., 1-14.
_____., ed. 1984. *Religion and Society in Early Modern Europe 1500-1800.* London.
Gurjewitsch, Aaron, J. 1972/1982. *Das Weltbild des mittelalterlichen Menschen.* München, 1982; originally published in Moscow, 1972.
Hefner, Robert W. 1993. "World Building and the Rationality of Conversion," in Hefner, ed. 1993, 3-44.
_____., ed. 1993. *Conversion to Christianity. Historical and Anthropological Perspectives on a Great Transformation.* Berkeley.
Hill, Jonathan D., ed. 1988. *Rethinking History and Myth.* Indigenous South American perspectives on the Past. Urbana,
Huisman, A.J. 1979. "Christianity and Germanic Religion," in Vrijhof and Waardenburg, eds., 55-70.
Isambert, François-André. 1982. *Le sens du sacré. Fête et religion populaire.* Paris.
Izard, Michel and Pierre Smith, eds. 1979. *La fonction symbolique.* Paris.
James, Mervyn. 1983. "Ritual, Drama and Social Body in the Late Medieval English Town." *Past and Present* 98: 3-29.
Jaritz, Gerhard. 1987. "Gemeinsamkeit und Widerspruch: Spätmittelalterliche Volkskultur aus der Sicht von Eliten," in Dinzelbacher and Mück, eds. 1987: 15-33.
Jarvis, Peter. 1980. "Towards a Sociological Understanding of Superstition." *Social Compass* 27: 285-295.
Kanagy, Conrad L. 1990. "The Formation and Development of a Protestant Conversion Movement among the Highland Quichua of Ecuador." *Sociological Analysis* 50: 205-217.
Kertzer, David I. 1988. *Ritual, Politics, and Power.* New Haven.
Kieckhefer, Richard. 1989. *Magic in the Middle Ages.* Cambridge.
Kselman, Thomas A. 1986. "Ambivalence and Assumption in the Concept of Popular Religion," in Levine, ed. 1986: 24-41.
Kudó, Tokihiro. 1980. *Práctica religiosa y proyecto histórico II, estudio sobre la religiosidad popular en dos barrios de Lima.* Lima.

La religion populaire. 1979. Paris [Table ronde, 395-408: interventions by Yves-Marie Hilaire, Serge Bonnet, Carlo Ginzburg, Fernand Dumont, Raould Manselli, Gabriele De Rosa, Vicent Josep Sastre García, Jacques Le Goff, Émile Poulat, André Vauchez, Pierre Chaunu; Discussions, 409-410].

Lancaster, Roger N. 1988. *Thanks to God and the Revolution. Popular Religion and Class Consciousness in the New Nicaragua.* New York.

Le Bot, Yvon. 1987. "Cent ans de protestantisme au Guatemala (1882-1982)." *Problèmes d'Amérique Latine* 86,4, 109-119.

Le Goff, Jacques. 1967. "Culture cléricale et traditions folkloriques dans la civilisation mérovingienne." *Annales E.S.C.* 780-791, reprinted in Le Goff, 1977, 223-235.

_____. 1977. *Pour un autre Moyen Age. Temps, travail et culture en Occident: 18 essais.* Paris.

Levine, Daniel H. 1990. "Popular Groups, Popular Culture, and Popular Religion" *Comparative Studies in Society and History* 32, 718-764.

_____., ed. 1986. *Religion and Political Conflict in Latin America.* Chapel Hill.

Lewellen, Ted C. 1979. "Deviant Religion and Cultural Evolution: the Aymara case." *Journal for the Scientific Study of Religion* 1979, 243-251.

Lewis, I.M. 1966. "Spirit Possession and Deprivation Cults." Man n.s. 1, 307-329, repr. in Lewis, 1986, ch. 2.

_____. 1986. *Religion in Context. Cults and Charisma.* Cambridge.

_____. 1989. *Ecstatic Religion. A Study of Shamanism and Spirit Possession.* 2nd. ed. London-New York.

Mann, Michael. 1986. *The Sources of Social Power,* vol 1. Cambridge.

Mannheim, Karl. 1936. *Ideology and Utopia.* New York; parts II-IV were originally published as *Idéologie und Utopie,* Bonn, 1929.

Martin, David. 1990. *Tongues of Fire. The Explosion of Protestantism in Latin America.* Oxford.

Marty, Martin E. and R. Scott Appleby, eds. 1991. *Fundamentalisms Observed* [The Fundamentalism Project 1], Chicago.

Marx, Karl. 1843/1844. "Zur Kritik der Hegelshen Rechtsphilosophie," reprinted in Karl Marx, Frühe Schriften, ed. by Hans-Joachim Lieber and Peter Furth, Darmstadt, 1962, I, 488.

Muratorio, Blanca. 1980. "Protestantism and Capitalism Revisited, in the Rural Highlands of Ecuador." *Journal of Peasant Studies* 8, 37-60.

———. 1981. "Protestantism, Ethnicity, and Class in Chimborazo," in Whitten, ed. 1981: 506-534.

O'Connor, Mary. 1979. "Two Kinds of Religious Movements Among the Mayo Indians of Sonora, Mexico." *Journal for the Scientific Study of Religion* 18: 260-268.

Pace, Enzo. 1987. "New Paradigms of Popular Religion." *Archives de Sciences Sociales des Religions* 64: 7-14.

Poole, Deborah A. 1981. "Social Hierarchy and Sacred Power in the Hindu and Andean Pilgrimage Tradition." *Journal of the Steward Anthropological Society* 13: 8-43.

Poulin, Joseph-Claude. 1979. "Entre magie et religion. Recherches sur les utilisations marginales de l'écrit dans la culture populaire du haut moyen âge," in Boglioni, ed. 1979, 121-143.

Prandi, Carlo. 1980. "La religion populaire: problèmes théoriques." *Annual Review of the Social Sciences of Religion* 4: 31-60.

Prat i Carós, Joan. 1983a. "'Religió popular' o experiència religiosa ordinária?: estat de la qüestió i hipótesis de treball." *Arxiu d'Etnografia de Catalunya* 2: 49-69.

———. 1983b. "L'experiéncia religiosa ordinária." *Arxiu d'Etnografia de Catalunya* 2: 45-170.

Rabenoro, Aubert. 1976. "Protestantisme et mobilité sociale au Chili," in *L'autre et l'ailleurs. Hommages à Roger Bastide*. Paris, 306-

Rasnake, Roger. 1986. "Carnaval in Yura: Ritual Reflections on Ayllu and State Relations." *American Ethnologist* 13, 1986: 662-680.

———. 1988. "Images of Resistance to Colonial Domination," in Hill, ed. 1988, 136-156.

Rei, Dario. 1974. "Note sul concetto di 'religione popolare.'" *Lares*. 265-280.

Riegelhaupt, Joyce Firstenberg. 1982. "O significado religioso do anticlericalismo popular." *Análise Social* 18: 1213-1230.

Rousseau, André. 1979. "Sur la 'religion populaire': une perspective sociologique." *La religion populaire*. 355-360.

Salomon, Frank. 1981. "Killing the Yumbo: a Ritual Drama of Northern Quito," in Whitten, ed. 1981: 162-208.

Sallnow, Michael J. 1987. *Pilgrims of the Andes. Regional Cults in Cusco*. Washington, D.C.-London.

Santana, Roberto. 1987. "Le Protestantisme chez les indiens du Chimborazo en êquateur." *Problèmes d'Amérique latine* 86, 4: 97-108.

Schieder, Wolfgang, ed. 1986. Volksreligiosität in der Modernen Sozialgeschichte [Geschichte und Gesellschaft, Sonderheft 11]. Gîttingen, 1986.

_____. 1986. "Einleitung," in Schieder, ed. 1986, 7-13.

Schmitt, Jean-Claude. 1976. "'Religion populaire' et culture folklorique." *Annales* 31, 941-953.

_____. 1990. "Der Mediävist und die Volkskultur," in Dinzelbacher and Bauer, eds. 1990, 29-40.

Schneider, Jane. 1990. "Spirits and the Spirit of Capitalism," in Badone, ed. 1990, 24-54.

Schreiner, Klaus. 1990. "Volkstümliche Bibelmagie und Volkssprachliche Bibellektüre. Theologische und soziale Probleme Mittelalterlicher Laienfrömmigkeit," in Dinzelbacher and Bauer, eds. 1990, 329-373.

Scott, James C. 1976. *The Moral Economy of the Peasant. Rebellion and Subsistence in Southeast Asia.* New Haven.

_____. 1977a. "Protest and Profanation: Agrarian Revolt and the Little Tradition." *Theory and Society* 4: 1-38, 211-246.

_____. 1977b. "Hegemony and the Peasantry." *Politics and Society* 7: 267-296.

_____.1979. "Revolution in the Revolution: Peasants and Commissars." *Theory and Society* 7: 97-134.

_____. 1985. *Weapons of the Weak. Everyday Forms of Peasant Resistance.* New Haven.

_____. 1990. *Domination and the Arts of Reistance: Hidden Transcripts.* New Haven.

Scribner, R.W. 1984a. "Ritual and Popular Religion in Catholic Germany at the time of the Reformation." *Journal of Ecclesiatical History* 35: 47-77.

_____. 1984b."Cosmic Order and Daily Life: Sacred and Secular in Pre-industrial German Society," in Greyerz, ed., 17-32.

_____. 1990. "Magie und Aberglaube. Zur Volkstümlichen Sakramentalischen Denkart in Deutschland am Ausgang des Mittelalters," in Dinzelbacher and Bauer, eds. 1990, 253-274.

Skar, Harald O. 1985. "Communitas and Schimogenesis: The Andean Pilgrimage reconsidered." *Ethnos* 50: 88-102.

Stoll, David. 1990. *Is Latin America turning Protestant? The Politics of Evangelical Growth.* Berkeley.

Taylor, William B. 1987. "The Virgin of Guadalupe in New Spain: An Inquiry into the Social History of Marian Devotion." *American Ethnologist* 14: 9-33.

Terdiman, Richard. 1985. *Discourse/Counter-Discourse. The Theory and Practice of Symbolic Resistance in Nineteenth-Century France.* Ithaca.

Trexler, Richard C. 1984. "Reverence and Profanity in the Study of Early Modern Religion," in Greyerz, ed. 1984, 245-269.

Trinkaus, Charles and Heiko A. Oberman, eds. 1974. *The Pursuit of Holiness in Late Mediaeval and Renaissance Religion* [Studies in Mediaeval and Renaissance Thought 10]. Leiden.

Turner, Paul R. 1979. "Religious Conversion and Community Development." *Journal for the Scientific Study of Religion* 18: 252-260.

Turner, Victor. 1973. "The Center Out There: Pilgrim's Goal." *History of Religions* 12: 191-230.

Turner, Victor and Edith Turner. 1978. *Image and Pilgrimage in Christian Culture. Anthropological Perspectives.* New York.

Voye, Liliane. 1979. "Religion populaire et culture régionale," *La religion populaire* 361-367.

Vrijhof, Pieter Hendrik. 1979a. "Introduction"; "Conclussion," in Vrijhof and Waardenburg, eds. 1979, 1-7, 668-699.

Vrijhof, P.H. 1979b. "Official and Popular Christianity in 20th Century Western Christianity," in Vrijhof and Waardenburg, eds., 217-243.

Vrijhof, P.H. and Jacques Waardenburg, eds. 1979. *Official and Popular Religion* [Religion and Society 19]. The Hague-Paris-New York.

Waardenburg, J.D.J. 1979. "Summaries of the contributions"; "Suggestions for Further Research," in Vrijhof and Waardenburg, eds., 631-667, 700-704.

Ward, Benedicta. 1987. *Miracles and the Medieval Mind. Theory, Record and Event 1000-1215.* Philadelphia.

Whitten, Jr., Norman E., ed. 1981. *Cultural Transformations and Ethnicity in Modern Ecuador.* Urbana.

Wolf, Eric R. 1966. *Peasants.* Englewood Cliffs.

Towards an Understanding of Synthesis in Iberian Hispanic American Popular Religiosity

3

JAIME R. VIDAL

The conquest and colonization of the central and southern portions of the Western Hemisphere has received very divergent moral and historical evaluations. Throughout the last five centuries, legends, both black and white, as well as more detached and nuanced positions have been used as interpretations. What is unquestionable is that a new civilization developed in these territories; a civilization transplanted from Spain into a different environment, grafted onto the civilizations of the various native peoples, influenced in many cases by the influx of African slaves, and affected in its development by the often divergent histories of the American viceroyalties and republics. Like any plant that is thus transplanted and grafted into such diverse environments, the civilization that started with the conquest evolved in different directions and produced a number of national and regional cultures which differ notably both from Spain and from each other. And yet, five hundred years later, the descendants of Aztecs, Incas and Taínos, of African slaves and Spanish conquistadors or farmers, still have in common certain crucial characteristics: a common language and common attitudes to life and death, to honor, love and work which—especially when we meet in a land with very different cultural presuppositions—make us realize that we are one people.

This is particularly true in the field of religion. The Spaniards, whether saints or sinners, conquistadors or friars, brought with them a medieval Latin Christianity which had already evolved specific characteristics as a result of its own history and geographical environment. This Iberian version of medieval Latin Christianity was in touch with the philosophical, theological and canonical developments of the rest of the Western Church, and these developments were brought to the new lands by men like the Dominican founders of the Antillean mission, who based their defense of the Indians' rights on Thomistic philosophy and canonical tradition,[1] like the Franciscan founders of the Colegio de Santa Cruz de Tlaltelolco, who trained young Aztec nobles in humanistic Latin,[2] and like Bishop Vasco de Quiroga of Michoacán, who tried to recreate in his diocese the *Utopia* of Thomas More.[3]

At the same time, like every other region of Western Christendom, Iberia had developed a rich *religiosidad popular;* a way of living the common faith which was less intellectual (although it did not contradict or ignore the dogmas of orthodox Catholicism) and more locally oriented (although it neither denied nor rejected the universality of Christendom); a religiosity which had instinctively incorporated the archetypes and images of Mediterranean religion into the praxis and imagery of monotheistic Christianity. This *religiosidad popular* was the religion of most of the conquistadors, and we hear of more than one instance of Spanish soldiers, in the absence of a friar, trying to share it with the native peoples.[4] But it was not a different religion from that of the friars, many of whom, at the emotional level approached the sacred in exactly the same terms. After all, they had learned to pray, not in the halls of Salamanca, but at their mother's knees, before their village's Virgin.

It is important to note that this Mediterranean *religiosidad popular* shared many archetypes and assumptions with the world view of the native civilizations, and that this made it much easier for the native Americans to accept it, and enter into it wholeheartedly. In some cases this may have resulted in a syncretism, by which the conquered peoples simply continued to consciously worship their gods under the guise of Catholic images.[5] But while such meshing of content has undoubtedly occurred in certain places in the Americas, I would like to suggest the possibility of another kind of meshing—one that would fall within the boundaries of orthodox Christian faith.

In many respects, the native religions and Iberian popular Catholicism **shared a common emotional and psychological "grammar"** in which their different religious contents were expressed. Religious expressions were rooted in agricultural cycles, kinship relations and rituals expressing joy, grief and other deeply felt human emotions; a sense of the special sacredness of certain times, places or persons, was found both in Iberian Catholicism and in the native religions. In the practice of their very different beliefs, both Spanish and native societies constructed meaning by ordering these experiences, like grammar is necessary to make coherent sense of nouns and verbs.

Thus, for instance, Spaniards celebrated the wheat harvest with festivals and *romerías* in honor of saints who were seen as "protectors" of the wheat, while in times of drought they would have implored Heaven for rain with penitential processions (Christian, 1981). The Aztec religion also celebrated the corn harvest with festivals in honor of the corn gods, and ensured the success of the harvest by collective penitential practices intended to propitiate the gods of rain and weather. Although the "nouns"—corn and wheat; Tlaloc and San Isidro Labrador—are different, the "grammar" of propitiating the heavenly powers or celebrating their protection with regard to the staple of communal nutrition is pretty much the same. The Spaniards, for example, might disapprove of dedicating processions to Tlaloc, but they had no doubt that they understood what the Aztecs were doing when they held such a procession. Thus, Christian saints and native gods— Catholic Mary and Aztec Tonantzin—are different nouns, but the similar "grammar" of religious expression with which both were honored allows for the replacement of one for the other with a minimum of psychological disorientation. Rather than *confusing* Mary with Tonantzin in a syncretism of content, the similar "grammar" of religious expression allows the native to *replace* Mary for Tonantzin. I believe that it is possible to limit syncretization to the "grammar" of religious expression, while at the theological level a true *conversion* (i. e., change in the *object* of one's worship) occurs.

Looked at from this perspective, the encounter of faith in the Americas was mediated by the conquered peoples' religious feelings. It may have been easier to give up one's previous gods when the Catholic worship of the new God was expressed in the same kind of behavior as in the old religion. Hence Christian chant and ritual, the use of incense, penances, pilgrimages to sacred places, etc., provide continuity, not change, with native religious practices in Latin America. The new Christian religion that came in the form of Iberian popular

Catholicism did require that the natives "worship what they had burned and burn what they had worshipped,"[6] but the point of the phrase is that the behavior remains recognizably similar; it is its *object* that is changed. This change of object, when expressed in the same worship behavior, does not require alienation from existing religious instincts or cultural dispositions.

This perspective is a theological way of describing a form of religious meshing which does not contaminate the orthodox content of the faith. For want of a better term, I would call this *"synthesization"* to distinguish it from *"syncretization,"* wherein both religions are effectively changed at the level of content. It is important not to confuse form with content when religious borrowings are in evidence. Catholicism has, throughout its history, been particularly fitted to unifying theological ideas while diversifying the cultural expressions of those beliefs.[7] Mediterranean Christianity in the millennium before 1492 repeatedly demonstrated such a pattern of synthesization, and, in addition to the experience at the time of the Spanish Conquest, it continues to the present, when the Mediterranean expression of Catholicism vies with a Northern European version. Moreover, much to the chagrin of some theologians and hierarchs, the "grammar" of ritual may provide more motivation in religious practice than the content of the belief. It may have been easier, one might suggest, for sixteenth century Aztecs, Mayas or Incas to convert to Iberian Catholicism from their ancestral religions than it is for Hispanic Catholics in the twentieth century United States to feel at home in a North American version of Catholicism.

Obviously, those aspects of Iberian *religiosidad popular* which shared the same emotional and psychological "grammar" with the native populations or with the slaves imported from sub-Saharan Africa had a much better chance of surviving and developing in the new environment to which they were transplanted. Other historical factors, such as scarcity or sufficiency of clergy, closeness to or distance from large cultural centers, and the religious policy of post-independence governments, have also affected the survival or developments of certain aspects of Iberian *religiosidad popular* in different areas of the Hispano-American world. What has died in one area may still be full of vitality in another, and customs or attitudes that share a common origin may have developed in different directions, even in regions within the same country.

In the remainder of this paper, I can discuss only a few religious aspects which display a significant continuity of the Iberian *religiosidad popular* brought to America in the sixteenth century to the *religiosidad popular* still lived by our people today. Because this religious culture is a côntinuum, and not a series of disparate items, these aspects will often overlap or intertwine with each other. It also goes without saying that the parameters of this paper do not allow for an exhaustive treatment of any of them; it only intends to point the way to further and deeper study. My explanations of these aspects of *religiosidad popular* will entertain the aforementioned process of *"synthesization,"* i. e., the eventual acceptance of the religious content of theologically orthodox Spanish Catholicism on the part of the native population, mediated by the psychological acceptability of the religious forms of Mediterranean Catholicism (popular and/or institutional) to this population. This psychological acceptability was based on the "grammatical compatibility" between Mediterranean Catholic and native expressions of worship. I recognize, however, that full proof of this phenomenon is also beyond the parameters of this paper.

Ritual

The great native cultures of Mesoamerica and the Inca empire had highly elaborate religious rituals, festivals, etc., which gave meaning and shape to the collective cycles of the year and to the cycles of birth, growth and death, and which consecrated both the social structures of the cultures in question and the social bonds which united the various strata of their hierarchical societies into one people. This sense of meeting the sacred in special times and places, through consecrated words, songs and gestures, was one of the factors that the native cultures shared with Iberian popular Catholicism at a time when the Erasmists both in northern Europe and in Spain were decrying ritual in favor of a more "spiritual" religion. It is well known that even those missionaries who were most committed to poverty and simplicity as a personal ideal drew the line on the issue of ritual (Ricard, 1974: 167-168, 289); the ceremonies of the new religion had to be celebrated in a way which would compare favorably with the converts' memories of the magnificent rituals of their old religion. This led them to emphasize the solemn celebration of the liturgy, especially of the Mass, Baptism and the Canonical Hours. Just a few years after the conquest, Fray Pedro de Gante could write to Charles V that the Indians' choir at *San José de los Naturales* in Mexico City could rival that of the Imperial Chapel in Flanders (McAndrew, 1965: 362-363),[8] and that an Indian had already composed a four-part polyphonic Mass (Ibid., 361, 363). This did not only go on at the capital; even a village chronicle describes the events of the conversion in terms of the friars coming to teach them "how to sing Mass and Vespers, and [how to sing] with organ and flute and plainsong, none of which did we know before" (Ibid., 361). Fray Juan de Zumárraga, first archbishop of Mexico, went so far as to comment in a letter to Emperor Charles V that music had made more converts than preaching had (Ricard, 1974: 168).[9]

The liturgy was also surrounded by a number of extra-liturgical enhancements, such as processions (Ricard, 1974: 179-181; McAndrew, 1965: 216) and mystery plays (Ricard, 1974: 194-206; McAndrew, 1965: 217-219), which were a long-accepted part of medieval piety. These had the added advantage of not having as strictly regulated a format as even the pre-Tridentine liturgy had; both in Europe and in America they presented an opportunity for the use of vernacular texts, local styles of music and even ritual dance, topical allusions, catechetical devices, etc. Extant descriptions of events such as the procession which brought the Image of Guadalupe from Bishop Zumárraga's private chapel to its newly built shrine at Tepeyac,[10] or the production of the Epiphany Play at Tlajomulco (Jalisco) before the Franciscan *Comisario General,* Fray Alonso Ponce,[11] show a prominent display of Aztec ceremonial costume and ceremonial dancing. The Epiphany Play was, of course, performed in Nahuatl (Ricard, 1974: 201),[12] and the "Song of the Drum" *(Pregón del Atabal),* traditionally associated with the dedication of the chapel at Tepeyac, skillfully weaves Marian devotion with the themes of classic Nahuatl poetry.[13]

Both processions and traditional religious plays are still very important, as is well known, in the *religiosidad popular* of Mexico and the American Southwest. One such play has been transcribed and translated, *Los Pastores* as played in San Antonio, Texas. This was brought to San Antonio from Mexico around 1900 by Don Leandro Granados in the form of an old manuscript *cuaderno,* whose incomplete text he supplemented from his childhood memories, and it has been played by groups of performers as a *devoción* since that time. A transcription of the text by Carmelo Tranchese, SJ, was published in San Antonio in 1949, and this was reprinted (with the addition of the music, transcribed by Carmela Montalvo, OSB) in 1976 by Our Lady of Guadalupe Church in San Antonio. The play is in verse, and its style and language reflect the Spanish taste of the seventeenth century, but, as anthropologist Richard Flores explains in his article in this volume, it continues to serve as a vehicle for social and cultural expression.

Flores' concept of "space" for religious expression finds confirmation in the historical experiences of colonial Latin America. Even in areas where scarcity of clergy and thinly- scattered population have made attendance at the Eucharist a rare event, this does not mean that the official liturgy has no importance in the religiosity of the people; it is simply reserved for special occasions—the kind of feast for which the *campesinos* would flock to the town, the city or the pilgrimage shrine to participate in the solemnities, sometimes camping in the streets or the outskirts for days. If the crowds from out of town overflowed the local church building, they would follow as best as they could from the plaza or the nearby streets. Furthermore, the processions associated with the greater feasts would bring the Host or the images of the Passion, Mary or the saints out of the church and into the midst of the crowds.

Even more important than the actual rituals or the importance given to them—which may vary from region to region—is the permanence of a sense of ritual in the religion of our people. This is a sense of the importance of traditional and symbolic action for the expression of joys and sorrows (enhancing the former and assuaging the latter), for giving meaning to the events of life (turning chaos into cosmos), and for creating and supporting the bonds of community.

A notable example of this occurred in New York in 1967, when *el Barrio* erupted into riots which neither Mayor John V. Lindsay nor Herman Badillo, the city's best known Puerto Rican political leader, were able to quell (based on Cole, 1968: 15-46; Díaz Ramírez, 1983: 229-237). At that point, Msgr. Robert Fox, director of the Archdiocese's Hispanic Apostolate, accepted the suggestion of a young Puerto Rican woman (Cole, 1968: 30) and organized a Peace Procession, which marched through the riot-torn streets bearing holy images, carrying candles, and singing the Rosary to the traditional tune of *Dios te salve, salve, María,* as well as old fashioned hymns such as *Oh, María, Madre Mía* (Cole, 1968: 42, 34, 36; Díaz Ramírez, 1983: 231). To Fox's own surprise (he had assumed he and the other marchers would be risking their lives) the procession pacified *el Barrio* in one night. The incident is particularly telling because Msgr. Fox himself had little use in his philosophy or methodology for either tradition or ritual (Cole, 1968: 41); the procession was characteristic of the very mentality he was trying to "wean" the Puerto Ricans away from, and indeed at its triumphant end he tried to reinterpret it by inviting the marchers into St. Paul's church, to "come in and rest," declaring furthermore that "tonight this is not a Catholic Church; it is a Temple to Man" (Cole, 1968: 46).[14] However, it was not secular values that succeeded in stopping the riot; it was instead a traditional and ritual invocation of the Sacred which was still powerful enough to elicit the reverence of the rioters—just as in Barcelona's *Corpus de Sangre* (June 7, 1640), Franciscan friars came in procession, bearing the Host, and brought to their knees the rioters who were trying to burn the Viceroy of Catalonia's palace over his head (Ignacio, 1974: 34- 35, 37, 41, 50).[15]

I believe that the power of ritual in Hispanic popular religiosity is one of its distinguishing characteristics in comparison with contemporary Catholicism as practiced among North American groups. Though different in form, both modes of religious expression are consonant with orthodox Catholic belief. Rather than judge either form as inferior, U.S. Catholicism might celebrate the diversity as evidence of religious vitality.

Marian Devotion

If the ritual manifestations of *religiosidad popular* are notable in the practice of Hispanic Catholicism, the Marian devotions are of particular importance within those manifestations. Even to the most casual observer, one of the most noticeable characteristics of *religiosidad popular* in both Spain and Hispanic America is the importance of Mary in the people's relationship with the sacred. In this, of course, the people are well within the mainstream of orthodox Catholicism. The central dogmatic definitions of Mary's role in the scheme of Salvation date from the fourth century, and form an essential part of the Mediterranean Christianity that was brought to the Americas by Iberian conquistadors, friars and colonists—as they would form an essential part of any Western Catholic or Eastern Orthodox expression of the Christian faith.

In order to explain how and why the devotion to Mary, as it is expressed in Hispanic *religiosidad popular,* is a case of synthesization rather than syncretization, I think it is important to point out in theological terms the place of Mary in the Christian faith of the more than 1,000 years from the end of the fourth century to the time of the encounter between Iberian and native American religions.

In orthodox Catholic theology, Mary is the *Theotokos;* the daughter of Adam and Eve who gave her flesh to the Word so that in the words of the Council of Chalcdeon the Wholly Other could become "a man like us in all things but sin" (Tanner, 1990: 86). In her womb, there took place the marriage of God and the human race—indeed, of God and matter—which sets Christianity apart from pure "radical monotheism" and makes it an incarnational religion, where Yahweh, the Wholly Other, can be found and worshipped in what is created. It is in Mary's Divine Motherhood—declared a dogma at the Council of Ephesus (Ibid., 58)—that matter becomes the vehicle for the hierophany, and earth is interpenetrated with heaven. This is essential not only for Catholic Mariology, but for Catholic Christology—and it is also essential to that Catholic "approach to reality" (what Rosemary Haughton (1979) calls "the Catholic Thing") which is instinctively shared by Catholics across the board, from theologians and prelates to *viejitas* and village priests. Without it, Teilhard de Chardin's cosmic Christology would be impossible, and so would the Sevillian gypsies' pilgrimage to El Rocío, or the Puerto Rican *jíbaros* climbing on their knees up the hill of Hormigueros. It is this "approach to reality," or this Faith, which is behind the theological propositions and conciliar definitions, and these do not create the Catholic *weltanschaung,* they only express it.

Because of this Divine Motherhood, and the consequences derived from it, it was possible for Mary, the woman of Nazareth, to take on the archetypal characteristics of the Mediterranean Earth Mother/Queen of Heaven, without compromising orthodox belief in the one God. It is not that "half-converted" or "imperfectly evangelized" Mediterranean pagans "used" Mary as a mask for the ancient goddesses. It was rather that with a perfectly Catholic instinct, they realized that what was foreshadowed in the Earth Mother was fulfilled in the historical peasant woman of Nazareth, just as what was foreshadowed in the Dying and Rising God was fulfilled in the carpenter of Galilee, and what was foreshadowed in the *hieros gamos* of Earth and Heaven was fulfilled when she bore him in her womb. She is not a goddess in competition with the Trinity, nor is she "the feminine face of God"; she is the daughter of Man who is also Mother of God. She made God human without losing of Divinity, and God makes her divine, but—and this is crucial—without losing her humanity. For the whole meaning of Mary, at both the archetypal and the theological levels, is that in her earth is transfigured, and matter divinized.

Because Mary, the historical woman of Nazareth, is also then the Earth Mother, Mediterranean religiosity has created the image of the Black Madonna; black as the earth, and often associated with a legend of being found in a cave,[16] but also black because the Sky God has burned her in his embrace: "do not look down on me for being swarthy, for the Sun has gazed on me" (Song of Songs 1:6). On her lap the Sky God is also black, for in her womb he became earth, and was found in a cave.

In the mystical commentaries of Bernard, and the lyrical Sequences of Adam of St. Victor—but also in the *sevillanas* you can hear in any street in Andalusia—she is the Bride of the Canticles; the virginal beloved of every man, the archetype of every girl who can love and be loved.

And in the Pietà—*Nuestra Señora de las Angustias*—she is the Bereaved Mother; the mother whose heart has been pierced by seven swords of sorrow, and who understands the fears of all men and the sorrows of all women. At the foot of the Cross, she becomes not just the Mother of God, but the Mother of us all.[17]

Thus, in her historical life and her role in the economy of salvation, Mary fulfills the triple archetype of the Mediterranean Earth Goddess. The historical peasant woman of Nazareth is truly "the Bride, the Mother and the Crone" of Mediterranean mythology; in her, as in her Son, the myth became history. She is also, by her relation to Christ, risen and ascended, the Queen of Heaven, and as such, she is the woman of mercy and of power, who listens to the problems of the oppressed and the suffering with a mother's heart, and helps them with the power of a queen.

This polyvalent image, at once rooted in psychological archetypes and orthodox theology, waved on the flags of the conquistadors, was carried within their hearts, and was enshrined by them on the altars of the Pyramid of Tenochtitlán and the Temple of the Sun in Cuzco. But she was no more alien to the Aztec and Inca neophytes than she had been to the Greeks who enshrined her in the Parthenon of Athena the Virgin, or the Gallo-Romans who placed her black image in the cave of the Earth Mother at Chartres. In America, too, the *Moreneta* of Montserrat is venerated at Hormigueros in Puerto Rico, and the Black Virgin of Guadalupe in Extremadura has given her name to the Indian-featured *Virgen Morena*. She was just as much *Tonantzin,* Our Lady and Our Mother. And yet, not the old *Tonantzin;* as in the Mediterranean, so also in America, she is the historical, the orthodox Mary, who replaces and fulfills the ancient archetypes. She is, as the *Nican Mopohua* claims she called herself, "the ever-virgin Mother of the One True God, through whom all live[18]." Not the old goddess, but she whom the old goddess foreshadowed; not the feminine face of God, but the *Theotokos:* the woman of this earth who gave birth to the Wholly Other, and thus manifests his paradoxical non-otherness; his union with earth and matter. The Virgin Bride, tanned with the Sun; the Mother of All, who awaits the oppressed and the afflicted "to listen to their woes, and to remedy their miseries and sorrows[19]"; the mighty queen before whom even Cortés trembles, and who will eventually be able to create a new people, neither Spanish nor Aztec, and yet both at once.

Explained in theological terms, this is all quite beyond the natives—and quite beyond the average Spaniard, for that matter. And I certainly would not wish to claim that any native convert ever articulated these notions in so many words. But conversion to Catholicism is conversion to a *faith* and a *world view,* not to the theological articulation of that world view. Catholicism views belief as endowed with a social or communal nature which allows a person to embrace Truth without fully understanding it in rational terms. An act of faith is assent to Truth on religious authority, or the acceptance of a world view whose ramifications one cannot necessarily spell out, even though these ramifications are in fact affecting one's attitudes to reality.

Within the context of the church's community, both peasant and theologian are expected to believe the same thing, but the theological explanation of the community's faith is the special responsibility of the theologian. Rationality in this relationship (i. e., being able to explain the belief) does not make the theologian "holier" than the peasant. In fact, if the theologian does not inwardly believe what he explains, he loses his soul, while the illiterate peasant who instinctively believes without being able to explain goes to heaven. Furthermore, it is important to realize that the theologian's task is not to impose his intellectual agendas on the people, but rather to articulate, spell out and explore the ramifications of the community's faith or world view. When the theologian's brilliant and original intellectual constructs do not accurately represent that faith, the theologian has fallen into heresy. The doctrine of the *sensus fidelium* means that ultimately the theologian is responsible, not to the hierarchy or to his academic peers, but to the *pueblo,* to the grass roots of the community, whose faith it is his job to express.

While all of this may not make sense to persons outside the realm of faith, I submit that the only way to appreciate the power of *religiosidad popular* within Catholicism is to recognize that at its core it is religious, and therefore, it cannot be ultimately understood from a non-religious standpoint.[20] Even if the observer is an atheist, he must set aside his own prejudice and recognize that religious people act religiously. The Italian Communist, Antonio Gramsci, confessed admiration for Catholicism's ability to connect uneducated believer and theologizing clergy in one community, and his explanations merit continued study (Díaz-Stevens, 1993: 119-125). Theologians—and intellectuals in general—tend to forget that a truly potent symbol, expressed in a symbolic language which is shared, can communicate a world view to simple people, and enable them to understand it and to work from it at a deep level. Just because they can't explain it in our jargon doesn't mean they don't understand.

The Passion of Christ

If Mary is the image of Earth glorified and raised up to Heaven, Jesus, in both Iberian and Hispanic American *religiosidad popular,* appears primarily as God made Man, as Heaven come down to Earth, as the Almighty who has emptied himself and became powerless. While the religiosity of the powerful, in a Byzantine imperial Church, stressed the image of the victorious *Pantokrator*—the All-Powerful Cosmic Ruler of apsidal and dome mosaics—Spain exalted the image of the Man of Sorrows, crowned with thorns, spat upon, bearing our burdens, healing us by his stripes, nailed to the cross. And yet, this image of the *kenosis* of God; of the Almighty made powerless by his own choice, is often referred to, paradoxically, by the Spanish translation of *Kyrios Pantokrator: El Señor del Gran Poder.*

This paradoxical image of power self-emptied into powerlessness, and of powerlessness which is stronger than coercion and might (the "weakness of God which is stronger than the strength of man," Corinthians 1:25), was also brought to the New World, and found a place in the hearts of the newly converted. They, too, had the archetype of the god who saves by suffering; it was a new God now, but not an alien symbol. And of course the image spoke powerfully to their oppressed condition. As Unamuno puts it: The lovely-fleshed and joyful gods of Hellas are all very fine for us when all goes well, but when sorrow, or oppression or tragedy strikes it is the racked body of Christ, the Christ of *agonía,* that can give comfort to sorrow and meaning to life.

> . . . but only you gave us a flesh that suffers,
> your white-bled flesh of pain, your very bowels,
> that was your gift: death-conquering bread for mortals;
> you, man and also God; the Son of Man!
> (Unamuno, Part I, VI: *Ecce Homo,* translation mine).

This "tragic sense of life" is present deep in the Iberian soul; when it met the tragedy of the conquered peoples it produced a shared sense—a sense for the mystery of the Incarnation as *kenosis* of God, which is the other side of the mystery shown in Mary: the Incarnation as *theosis,* as the divinization of creation and of Man.

In Mary, crowned and bejewelled, we see the results of the Incarnation for humanity whom she personifies; in Christ, bleeding and humiliated, we see the results of the Incarnation for the Almighty: we see his all-too-real humanness, and the price he paid for our glorification. Iberian and Hispanic *religiosidad popular* has often been criticized both for its glorification of Mary and for its "overemphasis" on the Christ of the Passion at the expense of the Risen Christ. And yet there is a deep theological wisdom—maybe too profound for professional theologians—in this inversion. Christ, who is God, is remembered chiefly in his sufferings, for the glorification of the Son of Man does not have to wait until Easter; he reigns from the Cross itself, as in the Gospel of John. It is in his very humiliation that his power is beheld. On the other hand, Mary, who is a creature, is exalted in glory. The power of the Incarnation makes the Godhead truly human and capable of suffering, even dying; it also makes created beings capable of divinization; capable of a glory which, before the Incarnation, it would have been idolatrous to ascribe to any being except God.

The first aspect of this is *kenosis,* literally "emptying out"; the second *theosis,* "the making of non-God into God." While Radical Monotheism, whether Hebrew, Islamic or classical Protestant, would find this unacceptable, orthodox Christian theology and spirituality, in both East and West, are centered on this exchange, which annihilates the *distance* between the divine and the human, though, without abolishing the *distinction* between them. This notion of *theosis* as the goal of the Christian life and the purpose of the Incarnation is a commonplace in the Eastern Fathers of the Church; the classic expression is St. Athanasius' *dictum* that "God became Man in order that men might become God." It is entirely orthodox, therefore, to see the power of the Incarnation and the Passion as shining out particularly in its capacity to divinize what is not God; to make a goddess out of Mary, as someday, it will make gods out of us all.[21]

Once again, the Sevillian gypsy kneeling before the *Señor del Gran Poder,* or the Andean Indian kneeling before the *Cristo de los Milagros,* cannot talk in terms of *kenosis* and *theosis,* but the symbols do speak; they speak as clearly to them as the Greek speaks to theologians. They understand it just as well, or better. It has been made difficult for the learned and the scholarly (who probably prefer it that way) but revealed plainly to the little ones.

Because of this, both in Spain and in Hispanic America, Holy Week is central to the people's calendar. It is a participation in the Passion, not only in liturgical rites and in processions, but also in a personally chosen share in Christ's sufferings, from the Caribbean *jíbaros* who fast all of Good Friday on a few sections of an orange to the *penitentes* of New Mexico[22]—for they know that we must "make up in our flesh what is lacking in the sufferings of Christ" (Colossians 1:24) but also that "if we suffer with him, we shall also reign with him" (II Timothy 2:12).

And yet, the Paschal dimension of the Cross is not—as is often said—entirely absent from the *religiosidad popular* of Iberia or Hispanic America. In the month of May, in Puerto Rico and Santo Domingo as in Seville or Granada, the Cross is decorated with flowers in *patio* or in *batey,* and is the center of singing, dancing and celebration. The tree of death suddenly bursts into flower and becomes the apocalyptic Tree of Life:

La Cruz que desea verse florecida,
entre tantas flores se halla convertida
(Garrido, 1952: 120).[23]

At least in Puerto Rico, the lyrics to some of the songs are pure theology, and some almost bring echoes of Byzantine hymnody.[24]

Laity and Church

It is well known that in the period between Trent and Vatican II, the Catholicism of the elites was expressed and dominated by the clergy, so that it was expressed primarily in hierarchical terms, and stressed institutional concerns. Similarly, its faith was expressed in theological and intellectual terms, and those who were not fluent in such terminology were assumed to be under-catechized, "half evangelized"; their faith, such as it was, was presumed to be not very orthodox. (Depending on the outlook of the commentator, this last statement was either an advantage or a disadvantage.) In the post-conciliar period, the importance of the laity has been stressed, sometimes even to the point of overcompensation. But the theory behind this rediscovery of the dignity of the laity has tended, in both liberal and conservative circles, to presuppose that the sacred is the province of the clergy, while the secular is the province of the laity. Conservatives, therefore, strive to keep priests out of politics and lay persons out of theology; liberals equate the re-evaluation of the laity with the re-discovery of the secular as a value in itself.

The *religiosidad popular* of both Iberia and Hispanic America does not fit well in this paradigm, because it tends to be run by and for the laity, but it is unabashedly sacral. This, in fact, is one of the reasons why it was given a negative value just as much by the liberals in the heady days immediately following the Council as by the pre-conciliar institutional clerics. If in New York, for example, Cardinal Spellman found the religion of the Puerto Ricans defective because it was not centered around institutional concerns and priorities, the liberal priests of the late 60s found it defective because it was not centered on social action or "building the earth" (Vidal, 1994). In terms of Avery Dulles' *Models of the Church* (1974), people like Spellman understood the church along the "institutional" model, while the new priests' vision was along the model of "the Church as servant." I am not sure if our *religiosidad popular* fits comfortably into *any* of Dulles' models; it may be a very modified hybrid of the "Church as sacrament" and "Church as mystical communion." But it certainly is too independent of the clergy to fit the institutional model, and too centered on the Sacred to fit the servant model.

On the whole, *religiosidad popular* is not anti-clerical; it is simply not controlled by the clergy. However, as we have mentioned before, the clergy performs necessary services for it; it is important, for example, to have one's religious articles blessed by a priest, even if one later uses them for one's own purposes and in one's own way. Rigid attendance at the Eucharist every Sunday is often not seen as important to one's relationship with God, but attendance on certain occasions (some of which may not be considered obligatory by the institution) is perceived as important. Having Masses said for one's dead, or in thanksgiving for favors, is very important in many areas.

In many cases scarcity of priests and distance from the parish churches led communities to give more importance, on a day-by-day basis, to religious events which did not need the presence of an ordained leader. But even in areas where priests were abundant, groups such as the *cofradías* arose which were run by the laity and for the laity. This was not a rebellion, and was not perceived as such by either clergy or laity; indeed membership in many *cofradías* was open to the clergy (Fernández Méndez, 1957: 213).[25] But priest *cofrades* had to accept, and in fact accepted, the leadership of the elected warden or mayordomo, who need not be, and in some cases could not be a cleric. Sometimes the *cofradía* would have a priest as its chaplain or spiritual director; other times it would simply hire a priest of its own choice, on a case by case basis, to sing the High Mass or to preach the "*panegírico*" on its feasts. In such cases, the *cofradía* would dictate to the priest the terms of the service;[26] there are cases when they even specified in the contract the minimum number of times that their saint had to be mentioned by name in the sermon, with extra payment for every mention beyond the minimum! (Sanchis, 1985: 275).[27]

To this day the great penitential processions of Holy Week in most Spanish towns are pretty much owned and operated by the lay *cofradías*. Indeed, there is evidence that, as post-conciliar priests discourage the processions, which do not fit in with their new vision of Christianity, those processions which are controlled by the clergy are slowly dying, but those controlled by the *cofradías* still thrive (Brandes,

1980: 196-198). In New Mexico too, the *Hermanos Penitentes* have kept alive a certain kind of Passion-piety which for more than a century has been discouraged by clerics because it did not fit with their new ideas, whether Tridentine or post-Vatican II.

Especially where priests were scarce and the parish churches were distant, the people would set up *altarcitos,* home altars akin to the Byzantine icon corner, where the family would gather for prayer. Once again, these altars were not set up in opposition to the altar in the parish, as if to say "we don't need the church, we have our own altar at home," but rather, an extension of the sacred space of the church into one's home, just as a procession extended the sacred space into the streets.[28] For this reason it was important to bring newly-carved *santos* to the church to be blessed, and to have a bowl of holy water or some blessed candles, or branches from the Palm Sunday procession, as part of the *altarcito* ensemble.

The prayers at the *altarcito* were usually led by the mother of the family, but if something more elaborate was required (e.g., for a *rosario de difuntos*) a *rezador* or *rezadora* would be asked to come and conduct the prayers. This was, obviously, not an official ministry; when a person was recognized in the community as having a skill in leading prayers, as well as knowing by heart a great number of prayer formulas, he or she would become known as a *rezador/a* and would be invited to lead prayers as needed.

It is to be noted that both in Spain and America, women who are barred from the ordained ministry play a very important role in *religiosidad popular.* The mother (or grandmother) is the great leader of prayer and transmitter of religious lore and religious values. *Rezadoras* are much more common than *rezadores.* The *beata,* although the object of much mockery as a "religious fanatic" and as a typical example of foolish religiosity, also has an important role. She is the direct descendant of the medieval *beguinas,* who led a religious life without formal vows or clerical control, often wearing some form of habit,[29] either at home or in a *beaterio* shared by a small group of them. Saint Catherine of Siena in Europe and Saint Rose of Lima in America were early examples of this kind of independent and uncloistered religious woman. There is also a little known example in seventeenth century Puerto Rico, the lay woman Gregoria Hernández (d. 1639) who set up an informal *beaterio* with a few other women, and whose virtues are extolled by canon Torres Vargas (1647, pp. 186-187).

Finally, it is interesting that the two great recent movements which have run like wildfire through the U.S. Hispanic Catholic community, are primarily lay movements. The *Cursillos de Cristiandad* were founded in Spain in the 1950s under hierarchical auspices with the purpose of regaining the Latin male for the Church. In Spain and in Latin America, the *Cursillo* is not necessarily a manifestation of *religiosidad popular,* since the participants at any given weekend form a cross-section of the local society. Indeed, the *rollo de piedad* in the standard format of the Cursillo has been described (by a *cursillista* leader) as "a frontal attack on popular religiosity."[30] But in the United States, where the Hispanic community comes almost exclusively from the popular classes, the *Cursillo,* which is run primarily by lay leaders, has become expressive of the attitudes and ethos of this class. It could be said that it is creating a new variety of *religiosidad popular,* more in touch with certain hierarchical attitudes, but translating these into popular terms and in the process transforming them.[31] One important service which the *Cursillos* have made to the U.S. Hispanic community is that they served as a vehicle by which the people preserved their own priorities and religious attitudes at a time when these were not appreciated by the American clergy, whether "institutionally oriented" or "renewed" (Vidal, 1994).

The Charismatic Renewal was founded as a Catholic movement by theologically educated American laypersons; professors and theology majors at Duquesne and Notre Dame[32]. In its early days its catechesis was in English, and presupposed some theological sophistication, and for both of those reasons at that time it held no attraction for U.S. Hispanics. It was only when the movement spread to their lands of origin—a development which began in 1971 with a Charismatic retreat in Aguas Buenas, P.R.—that it could be brought back to the mainland in Spanish, and in a format attractive to the U.S. Hispanic community. Since then, it has spread significantly in the community, although its high visibility should not blind us to the fact that the *Cursillos* have had more of an impact (Doyle, et al., 1982: 91).[33] Once again, the lay character of the prayer groups has made it possible for the Charismatic Renewal to be transformed into a popular Hispanic movement; this has been crucial to the movement's style and to its popularity among Hispanics (Vidal, 1988: 313-329).

Conclusion

In conclusion, we may say that in many respects the *religiosidad popular* of Latin America and of the Hispanic peoples of the United States is a continuation and adaptation of the Mediterranean version of orthodox Catholicism as lived by the *pueblo* of the Iberian Peninsula—a plant transplanted to a new but not altogether alien environment, grafted onto peoples whose cultures were not ultimately incompatible with it, and naturally growing and developing under the influence of its new circumstances,[34] but still in continuity with its Iberian and Mediterranean origins.

It has been a common belief in this country that the cultural conflict between the Catholicism of the "mainstream" U.S. Catholic Church and the Catholicism of U.S. Hispanics is a conflict between a "European" or "Euro-American" understanding of Christianity and a "native American" or "Indigenous" understanding. This assumption has been shared by the "liberals"—for whom it signified the "superiority" of the Hispanic religiosity—and by the "conservatives"—for whom it signified its basic "inferiority" as a product of "religious ignorance" and "defective evangelization."

It would seem to me, on the basis of the continuities we have seen in this essay, and of the many others which its limitations of space have precluded us from mentioning, that a case may be made for a different paradigm. In this view which I propose, *both* the "mainstream" American and the Hispanic versions of lived Catholicism are legitimately variant expressions of orthodox Catholicism, and *both* are basically European plants transplanted to a New World environment—each in its own way affected by its new environment, but still in basic continuity with their European roots. Some of the differences between these two ways of being Catholic stem from the differences in the two environments; American Catholicism has been shaped to a great degree, for example, by the immigrant experience and the experience of being a minority faith in a Protestant culture.

The great difference between them, however, is that while Hispanic Catholicism is in continuity with Mediterranean Catholicism, the "mainstream" American version of Catholicism is in continuity with the northern European Catholicism which was brought to Maryland by the English Catholic settlers and which was also the religion of the leaders among the Irish immigrant clergy and the German immigrants.

By the time large numbers of Italian and Polish Catholics came to the United States, that form of Catholicism was already in possession of the field, and partly by imposition from the hierarchy and partly by natural processes of adaptation, these groups had to adapt their Mediterranean or Slavic Catholicism to the ethos practiced and advocated by the Church in their new environment. But for reasons which are beyond the scope of this essay, the Hispanic peoples of the United States have been in a position to passively resist this assimilation and hold on to their traditional way of being Catholic to a much greater degree than other ethnic groups.

Endnotes

1. The classic work for the Dominican philosophical position on the human rights of the Native Americans is Francisco de Vitoria's *Relectio de Indis,* of which the most recent edition (Latin text with Spanish translation) is in *Obras de Francisco de Vitoria* (Madrid: Biblioteca de Autores Cristianos, 1960). The stages of the philosophical controversy between the Dominicans and their opponents can be followed in Lewis Hanke, *The Spanish Struggle for Justice in the Conquest of America.* (Boston: Little, Brown, 1965). Antecedents in the canonical tradition are discussed in James Muldoon, *Popes, Lawyers and Infidels: the Church and the Non-Christian World, 1250-1550* (Philadelphia: University of Pennsylvania Press, 1979) whose final chapter deals specifically with the application of this tradition in the Spanish conquest of the Indies.

2. The development of this college is described in Robert Ricard, *The Spiritual Conquest of Mexico* (Berkeley: University of California Press, 1974) pp. 219-231. An opponent of the college is quoted as admitting that the Aztec students at Tlaltelolco "hablan tan elegante el latín como Tulio" ("speak Latin with the elegance of Cicero"), p.222. On p. 223 Ricard also gives the text of a short letter written in his old age by Antonio Valeriano, the most famous of the college's alumni, whose humanistic Latin is indeed most elegant, *simplex munditiis.*

3. Ricard, *Spiritual Conquest,* p. 299, basing himself on M. Bataillon, *Erasme en Espagne* (Paris, 1937) pp. 580-590, and on Silvio Zavala, *La Utopía de Tomás Moro en la Nueva España* (Mexico, 1937).

4. Cortés himself made great efforts to catechize and convert the towns through which he passed on his way to Tenochtitlán, and had to be restrained by the expedition's chaplain Fray Bartolomé de Olmedo, who felt his zeal was imprudent; during Moctezuma's captivity the Spaniards (especially the page boy Orteguilla) tried strenuously to convert him, and were genuinely sorry when he died refusing Baptism. During their trek across the southern United States Cabeza de Vaca and his soldiers healed a number of natives by signing them with the Cross (*santiguar,* a method of healing still practiced in Hispanic popular religion) and reciting the *Pater* and *Ave* over them. They were so successful that their fame as healers preceded them from tribe to tribe, assuring them of welcome and food. In his edition of *Los naufragios* (Madrid: Editorial Castalia, 1992) Enrique Pupo-Walter actually refers to Cabeza de Vaca as *el chamán evangelizador;* "the evangelizing shaman." (p. 122).

5. The best known and clearest examples are the syncretizations of a sancto-centric Catholicism with the religion of the imported Yoruba slaves known as *Santería* in Cuba and as *Candomblé* in Brazil. Cases are also known in which Mesoamerican natives hid their idols behind or underneath the altar of a mission church, so as to continue worshipping the old gods under the appearance of Christian observance.

6. The phrase is attributed to St. Remy of Rheims at the baptism of Clovis, first Barbarian chieftain to convert to Catholicism.

7. I recognize the similarity of this term to "*inculturation*", but discussion of how that concept is used by others is beyond the parameters of this article. Persons interested in such a discussion may consult Anscar J. Chupungco, OSB, *Liturgical Inculturation* (Collegeville, MN: The Liturgical Press, 1992) pp. 13-31.

8. This was the Chapel of Burgundy, one of the most musically advanced choirs in Europe; Fray Pedro would be familiar with its performance standards since he had been personally close to the Emperor, and may have been his illegitimate half-brother.

9. Letter to Emperor Charles V, April 17, 1540, quoted in Ricard, *The Spiritual Conquest,* p.168. For a detailed treatment of music in the early mendicant missions of Mexico see McAndrew, *The Open Air Churches,* pp. 359-367, and Ricard, pp. 176-179.

10. This procession is described in the Nahuatl work *Huei Tlamahuizoltica,* first published in 1649, but probably written much earlier by Fernando de Alva Ixtlilxóchitl, one of the Aztec aristocrats

who had studied at the Colegio de Tlaltelolco. Because the first miracle attributed to the Image of Guadalupe occurred during this procession, it is also described in other sources, especially Miguel Sánchez, *Imagen de la Virgen María*... (1648) and by three of the elderly Aztecs who made depositions in the *Informaciones* of 1666, some of whom were children or grandchildren of persons who had been present at the procession. Since the miracle occurred to one of the dancers, who was accidentally wounded with an arrow in a mock battle, all the narratives stress the presence of such dancing and music in the Aztec tradition. The descriptions may be found in E. de la Torre Villar and R. Navarro de Anda,eds., *Testimonios históricos guadalupanos* (Mexico: Fondo de Cultura Económica, 1982) pp. 245- 246, 277, 299, 1352, 1353 and 1356.

11. January 6, 1587; but there is contemporary evidence that the play was at least thirty years old at that time. It is described in detail in Ricard, *The Spiritual Conquest,* pp. 199-202, from a description by a friar in the *Comisario's* staff. Ricard also describes (pp. 196-198) a play presented at Tlaxcala on Corpus Christi Day in 1538, where different native nations (led, of course, by the Tlaxcaltecs) join the Spaniards in capturing Jerusalem from the Turks.

12. The anonymous source keeps repeating that each of the speeches is being made in *lengua mexicana.*

13. This Nahuatl poem is found in the manuscript known as *Cantares Mexicanos,* in the National Library of Mexico; it is attributed to Francisco Plácido, Lord of Azcapotzalco, and is believed to have been sung to the beat of the *teponaztli* drums at the procession that transferred the Image of Guadalupe to its shrine, Dec. 26, 1531. A Spanish translation is found in *Testimonios históricos guadalupanos,* p. 23.

14. A priest more in touch with the spiritual/emotional forces Msgr. Fox had used that night would have invited them in to close the event with a solemn and heartfelt *Salve* to the Blessed Virgin in thanksgiving for the achievements of the night, or some other overtly religious act.

15. The Viceroy escaped the palace, and was later caught in the streets and murdered.

16. In Montserrat, for example,the legend of finding the statue in a cave of the mountain, where it had been hidden at the Moorish invasion, had become accepted by the XVIth century, when a chapel was erected over the mouth of the santa cova. (F. P. Verrié, *Montserrat*

[Madrid: Plus Ultra, n.d.] p.148). The legend as traditionally told is found in the Catalan-language *Goigs* (a type of song of praise with refrain, known in Spanish as *Gozos*) in honor of Our Lady of Montserrat, a broadside of which is reproduced in O. Cardona and R. Camprubí, *Montserrat* (Barcelona: Ediciónes Destino, 1977) p.163. Since the style of the statue is XIIth century Romanesque, the legend of its being hidden in the VIIIth century and discovered in the IXth is historically impossible, but the fact that such a legend arose is psychologically and anthropologically significant.

17. This is the traditional Catholic interpretation of John XIX: 26-27; in the person of the Beloved Disciple Christ gives Mary as a Mother to the whole human race, or at least to all believers.

18. *"Sabe y ten entendido...que yo soy la siempre Virgen Santa María, Madre del verdadero Dios por quien se vive; del Creador que sabe donde está todo; Señor del cielo y de la tierra."* Nican Mopohua, the original Nahuatl narrative of the apparition of Guadalupe, in the classic translation of Primo Feliciano Velázquez. *Testimonios históricos guadalupanos*, p. 28. The *Nican Mopohua* is attributed to Antonio Valeriano (c.1531-1605) the most learned of the alumni of the college of Tlaltelolco.

19. *"...[para] oír allí sus lamentos, y remediar todas sus miserias, penas y dolores."* Nican Mopohua, p.28.

20. I do not, of course, mean that non-religious disciplines or approaches, such as economics or politics, have no light to cast on the phenomenon, but only that the phenomenon can not ultimately be understood from a reductionistically non-religious standpoint.

21. It is important to realize that the so-called "Marian privileges" in Catholic theology are simply cases of Mary getting beforehand (as "firstfruits" or "earnest") the fruits of the Incarnation and the Passion/Resurrection which we all are to get at a later date. Thus the Assumption, for example, is simply the Resurrection of the Dead promised to all as a result of Christ's Resurrection, which in her case is not reserved to the Last Day. Rather than being "alone of all her sex," Mary is thus the front runner of all her sex, and indeed of all the human race, into the divinization won for us all by her Son.

22. Such flagellant *cofradías* were extremely common in Spain from the late Middle Ages, and a few have survived the decree of the enlightened despot Carlos III (1767) prohibiting public flagellation; other forms of penance, such as walking the procession barefoot, or

in leg-irons, or carrying a heavy cross, are still common. (See Christian, 1981: 185-190, 204, and photo of a 1974 flagellant procession in San Vicente de la Sonsierra, province of Logroño, p. 205.) These facts help us to see the *penitentes* as neither an "aberration" or a "creative invention" of the New Mexican Indians, but as a local survival of something that was at one time shared by elite and *pueblo* in both Spain and Hispanic America.

23. The full text and music of the *Fiesta de Cruz* as sung in Puerto Rico is transcribed in Pablo Garrido, *Esoteria y fervor populares de Puerto Rico* (Madrid: Ediciones Cultura Hispánica, 1952) pp. 89-123; textual and musical variants, pp.127-148.

24. The Puerto Rican version of the *Fiesta de Cruz* seems to come from the Canary Islands, and especially from Santa Cruz de Tenerife; Canarian scholars who attended the feast in Puerto Rico recognized many of the tunes as coming from their homeland (Verbal communication from Anthony Stevens-Arroyo). I do not know to what degree this may also apply to the texts as sung in Puerto Rico.

25. In seventeenth century San Juan, for example, the statutes of the *Cofradía del Santísimo Sacramento* specified that the members had to be fifty percent clerics and fifty percent laymen. *Descripción de la Isla y Ciudad de Puerto Rico...Enviada por el Licenciado Don Diego de Torres Vargas, Canónigo de la Santa Iglesia de Esta Isla* (1647) in Eugenio Fern†ndez Méndez, *Crónicas de Puerto Rico* Vol. I: 213. The secular Third Orders of the mendicant friars accept secular clerics, lay men and lay women, with no distinction made among them within the Fraternity, all authority being based on elected office.

26. It should be noted that while a scarcity of priests forces the laity to create their own alternative forms of worship, and thus, makes their religion less dependent on clerical leadership, a surplus of priests (which often existed in the larger cities of colonial Latin America) puts many priests at the mercy of the laity, since those who could not obtain a benefice must make a living as tutors, independent schoolmasters, private chaplains, etc. Such priests would often be treated as employees rather than superiors.

27. Sanchis tells of the people who have commissioned a sermon promising "a few coins more for every time the preacher pronounces the name of St. Peter." There are a number of jokes in the Iberian oral tradition about the efforts of priests in such a situation to add mentions of the saint's name at any price.

28. When home Masses became popular in the 1960s, a similar attitude became evident. Priests often encouraged these in order to bring the Eucharist out of the sacred space into a secular context, only to find that their hosts had rearranged their living room or dining room to look like a church; for them the significance of the home Mass was that the Sacred had come into their house, and taken it over for a short space. I know of a Colombian family in Jersey City who refuse to consider moving to a better apartment because a Mass which was very significant to their community was celebrated in their living room—it is now "sacred space" to them.

29. The habit could indicate a loose connection to a religious order, or even membership in its lay branch (Third Order Secular) but it might indicate no more than a personal devotion to that order's patron or founder. The *hábito del Carmen,* for example, was extremely popular in Puerto Rico long before there were any Carmelite friars on the island.

30. Interview with Mr. Hilvic Ferrer, former secretary of the *Cursillo* Movement for the diocese of Metuchen.

31. For a more detailed treatment of the *Cursillos* in the context of *religiosidad popular* see J. Vidal, 1988: 302-308.

32. A primary source for the origins of the Charismatics as a Catholic movement is Ranaghan, 1969. The book was published within three years of the movement's inception by two of its founders.

33. In the survey of Hispanics sponsored by the Archdiocese of New York in 1982, 43% of the respondents considered the *Cursillos* important in their lives, and 28.8% considered the Charismatic Renewal important; 41.9% had never heard of the Charismatics, while only 31.2% had never heard of the *Cursillos.*

34. Some of these New World developments, such as the *Sermón de las Siete Palabras* combined with devotions lasting from 1 to 3 PM on Good Friday (an arrangement invented in the XVIIth century by a Jesuit in Peru) were exported back to Europe and became popular there.

Bibliography

Anonymous, 1976. *Los Pastores,* Spanish text, with English translation by Carmelo Tranchese, sj., and musical notation by Carmela Montalvo, OSB. San Antonio, Our Lady of Guadalupe Church.

Bataillon, M. 1937. *Erasme en Espagne.* Paris.

Brandes, Stanley. 1980. *Metaphors of Masculinity: Sex and Status in Andalusian Folklore.* Philadelphia: University of Pennsylvania Press.
Cabeza de Vaca, Alvar Núñez. 1992. *Los naufragios.* ed. by Enrique Pupo-Walter. Madrid: Editorial Castalia.
Cardona, O. and R. Camprubí. 1979. Montserrat. Barcelona: Ediciónes Destino.
Christian, W.A. 1981. *Local Religion in Sixteenth Century Spain.* Princeton: Princeton University Press.
Cole, Mary. 1968. *Summer in the City.* New York: Kenedy.
De la Torre Villar, E. and R. Navarro de Anda, eds., 1982. *Testimonios Históricos Guadalupanos.* Mexico: Fondo de Cultura Económica.
Díaz Ramírez, Ana María. 1983. *The Roman Catholic Archdiocese of New York and the Puerto Rican Migration.* Doctoral dissertation, Fordham University.
Díaz-Stevens, Ana María. 1993. *Oxcart Catholicism on Fifth Avenue: the Impact of the Puerto Rican Migration Upon the Archdiocese of New York.* Notre Dame: Notre Dame University Press.
Dolan, Jay P. and Vidal, Jaime R., eds. 1994. *Puerto Rican and Cuban Catholics in the US, 1900-1965.* Notre Dame, Indiana: University of Notre Dame Press,
Doyle, Ruth et al., 1982. *Hispanics in New York: Religious, Cultural and Social Experiences.* New York: Office of Pastoral Research.
Dulles, Avery, SJ. 1974. *Models of the Church.* Garden City, NY: Doubleday.
Fernández Méndez, Eugenio. 1957. *Crónicas de Puerto Rico.* San Juan: Ediciones del Gobierno, Vol. I.
Garrido, Pablo. 1952. *Esotería y fervor populares de Puerto Rico.* Madrid: Ediciones Cultura Hispánica.
Hanke, Lewis. 1965. *The Spanish Struggle for Justice in the Conquest of America.* Boston: Little, Brown.
Haughton, R. 1979. *The Catholic Thing.* Springfield, IL: Templegate.
Ignacio, León. 1974. *Corpus de Sangre: la Rebelión de los Segadores en Barcelona.* Barcelona: Plaza y Janés.
McAndrew, John. 1965. *The Open Air Churches of Sixteenth Century Mexico.* Cambridge, MA: Harvard University Press
Muldoon, James. 1979. *Popes, Lawyers and Infidels: the Church and the Non-Christian World, 1250-1550.* Philadelphia: University of Pennsylvania Press.

Ranaghan, Kevin and Dorothy. 1969. *Catholic Pentecostals*. New York: Paulist.
Ricard, Robert. 1974. *The Spiritual Conquest of Mexico*. Berkeley: University of California Press.
Sanchis, Pierre. 1985. "The Portuguese *Romarías*" in Stephen Wilson, ed., *Saints and their Cults*. Cambridge: Cambridge University Press.
Tanner, Norman P. SJ ed. 1990. *Decrees of the Ecumenical Councils*. Vol. 1 London and Washington: Sheed and Ward/Georgetown University Press.
Torres Vargas, Diego de. 1647. "Descripción de la Isla y Ciudad de Puerto Rico," in Fernández Méndez, 1957.
Tranchese. Rev. Carmelo. 1976. *Los Pastores,* Spanish text, with English translation by Carmela Montalvo, OSB. San Antonio: Our Lady of Guadalupe Church.
Unamuno, Miguel de. *El Cristo de Velázquez*.
Verrié, F.P.M. *Montserrat*. Madrid: Plus Ultra.
Vidal, Jaime R. 1988. "Popular Religion Among Hispanics in the General Area of the Archdiocese of Newark," *Presencia Nueva* Newark, NJ: Archdiocesan Office of Research and Planning.
_____. 1994. "Citizens, yet Strangers: The Puerto Rican Experience, 1898-1965" in Dolan and Vidal, eds. *Puerto Rican and Cuban Catholics: the US, 1900-1965*. Notre Dame, Indiana: University of Notre Dame Press. 1994.
Vitoria, Francisco de. 1960. *Relectio de Indis in Obras de Francisco de Vitoria*. Madrid: Biblioteca de Autores Cristianos.
Zavala, Silvio. 1937. *La Utopía de Tomás Moro en la Nueva España*. Mexico.

The Penitential Doctrine of Restitution: Its Use by Bartolomé de Las Casas to Liberate Popular Religiosity during the Conquest of America

LUIS N. RIVERA PAGÁN

Translation by
ANTHONY M. STEVENS-ARROYO

Popular religiosity has special significance for Latinos living under the United States's flag today, partly because it represents an alternative form of Christian belief and practice that responds to our particular circumstances as peoples still searching for self-determination. But the capacity of popular religiosity to protest a Christianity too closely identified with an oppressive socio-economic regime antedates the encounter with the indigenous religions of the Americas. This critical capacity is derived largely from the very nature of popular religiosity as brought by the Spanish conquistadors and colonists. This article traces through the writings of Bartolomé de Las Casas the struggle within sixteenth century Catholicism for control of Spanish popular religiosity. It was a tug of war between opposing groups over the political implications of the Gospel for the Spaniards of that time.

It is important to stress that this struggle over the religious meaning of the conquest was not an incidental, subordinate dimension of Spanish colonization. Religious purpose was articulated by virtually every protagonist during the conquest and played out a centralizing role in the popular religiosity of the soliders, sailors and settlers who came to the Americas under the banners of the Spanish monarchy. Take, for instance, the harangue by Hernán Cortés to his troops on December 20, 1520 in Tlaxcala Province on the eve of his seige of

Tenochtitlán, one of the most famous battles between the Spaniards and the natives during the epoch-marking conquest of America. He confirmed a tight linkage between his military enterprise and the evangelization of the indigenous peoples. In his military instructions at Tlaxcala, he proclaimed:

> *The people of these parts place so much watchful care in their worship and veneration of idols that Our Lord God is done a great disservice. The devil is much adored because of the blinding deceit he works on them. He leads them off into great error and idolatry, reducing for them the knowledge of our holy Catholic faith... I heartily implore all Spaniards in my troops who have come to wage this war, and all others that have had to proceed under my command in the name of His Majesty that their principal motive and intention may be to uproot all such idolatries and lead every native here away from them...bringing back the knowledge of God and His holy Catholic faith. Because if this war were to be made with any other intention, it would be unjust (Cortés: 165).*

Echoing the rhetoric of courtly discourse, war was waged against the Mexican natives for reasons that were strictly evangelizing and missionary in order to combat idolatry and to promote the expansion of the one true Catholic faith. The theological paradigm was converted into a normative criterion that validated the military enterprise as a just one. It also neutralized the blatant fact that Christians were the agressors and the unbelievers, the victims (Rivera, 1992).

Fulfilling the missionary command of the resurrected Jesus by means of military conquest did not sound so paradoxical nor particularly strange to Spaniards raised during centuries of the religious-military ideology of the Reconquest. It is not mere coincidence that Cortés calls the native temples, "mosques" or that he bore a standard with a cross containing the Latin inscription: *Amici, sequamor crucem: si nos fidem habuerimus, in hoc signo vincemos* (Friends, let us follow the Cross and if we have faith in this sign, we shall be victorious).[1] The bearing of the cross was the symbolic accoutrement of the Crusades in accord with medieval canon law (Brundage, 1969). In this way, the military enterprise acquired its missionary nature.

The intimate link between spreading the gospel and theologizing a just war does not manage, however, to hide the overriding desire for riches. Avarice is not always far removed from piety. While emphasizing the missionary character of his military daring, Cortés includes the possible pecuniary benefits to booty in his military orders as pleasing the monarchy: "Because if this war were waged with another purpose, it would be unjust and everything in the war would be vitiated and restitution would be called for. And his Majesty would have no reason to mandate the rewarding of those who served in it"(Cortés: 165).

It is interesting that in the middle of a military escapade, the sacramental concept of restitution comes into Cortés's head.[2] If the war were waged exclusively for pecuniary ends it becomes unjust and the booty would fall in the category of theft, of ill-acquired goods, subject to restitution according to canon law. What a strange context for ennuciating the stipulations that belong to the doctrine of restitution! What does this tell us about the popular religious mind of Spanish Catholicism in the sixteenth century?

Certainly it tells us that the Spanish Catholic popular religious mindset never was divorced drastically from the theological traditions of the medieval church, although some scholars have asserted this— be it to criticize popular religiosity or to praise its alleged rectitude. One finds these traditional concepts behind the relation Cortés established between correct intention of a just war for his troops setting seige to Tenochtitlán, and the waiver of a need to return booty. St. Thomas Aquinas had postulated in the *Summa Theologica* that plunder in an unjust war, or even malicious robbery in a just battle, constitutes a grave sin that incurs the need for restitution of what has been taken.

> *If those who plunder their enemies wage a just war.. they are not obliged to restitution. However, even if they wage a just war they can sin by craving to take booty. If their intention is evil, that is, if they fight not for justice but principally for booty.. and if those who take booty do it in an unjust war, they commit robbery and are obliged to restitution.* (Summa theologica: II-II, ques. 66, art. 8 ad 1.)

It is suprising that before the conflict a military commander and secular conquistador would incorporate into his planning the idea of restitution. In the mind of the speaker and of the listeners, this idea had to be accompanied by the complicated sacramental notions of penance, satisfaction, and absolution. It shows the importance that religious practice had for the internal conscience of a sixteenth century Spaniard. Violence could acquire its capacity of feudal subjugation, but only if it managed to link itself to popular piety. Those who proposed military conquest had to be able to unfurl religious imagination as if it were a symbolic synecdoche in a global enterprise of empire building.

However, it was not chiefly the conquistadores à la Cortés who invoked the theological principles of the doctrine of restitution. During the whole long and violent process of conquest of the native American communities, different efforts were made to withhold absolution, a chief part of the sacrament of penance, from the conquistadors and *encomenderos* (serf-holders) who exploited and plundered the indigenous peoples.

No one gained more fame for upholding this principle[3] than Bartolomé de las Casas, the cleric *encomendero* who was converted into the defender of the Indians and became an influential Dominican friar. He made the liberation of the natives and restitution with satisfaction for the damage done to them an indispensible condition before the penitent would receive the *ego te absolvo*. This included the treatment of a dying man, in which case a notarized testament was required for the desired effects. "Everyone is obligated to restitution *in solidum*. And none can be saved if they did not make restitution and satisfaction when it was possible..."[4] Las Casas concludes his extensive missiological treatise, *The Only Way*, with this penitential consequence:

> *All men who are, or might be, cause of the aforementioned war because of any of the means of cooperation listed, are obliged as a necessary means of salvation to restore to all these agrieved unbelievers everything that has been seized from them... and to satisfy them by solidarity, that is, totally, for the harm done to them (Las Casas, 1942: 541).*

The "advice to confessors" that he wrote as Bishop of Chiapas reveals las Casas's campaign to use his religious sacramental authority to free the oppressed:

> Concerning the Indians who are held as slaves... the confessor ought command the penitent that without repair he is to set them free by a public edict before a clerk and that he pay them each year or each month what they deserve for their services and work. This is to be done before entering the confessional. Likewise he is to ask forgiveness for the injury he has caused...because he ought to hold it certain and sure ... that in all the Indies from the discovery until today, there has not been nor is there now even one Indian who justly has been made a slave (Las Casas, 1965: 879).

There had been a recent precedent. The famous renaissance humanist, Desiderius Erasmus, in his popular anti-war tract, *Querela pacis* (1517) had suggested that priests not minister to dying soliders, nor permit them to be buried in church cemeteries. "Those wounded in battle have to be content with secular burial... The priests consecrated to God do not minister to places where war is waged..."(Erasmus, 1964:986-987). Las Casas did not cite Erasmus, but this ommission can be attributed to the campaign against the eminent humanist that was underway in Spain. It is very likely that las Casas had read *Querela pacis,* which had gone through ten editions in the first year it was published and was promptly translated into various languages, among them, Spanish (1520). The theoretic approximations are evident, above all the emphasis on the pacific nature of the Gospel.[5]

The refusal of Las Casas as Bishop of Chiapas to grant absolution from sin to those who had been involved in war or with the *encomiendas* was not something new in his thought. He did not affirm anything that he had not previously insisted upon publicly, in an official capacity. According to his own autobiographical reflexions, at the start of his conversion he set free the Indians he had consigned to him. He categorically stated the need for restitution in his sermon preached on the Day of the Assumption of Our Lady (August 15, 1514). The tone of his homily made it clear that he intended his own act to have a paradigmatic nature that might become a general norm of conduct.

In 1531, after spending many years in the cloistered Dominican monastery on Española, he wrote to the Council of the Indies:

> ... universally speaking, there has never been a just war waged by the Christians .. and so it follows that neither the King nor anyone who has come or stayed here has been engaged in any just affair nor rightly won anything. All are obligated to restitution...And it is so true, that there is no more doubt about this than about the Holy Gospel (Fabié: 483).

It must be noted that in this formal letter of official character, the depravity of the acquistions and the obligation to full restitution apply to the monarchy as well. The Spanish authorities who had jurisdiction over administration in the Indies are responsible for restitution of ill gains, even if they had not participated in such illicit profits. "You are obliged to restitution of all these goods and riches that others stole from these peoples even if not a single penny came to you." (Fabié:478). This idea would not be abandoned. It is reiterated in 1555 by Las Casas to Bartolomé Carranza, a ranking ecclesiastic very close to the crown: "the Kings of Castile are bound by reasonable grounds of necessary restitution and satisfaction."(Fabié, 1966:71:418.). In his final communication to the Council of the Indies, Las Casas wrote:

> All the sins committed throughout the Indies are tied to this. The damage of countless problems that have followed ever since and the obligation to make resitution, fall upon the conscience of His Royal Majesty and upon this Royal Council. You cannot take a single maravedi of profit from those kingdoms without the obligation of restitution (Las Casas, 1969: 280-281).

More than angry denunciation, this is an admonition to the monarchy to put imperial rule back on the track of justice. It is Las Casas's perennial quest, always frustrated by an imperial regime.

The effort of Las Casas to make absolution of sins dependent upon restitution for the evils done against the natives seems anachronistic and useless to us today. It should not be forgotten, however, that in the sixteenth century, absolution was considered an ecclesiastical favor that was indispensible at the time of imminent death. It was common among the Catholic masses to believe that if one confessed their sins before dying, sacramental forgiveness may be secured. Even when the sins were the most horrendous imaginable, one's soul could escape the perpetual torments of Hell. The contemporary religious mindset, what was at stake was the transcendental meaning of one's personal eternal destiny.

Because Las Casas targeted the pastoral practice of confession as the mode of affecting the Spanish popular conscience, the efforts to stop him centered upon the confessionary. It became an object of intense controversy, bitterly criticized by persons as dissimilar as the Franciscan missionary, Fray Toribio de Benavente (Motolinía); the court humanist, Juan Ginés de Sepúlveda (who was a friend of Cortés); and the Jesuit theologian, José de Acosta.

Motolinía was one of the famous twelve Franciscan missionaries who were given the task of converting millions of native Mexicans to Catholicism. In a letter to the Emperor Charles V, he accused Las Casas of being "hard to take, nervous and pushy and noisy and a trouble maker, of being unhappy in the religious life, of being rude and offensive and prejudiced... who has dishonored and defamed most gravely, and has injured and offended most terribly the Spanish nation and its prince.." (Motolinía: 208, 214).[6] He requested the monarch to consult with the highest church and theological authorities to untangle the spiritual confusion of conscience that Las Casas has created with his strict rules about the obligation to restitution. Not far from the theological dispute, however, lies a political one. There is a radically different evaluation of the achievements of the conquistador, Hernán Cortés. For Motolinía, Cortés was the originator and patron of an apostolic work of Providence. "Through this captain, God opened up for us the door to preach the Holy Gospel.."(Motolinía:221) The favoritism for Cortés is expressed without hedging in the work of Motolinía as well as in what was written by his successor, Mendieta (Lejarza: 43-136). Theirs was a history in which the passion for evangelizing went hand in hand with an apology for Cortés.

For his part, Sepúlveda, court historian and very close friend of Hernán Cortés as well, conspired to have Las Casas accused of treason before the Council of the Indies and of heresy before the Inquisition.(Fabié: 71, 335-351). In a letter to Prince Philip on September 23, 1549, he wrote about his bitter enemy in a delightful collage of Spanish and Latin:

> *The matter of the Confessionary of the Bishop of Chiapa[s] and of my book [Demócrates segundo] is coming to be the business of two opposing parties; one is the Kings of Spain, whose most just cause supports my book and the other the fevered men in this business whose chief is the Bishop of Chiapa[s]. As in other similar issues, it is* ut est homo natura factiosus, et turbulentus *[because he is a man of factious and disturbing nature.] (Losada: 202).*

In particular, he attacked the seventh rule of Las Casas confessionary, which proposed:

> *Everything that has been done in the Indies from the entry of the Spaniards into each of their provinces to the subjection and servitude imposed on the people... has been against every natural right, all international laws and against divine law as well. Thus, every such action is totally unjust, evil, tyrannical and worthy of hell fire and consequently, also null, invalid and without any value or legal effect (Las Casas, 1965: 2, 873).*

Writing several years after the death of Las Casas, the Jesuit theologian, Acosta, attacked Las Casas's position on restitution without mention of his name. Acosta censured those who "under a pretext such as piety doubt the right of our kings and of their governmental administration and who promote disputes about the rightful title with which the Spanish rule the Indies." Acosta was not content with theological response. He exhorted the authorities to set a hard hand against such complainers, because if they were allowed to disseminate their criticisms without reprisals, "there is no telling what evils and universal ruin will follow" (Acosta: 185ff.).

It is typical of the thought of Acosta to insist that God acts in history making violence and injustice the paradoxical channels for pouring out His grace. The Roman Empire was oppressive and exploitative, but having subdued many peoples violently it created the necessary context for the rapid expansion of the Gospel throughout the entire civilized world of classical antiquity. Likewise, the Spanish Empire, through the instrument of deviant violence by someone like Pizarro, permitted the efficient and rapid dissemination of Christianity among the American unbelievers.

More than anything, Acosta was worried by the problem Las Casas created with restitution, since it mattered to the popular Catholic conscience. He insisted that "Neither can one now provide restitution, because there is no one to make restitution to, nor any way to perform it efficiently" (Acosta: 185-188). In sum, the obligation to restitution, if it ever had existed, was now invalid. Even more, nothing should be done to weaken Spanish hegemony in America since the stability of the Christian faith in the conquered territories depended upon that rule.

Although the controversy about his confessionary was scarcely an agreeable moment for the insistent Las Casas, neither of the two charges of heresy and treason prospered. However, he was not able to prevent a royal decree of November 28, 1548 to the court of New Spain mandating the confiscation of all copies of the confessionary (Manzano: 166). Las Casas had never faced such a precarious situation.

The prohibition of Las Casas's confessionary did not dispel the notion of using sacramental power against conquistadors, serf-holders and colonists. Marcel Bataillon found in the National Historical Archive of Spain a letter that was written July 3, 1565 by a Dominican friar, Bartolomé de la Vega to the interim vicar of the Diocese of Cuzco, Fray Pedro de Toro. Vega repeats forcefully the idea of prohibiting absolution when there is no accompanying repentance and restitution by those who have participated in the oppression of the natives of Peru.

> *It is not permitted to absolve any of the aforementioned any more than one can absolve Judas...*Omnes praefati indigni sunt absolutione...*[All of those listed are unworthy of absolution] As a result, it is in the hands of Your Paternity to restore Peru by not granting permission to any cleric or friar to absolve any of these persons.. The reason is because they have taken the lands, the dominion and the freedom of the Indians without justification. (Bataillon: 311-314)*[7]

Until the end of his life, Las Casas maintained without reservation, his theological and moral position on the doctrine of restitution (Las Casas, 1969:235-250). It was for him the crucial guide for sacramental practice in the American church.[8] In his "Treatise of the Twelve Doubts," he developed vigorously the thesis that the Church's posture should be judged primarily in reference to this issue. He also urged that reception of the Eucharist and the rites of Christian burial be regulated by the same norm (Las Casas, 1958: 517-522).

We find, in this point, the thematic axis that gives unity to the pastoral activity of Las Casas. From his sermon in Cuba in 1514 before Diego Velázquez on the Feast of the Assumption of Our Lady, to his pistle to Pope Pius V in 1566, he presented restitution as the indispensible requirement for finding justice on earth and eternal salvation. In his petition to the pope, he requested that the Supreme Pontiff remind "the bishops, friars and clergy (who had grown rich in America) that they were obliged by natural and divine law ...to return all the gold, silver and precious gems that they had acquired..."(Las Casas, 1951: 3, 95). Here was the cutting edge of the sacramental doctrine that was applied unremittingly to the ecclesiastical institution itself. Las Casas sought from the church a strict austerity in material matters that would be a symbol of solidarity with those he called "the most poor of the poor of Christ".

The aggrandizement of ecclesiastical institutions was a scandalous matter for the Bishop of Chiapas. Among other things, it loomed large because canon law allowed a custom that made the church an alternative for restitution. When the victim was not accurately identifiable, or no longer alive, the obligation to pay back the damages incurred could be made to holy places. The guilty consciences of the conquistadors and colonists could be assuaged by making donations, often substantial ones, to church agencies.

In his writings, Las Casas sharpened the principle mentioned above that was taken from St. Thomas Aquinas about pillage in an unjust war or even about ill-intentioned plunder in a just conflict. Such constituted mortal sin that requires restitution of what had been stolen. Las Casas changed the context of the Thomist principle and placed it at the origin of the colosal epoch of imperial domination that Christian Europe would achieve over the rest of the planet in a few short centuries. In this way, Las Casas confronted a modernity that subjected different peoples and their cultures. He claimed a divine authority that seemed out of place and obsolete in the intolerant view of an empire that claimed evangelization as its ideological aegis.

By using the sacramental concept of restitution to confront, ecclesiastically, the subjugating character of the conquest, Las Casas— more than anyone else in the sixteenth century—drew close to the threshold of a theology that negates identification between the Christianization of the global community and European colonial rule. His intention was to do so from within the very interior of a popular religious conscience. This was his titanic, frustrating task in the model of Sisiphus. The idea of restitution of goods unjustly stolen was transformed especially in his last polemic writings, into the idea of the restitution of the sovereignty and the right to self-determination for the native peoples. It was an idea whose time had not yet come, but it bestowed immortality upon his writings (Rivera, 1992:63ff).[9]

The restriction placed on the absolution of conquistadors and serf-holders carried one central idea, basic both to various biblical texts and to the critical reflections of any theology focused upon the emancipation of the exploited. It was incompatible to oppress the poor and to participate in the sacraments. Las Casas and the other friars echoed the gospel and prophetic theme, "I desire mercy and not sacrifice" (Hosea 6:6; Matthew 9:13). The policy of oppression contradicts the soteriological purpose professed by worship. On this point the friars waged a battle destined for defeat, but one that became a dramatic and indelible memorial of gospel solidarity.

This detailed examination of the doctrine of restitution in the writings of Las Casas and his contemporaries shows that Spanish popular religiosity played a crucial role in the conquest. But popular religiosity acquired its political and liberating function because of linkage to sacramental ministry. The desire for salvation, an impulse that permeates popular religiosity, led inevitably to reception of the sacraments which were under the control of the clergy. Las Casas sought to influence the popular religiosity of the Spaniards in the Americas by bringing the weight of Christian theology about restitution to bear upon the everday practice of religion. It was this connection between theological principle and pastoral application that his opponents sought to debilitate.

The sixteenth-century struggle within Christianity between those radically identified with the cause of the poor and those who temporized with the dominant political power, continued in Latin America until our own times. It was this connection between a Christianity in defense of the poor that is echoed by Padre Hidalgo in the cry of Mexican independence in the 19th century, and is suggested in the notion of the Cosmic Race by Vasconcelos in the 20th. The clash of institutional interests against popular faith resonates in the identification of Puerto

Rican nationalism with Catholicism by José de Diego and Pedro Albizu Campos. It reaches out to include the son of a Protestant minister, Frank País, in the struggle against Cuba's dictator, Fulgencio Batista. It was heard in the Delano Valley with the call for social justice by César Chávez. In Nicaragua, El Salvador and many other parts of the hemisphere, the contradictions between the Christianity of the political establishment and the Gospel call to social justice are issues of life and death.

Indeed, much of this century's politics in the United States and Latin America hinge upon religious perception. The role of popular religiosity is one that is not frequently taken into account by historians, even those of Christian affiliation. It is a tendency that begins even with the origins of Latin America and the Latino reality in the sixteenth century. For example, by accentuating the beginnings of modernity with the discovery and the conquest of the Americas, Enrique Dussel neglects a signficant fact: this modernity had not achieved full awareness of its secularity (Dussel).[10] It felt the need to understand and express itself with symbols, images and concepts that appealed to the conscience and the religious imagination of the people. The typical social imagery of that time was still shaped by the religious traditions of the Middle Ages. A peculiar paradox was played out in this modernity because it evolved and defended itself on the altar of religious traditions. The struggle of Latinos today reflects much of this same pattern. It would be tragic to attempt to address the problems we now face while ignoring the key role of religious conscience among our peoples.

Endnotes

1. The Latin slogan of Cortés is referred to by Fray Gerónimo de Mendieta: 176. Robert Ricard gives a slightly different version: 75. I derive my translation from the text provided by Francisco López de Gómara: 301. Bernal Díaz del Castillo has still a different rendition: 33.

2. For the doctrine of restitution, see N. Jung, "Restitution" in *Dictionnaire de théologie catholique, contenant l'exposé des doctrines de la théologie catholique, leurs preuves et leur histoire*, A. Vacant, E. Mangenot and E. Amann, eds. Paris: Librairie Letouzey (1937) columns 2466-2502.

3. Something similar was stated in 1518 by the Dominicans on Espñola to the Jeronymite fathers. "Because the acquisitions of the

Christians and the goods that they have attained from the work of the Indians have been and continue to be great, we believe that they are obnoxious and restitution would seem to be in order." This is found in *Colección de documentos inéditos relativos al descubrimiento, conquista y organización de las antiguas posesiones españolas de América y Oceanía, sacados de los Archivos del Reino y muy especialmente del de Indias,* Joaquín Pacheco, Francisco Cárdenas y Luis Torres de Mendoza, eds. 42 vols. Madrid: Imprenta de Quirós, 1864-1884, vol. 26:213. See also *Historia de la Indias:* 3:79, vol. 3:95.

4. The phrase, *in solidum* that las Casas constantly repeats means that the obligation of restitution refers not only to the private gain that each conquistador, settler or encomendero obtains, but to the benefits aquired by all. See Las Casas, 1965:1, 439.

5. It is difficult to avoid the impression of a probable influence over Las Casas of the other writings of Erasmus, like his treatises, "Most Useful Advice about the Declaration of War Against the Turk" (1530) in which he notes that behind the religious and pious motives to wage war against the Ottoman empire, can be hidden avarice and the desire for riches. Also in *Ecclesiastes sive conciator evangelicus* (1535) in which he disputes the apostolic and pacific method of evangelizing. In this regard, see the excellent work of Marcel Bataillon, *Erasmo y España: Estudios sobre la historia espiritual de siglo SVI* Mexico; Fondo de Cultura Económica, 1966.

6. Note however, that in a work previous to his bitter letter against las Casas, Motolinía had emphasized in an intense tone, the obligation that rested upon the conquistatores and settlers of restituting what they had obtained with an evil conscience from the blood, sweat and tears of the natives: *"porque todas estas cosas serán traídas y presentadas en el día de la muerte, si acá primero no se restituyen..."*. (Motolinía:167).

7. Las Casas' position on the obligation for restitution as an indispensable condition for receiving sacramental absolution influenced some sectors of the Latin American church. See Guillermo Lohmann Villena, "La restitución por conquistadores y encomenderos: Un aspecto de la incidencia lascasiana en el Perú", *Anuario de estudios americanos* 23 (1966) 21-89. It seems to me, however, that Lohmann exaggerates the "ethic beauty" and the "extreme virtue" of the "Christian knights" who showed remorse for their misdeeds by acts of restitution, reparation and compensation as their hour of death drew

near. Lohmann does not take into account the stylistic character, empty and repetitive, of these expressions of contrition, all of which are suspiciously similar. Nor does he bother to investigate if such promises were fulfilled to the letter of the law by the heirs and successors. Certainly, this would be an extremely taxing task of research, but methodologically essential. I am not certain that these formulas were expressive of "ethical sensitivity." There is another perspective possible, somewhat more skeptical or perhaps cynical: Those who lacked scruples in doing whatever was necessary to seize a temporal kingdom, fame and riches would likewise struggle in their last hour to win heavenly bliss. Certainly, this would be a paradoxical mode of reaffirming the crucial importance of religious symbols to the popular Catholic conscience of the 16th century.

8. He was not the only Spanish theologian of the 16th century to be interested in the doctrine of restitution. See, for example, the extensive treatment that Domingo de Soto dedicates to this topic: *De la justicia y del derecho* (1556) 4 vols. Venancio Diego Carro, introduction: Marcelino González Ordoñez, translator. Madrid: Instituto de Estudios Políticos, 1967-68; 2:327-381. His chief conclusion is: "Restitution of what has been stolen is so necessary, that without it, no one can remain in the state of grace nor recover it." (331).

9. Important to developing this idea is the work of Vidal Abril-Castelló, "La bipolarización Sepúlveda-Las Casas y sus consecuencias: La revolución de la duodécima réplica," in Demetrio Ramos, et al. *La ética en la conquista de América,* Corpus Hispanoroum de Pace, Vol. 25. Madrid: Consejo Superior de Investigaciones Científicas, 1984:229-288.

10. A better awareness of this paradox wherein modernity needs to sacralize the incipient capitalist accumulation with traditional religious symbols and images can be found in the conclusion to the erudite work of Alain Milhou, dedicated to clarifying the religious context of Spain at the time of discovery and conquest.

Bibliography

Acosta, José de. 1952. *De procuranda indorum salute (1589).* Madrid: Consejo Superior de Investigaciones Científicas.

Bataillon, Marcel. 1976. *Estudios sobre Bartolomé de las Casas.* Barcelona: Península.

Brundage, James A. 1969. *Medieval Canon Law and the Crusader.* Madison: University of Wisconsin Press.

Cortés, Hernán. 1990. *Documentos cortesianos, 1518-1528 José Luis Martínez.* Mexico: Universidad Nacional Autónoma de México.

Díaz del Castillo, Bernal. 1986. *Historia verdadera de la conquista de la Nueva España.* Mexico: Editorial Porrúa.

Dussel, Enrique. 1992. *1492: El encubrimiento del otro: Hacia el origen del "mito de la modernidad.* Santa fé de Bogotá: Ediciones Antropos.

Erasmus, Desiderius. 1964. "Querella de la paz" (1530) in *Obras escogidas.* Lorenzo Riber, ed. Madrid: Aguilar, 963-994.

_____. "Ecclesiastes sive concionator evangelicus" (1535) in *Opera omnia* 1704, n.p. vol. 5:769-1099.

Fabié, Antonio María. 1879. *Vida y escritos de don Fray Bartolomé de Las Casas, Obispo de Chiapa* Madrid: Imprenta de Miguel Ginesta. Republished as *Colección de documentos inéditos pra la historia de España.* Kraus Reprint, 1966, 70, 71.

Gutiérrez, Gustavo. 1992. *En busca de los pobres de Jesucristo: El pensamiento de Bartolomé de las Casas.* Lima: Instituto Bartolomé de las Casas.

Las Casas, Bartolomé. 1942. *Del único modo de atraer a todos los pueblos a la verdadera religión.* Mexico: Fondo de Cultura Económica.

_____. 1965. *Tratados.* Juan Pérez de Tudela Bueso, Agustín Millares Calvo y Rafael Moreno, trans. 2 vols. Mexico: Fondo de Cultura Económica.

_____. 1969. *De regia potestate o derecho de autodeterminación* Luciano Pereña et al. eds. in Corpus Hispanoroum de Pace, Vol. VIII, Madrid: Consejo Superior de Investigaciones Científicas.

Lejarza, Fidel de. 1948. "Franciscanismo de Cortés y cortesianismo de los franciscanos" *Missionalia hispánica* 5: 43-136.

López de Gómara, Francisco. 1946. *Conquista de Méjico. Segunda parte de la crónica general de las Indias.* Madrid: Biblioteca de Autores Españoles (volume 22).

Losada, Angel. 1949. *Juan Ginés de Sepúlvda a través de su "Epistolario" y nuevos documentos* Madrid: Consejo Superior de Investigaciones Científicas.

Manzano Manzano, Juan. 1948. *La incorporación de las Indias a la corona de Castilla.* Madrid: Ediciones Cultura Hispánica.

Mendieta, Fray Gerónimo de. 1980. *Historia eclesiástica indiana* (1596) Third facsimile edition. Mexico: Editorial Porrúa.

Milhou, Alain. 1983. *Colón y su mentalidad mesiánica en el ambiente franciscanista español. Cuadernos colombinos,* No. 9. Valladolid: Casa-Museo de Colón/Seminario Americanista de la Universidad de Valladolid.

Motolinía. (Fray Toribio de Benavente). 1984. *Historia de los indios de la Nueva España: Relación de los ritos antiguos, idolatrías y sacrificios de los indios de la Nueva España, y de la maravillosa conversión que Dios en ella ha obrado.* Edmundo O'Gorman, ed. Mexico: Editorial Porrúa.

Ricard, Robert. 1986. *La conquista espiritual de México. Ensayo sobre el apostolado y los métodos misioneros de las ordenes mendicantes en la Nueva España de 1523-24 a 1572.* Mexico: Fondo de Cultura Económica.

Rivera, Luis N. 1992. *A Violent Evangelism: The Political and Religious Conquest of the Americas.* Louisville: Westminster/John Knox Press.

Popular Religion as the Core of Cultural Identity Based on the Mexican American Experience in the United States

VIRGILIO ELIZONDO

Introduction

I am a native-born Mexican American Tejano from San Antonio, Texas. I have always lived and worked among my own people— except for brief periods of time when I went away to do advanced studies or was on special assignments in different parts of the world. My own family and the people from my barrio have been my basic formation team and it is from them that I have received my most cherished values, beliefs and religious expressions. It is through them and with them that I have experienced God, Jesus and the communion of saints— the extended family of my people.

Today, I am a grass-roots pastor with a doctorate in theology working in the parish where my parents were married, and where the people who nourished me as a child are the senior citizens I minister to every day. I could have left to become a university professor as I have had some very attractive offers from various universities and certainly enjoy going for brief periods as a visiting professor, but I have chosen to do what I can— academically and pastorally—with my people in their daily life and struggles. As I practice and reflect on the popular faith tradition of my own Mexican American people, I become more and more fascinated with its meaning and function in our everyday lives and the enriching contribution that our faith tradition can make to the universal church and to society in general.

Since 1731, my people have been living, transmitting and celebrating our Christian faith in continuity with the ways of our ancestors in the very same spot where I minister today, and we know that future generations will continue to find identity, solidarity and life in these *mestizo* traditions of deeply inculturated faith. The *Benditos* and *Alabados* will continue to be the common songs of the spiritual homeland within us that nobody can abolish, while our processions and fiestas will continue to celebrate ritually the painful and arduous way of the immigrants, undocumented, unjustly condemned, exploited and ridiculed of today's society who refuse to be eliminated or destroyed.

Many have tried to suppress our language, culture and even the religious expressions of our faith. But we have resisted and to the degree that we have resisted, we continue to be *el pueblo... la raza...* What ultimately makes us who we are? We continue to recreate annually the ancient traditions which are the substance of our collective soul. I became a priest to work with my people; to maintain alive that which had given our lives meaning in an otherwise meaningless and alien cultural world; to animate the struggle for justice, equality and liberty in a world where "law and order"—even in the Church—worked to justify and mask segregation and the exploitation of the poor; to celebrate life despite the many death threats; to transmit to the coming generations the basic elements of our common soul which are the substance of our identity as a people—as a *pueblo*.

Formation of Mexican American Religious Tradition

Religion and religious expression is power—but will it be a power unto life or a power of sacralized and legitimized oppression, margination, exclusion, ethnocide and even genocide? I am involved in the praxis of what theologians and social scientists tend to call "popular religiosity." And from within the praxis of "popular religiosity" I find few authors that seem to know what they are really talking about—they always seem to be speaking about the faith expressions of someone else who does not have the "pure faith" the author seems to presuppose about him/herself. I do not believe that anyone can penetrate the deep mystery of the religious expressions of a people from the outside. Outsiders can describe it and analyze it, but they will never know it for what it truly is. To the outsider, the ways in which people express their faith will always appear as "religiosity", but to the people themselves, their religious practices are the tangible expressions of the ultimately inexpressible: the mystery of God present and acting in our midst.

Our Mexican American religious expressions started with the prodigious *mestizaje* of Iberian Catholicism with the native religions which were already here. This rich and original synthesis did not take place in the theological universities or the councils of the Church, but in the very ordinary crossroads of daily life. This mestizising process started in 1519 and is still going on today. It is in the context of these religious symbols and rituals that the Mexican American experiences the deepest belonging and cultural communion. Our faith expressions need no explanation for those of us for whom they are meaningful, and no explanation will suffice for those who live and operate in a world of different religious symbols. We Mexican Americans do not need or seek explanations about *Our Lady of Guadalupe, Nuestra Señora de los Lagos, el Cristo Negro de Esquipulas, San Martín de Porres...* we know them well as living persons. In them, we experience the mystery of our own identity. They are our collective *alter ego*.

The Christian word of God was inculturated deeply within the collective soul of Mexico not by the intention of the missionaries, but by the process of symbolic interchange which took place in a very natural way in the *cocinas, mercados, plazas, hogares, tamaladas, panteones, milpas y fiestas del pueblo...* Although no one planned or organized it, it was in these places that the free interchange of life and ideas between the Iberians and the Nahuatls took place as naturally as the new flowers blossom in spring time.

The ordinary Spaniards of that period were mostly illiterate and came from a Catholic culture which was rich in imagery, and the native world of the Americas communicated mainly through an image-language, as well. Thus it was much more at the level of the image-word than of the alphabetic spoken word that the new synthesis of Iberian Catholicism and the native religions took place and continues to take place today. This synthesis became flesh in the gastronomic world which produced the new foods for which Mexico is famous today. Our cuisine, rich in contradictory flavors, is the earthly expression of the heavenly banquet referred to in the Scriptures. As Mexican cuisine emerged, so did the Mexican soul. Our mothers struggled to prepare tasty dishes out of the little or nothing they had available. They managed to nourish both our bodies and our spirit out of the same domestic tabernacles of life: *Las cocinas*.[1] Here they were free to talk, discuss, imagine, think, formulate and understand without coercion or control from higher authorities. This interchange at the grass-roots level has gradually given birth to Mexican Christianity.[2]

Ritual, mystery and image might well be called the trinity of the Mexican and Mexican American cultural-religious identity. Dogma and doctrines seem to be so Western, while ritual and mystery seem to be so *mestizo* Mexican. It is only in Our Lady of Guadalupe that the dichotomy is both assumed and transformed into synthesis. It would be the *madrecitas* in the *cocinas* who would gradually unfold and transmit the innermost meaning of this teophany which ushered in the new Christian tradition of the Americas. The male theologians have imposed western Marian categories on Guadalupe and have missed the creative and generative power of Guadalupe which has been articulated, developed and transmitted by the *abuelitas,* story-tellers and artists.[3] This articulation, development, and transmission is the starting point of our own indigenous Christian tradition—or what some people call "popular religiosity."

Function of Religious Tradition

Popular religiosity is simply the religious tradition of the local church (Tillard, 1976). The term "popular religiosity" is also what others call the religious expressions of my people. For us, these expressions are simply *¡nuestra vida de fe!* They are our own sacramental life which has arisen out of the common priesthood of the people acting in the power of the Spirit. The Word has become flesh in us in the form of our religious practices and traditions. They are the visible expressions of our collective soul through which we affirm ourselves in our relationship to each other and to God. Others may take everything else away from us, but they cannot destroy our expressions of the divine. Through these practices we not only affirm ourselves as a people, we also resist ultimate assimilation. Thus our religious practices are not only affirmations of faith, but the language of defiance and ultimate resistance. In our collective celebrations, we rise above the forces which oppress us or even seek to destroy us, and we celebrate our survival publicly. But it is much more than survival:

through our communal rituals and symbols the new born babies and growing children are initiated into the God-language of our people and thus we are assured that life will continue unto the next generation and generations to come.

By popular expressions of the faith I do not refer to the private or individual devotions of a few people but to the ensemble of beliefs, rituals, ceremonies, devotions and prayers which are publicly practiced by the people at large. It is my contention, which is beyond the scope of this paper to develop but which will be its point of departure, that the deepest identity of the people is expressed in those expressions of faith which are celebrated voluntarily by the majority of the people, transmitted from generation to generation by the people themselves, and go on with the Church, without it, or even in spite of it.

Popular faith expressions function in different ways for various peoples depending on their history and socio-cultural status. For the dominant culture, these expressions serve to legitimize their way of life as God's true way for humanity. They will tranquilize the moral conscience and blind people from seeing the injustices which exist in daily life. For a colonized/oppressed/dominated group, they are the ultimate resistance to the attempts of the dominant culture to destroy them as a distinct group either through annihilation or through absorption and assimilation. They will maintain alive the sense of injustice which the people experience in their daily lives.

These religious practices are the ultimate foundation of the people's innermost being and the common expression of their collective soul. They are supremely meaningful for the people who celebrate them, but often appear meaningless to the outsider. To the people whose very life-source they are, no explanation is necessary, but to the casual or scientific spectator no explanation will ever express or communicate their full meaning. Without them, there might be associations of individuals bound together by common interest (e.g. the corporation, the state, etc...), but there will never be the experience of being a people, *un pueblo*.

It is within the context of the group's tradition that one experiences both a sense of selfhood and a sense of belonging. Furthermore, it is within the tradition that one remains in contact both with one's beginnings, the stories of origins and with one's ultimate end. We are born into them and within them we discover our full and ultimate being. I might enjoy and admire other traditions very much, but I will never be fully at home within them. No matter how much I get into them, I will always have a sense of being other.

In the very beginning, those who followed the way of Jesus presented a very unique way of universalizing peoples without destroying their localized identity. This in fact was the genius and grace of the "Good News." People could now become members of the same family without ceasing to be who they were ethnically, even without giving up the symbols which were sacred to them. St. Paul at Athens does not ask the people to tear down their gods, but to recognize the one who was already there but had not yet been named. People would neither have to disappear through assimilation nor be segregated as inferior. The Christian message interwove with the local religious traditions so as to give the people a deeper sense of local identity (a sense of rootedness) while at the same time breaking down the psycho-sociological barriers that kept nationalities separate and apart from each other so as to allow for a truly universal fellowship (a sense of universality).

This process was the very core of the evangelizing process of the various European tribes. In fact that is precisely why today's Europe is so deeply united as Western culture and yet so diversified linguistically, culturally, gastronomically and in so many other exciting ways. Early Christianity affirmed the local identity while providing truly universalizing rites, words and symbols. In other words, it affirmed rootedness while destroying ghettoishness. Christianity changed peoples and cultures not by destroying them, but by re-interpreting their core rituals and myths through the foundational ritual and myth of Christianity. Thus, now a Jew could still be a faithful Jew and yet belong fully to the new universal fellowship and equally a Greek or a Roman could still be fully Greek or Roman and equally belong to the new universal group.

Unfortunately, once Christian Europe went out to conquer and evangelize other peoples, the missioners so identified the Gospel with their own Western culture that for the most part, they ignored the original genius of the Gospel and used it to destroy differences rather than bringing them into the whole of the Christian family which has room for all of the peoples—nations—of the world. It would take hundreds of years before the Second Vatican Council would begin to rectify these historical deviations. Thus, today, the greatest challenge of the Church has become the process of inculturation.

In ways similar to that of early Christians, Christianity without destroying our ancient rootedness, allowed us to enter into a universal family by sharing in a new common faith and in universal religious symbols. The missioners tried desperately to uproot all the ancient religions, but the laity—Spanish and Natives—simply constructed a new synthesis. This synthesis changed our native ancestors and their *mestizo* descendants not by the elimination of our religious ways, but by combining them with the Iberian-Christian ways to the mutual enrichment of both. This has been the basic way of the Christian tradition as it has historically made its way from Galilee, to Jerusalem, through Europe, Asia and North Africa and to the ends of the earth (Aragon, 1976). Without ceasing to be who we had been, we have become part of a broader human group—the Christian family which takes its members from all the nations of the world without destroying their cultural genius.

Two Distinct American Religious Traditions

The beginning of the Americas reflects two radically distinct images/myth representations of the Christian tradition. The United States was born as a secular enterprise with a deep sense of religious mission. The native religions were eliminated and supplanted by a new type of religion. Puritan moralism, Presbyterian righteousness and Methodist social consciousness coupled with deism and the spirit of rugged individualism to provide a sound basis for the new nationalism which would function as the core religion of the land. It was quite different in Latin America where the religion of the old European world clashed with native religious traditions. In their efforts to uproot the native religions, the conquerors found themselves assumed into them. Iberian Catholicism with its emphasis on orthodoxy, rituals and the divinely established monarchical nature of all society conquered physically. But it was absorbed by the pare-Colombian spirituality with its emphasis on the cosmic rituals expressing the harmonious unity of opposing tensions: male and female, suffering and happiness, self-immanence and transcendence, individual and group, sacred and profane, life and death.

In the secular based culture of the United States, it is the one who succeeds materially who appears to be the upright and righteous person—the good and saintly. The myth of Prometheus continues to be the underlying myth through which religions of the United States are reinterpreted and reshaped. In the pare-Colombian/ Iberian-Catholic *mestizo* based culture of Mexico it is the one who can endure all of the opposing tensions of life and not lose one's interior harmony who appears to be the upright and righteous one. Our religion and culture is constantly reinterpreted and reshaped through the combined myths of the suffering and crucified Jesus—as Jaime Vidal has stated: *El Señor del Gran Poder*—combined with the myths of Cuatemoc (the young Aztec prince whom the Spaniards killed because he refused to release Aztec gold) and Quetzalcoatl (who sacrificed himself for the good of his people).

Prometheus sacralized the power to conquer for self-gain while *El Señor del Gran Poder* and Quetzalcoatl sacralized the power to endure any and all suffering for the sake of the salvation of others—two very distinct foundations for the main religions of the Americas.

The Catholicism of the United States and the Catholicism of Mexico accept the same creed, ecclesiology, sacraments, commandments and official prayer. But the ways these are interpreted, imaged, and lived are quite different. The use of sacramentals and prayer forms and the relationship of people to the institutional Church is different in Mexican and Mexican American Catholicism than in the United States. For example, in the United States, many Anglo-Americans tend to see the Pope more as the President/CEO of our giant, world-wide Catholic "multinational", while in the Mexican American group, we love and reverence him as the *"papa grande"* of our big family. The implications of this are quite vast! In the United States, the sacraments have been the ordinary way of Church life, while in Mexico it has been the sacramentals. The written and spoken alphabetic -word (dogmas, doctrines and papal documents) are most important in U.S. Catholicism while the ritual and devotional image-word have been the mainstay of Mexican Catholicism. The United States has been parish-centered while the Mexican Church has been home, town and shrine centered.

With the great Western expansion of the United States in the 1800's, the two religious traditions of the Americas came into contact and conflict. During this period, the United States conquered fifty percent of northern Mexico. The Mexicans living in that vast region spanning a territory of over 3500 kilometers from California to Texas, suddenly became aliens in their own land... foreigners who never left home. Their entire way of life was despised. The Mexican *mestizo* was abhorred as a mongrel who was good only for cheap labor. Efforts were instituted to suppress everything Mexican: customs, language and Mexican Catholicism. The fair-skinned/blond Mexicans who remained had the choice of assimilating to the White, Anglo-Saxon, Protestant culture of the United States or be ostracized as inferior human beings. The dark-skinned had no choice! They were marked as an inferior race destined to be the servants of the White master race.

Today, social unrest and dire poverty forces many people from Mexico to relocate in the former Mexican territories which politically are part of the United States. Newcomers are harassed by the immigration services of the United States as illegal intruders—a curious irony since it was the United States citizens who originally entered this region illegally and stole it from Mexico. Yet the Mexican American descendants of the original European settlers in this region, along with recent Mexican immigrants, continue to feel at home, to resist efforts of destruction through assimilation, and to celebrate their legitimacy as a people.

Religious Symbols of Mexican American Communities

The Mexican Americans living in that vast borderland between the United States and Mexico have not only survived as a people but have even maintained good mental health in spite of the countless insults and put-downs suffered throughout their history and continuing to the present (Acuña, 1972). Anyone who has suffered such a long history of segregation, degradation and exploitation could easily be a mental wreck (Jiménez, 1985). Yet, despite this on-going suffering, not only are the numbers of Mexican Americans increasing, but in general Mexican Americans are prospering, joyful and healthy thanks to our profound faith as lived and expressed through group religious practices. I could explore many of them,[4] but I will limit myself to what I consider to be the three sets of related core expressions which mark the ultimate ground, the perimeters and the final aspirations of the Mexican American people: Guadalupe/Baptism; *polvo/agua bendita;* crucifixion/*los muertos.* They are the symbols in which the apparently destructive forces of life are assumed, transcended and united. In them, we experience the ultimate meaning and destiny of our life pilgrimage.

Guadalupe/Baptism

There is no greater and more persistent symbol of Mexican and Mexican American identity than devotion to Our Lady of Guadalupe. Thousands visit her home at Tepeyac each day and she keeps reappearing daily throughout the Americas in the spontaneous prayers and artistic expressions of the people. In her, the people experience acceptance, dignity, love and protection...they dare to affirm life even when all others deny them life. Since her apparition she has been the banner of Mexican and Mexican American movements of independence, reform and liberty.

Were it not for Our Lady of Guadalupe[5] there would be no Mexican or Mexican American people today. The great Mexican nations had been defeated by the Spanish invasion which came to a violent and bloody climax in 1521. The native peoples who had not been killed no longer wanted to live. Everything of value to them, including their gods, had been destroyed. Nothing was worth living for. With this colossal catastrophe, their entire past became irrelevant. New diseases exacerbated the trauma and collective death-wish of the people, and the native population decreased enormously.

It was in the brown Virgin of Guadalupe that Mexicanity was born and through her that the people have survived and developed. At the very moment when the pre-Colombian world had come to a drastic end, a totally unsuspected eruption took place in 1531 when, in the ancient site of the goddess Tonantzin, a dark-skinned woman appeared to announce a new era for "all the inhabitants of this land." Guadalupe provided the spark which allowed the people to arise out of the realm of death like the rising Phoenix arising out of the ashes of the past -- not just a return to the past but the emergence of a spectacular newness (Ruffle, 1976: 247-252). In sharp contrast to the total rupture with the past which was initiated by the conquest-evangelization enterprise, Guadalupe provided the necessary sense of continuity which is basic to human existence. Since the apparition took place at Tepeyac, the long venerated site of Tonanzin, mother of the Gods, it put people in direct contact with their ancient past and in communion with their own foundational mythology. It validated their ancestry while initiating them into something new. The missioners claimed their ancestors were wrong and that the diabolical past had to be totally eradicated. But the lady who introduced herself as the mother of the true God was now appearing among them and asking that a temple be built on this sacred site. She was one of them, she was clothed with the colors of divinity, but she definitely was not one of their goddesses. In her, there was continuity and newness, rootedness and breakthrough. Out of their own past and in close continuity with it, something truly new and sacred was now emerging.

Furthermore, she was giving meaning to the present moment in several ways for she was promising them love, defense and protection. At a time when the people had experienced the abandonment of their gods, the mother of the true God was now offering them her personal intervention. At a time when new racial and ethnic divisions were emerging, she was offering the basis of a new unity as the mother of all the inhabitants of the land. At a time when the natives were being instructed and told what to do by the Spaniards, she chose a low-class native to be her trusted messenger and to instruct the Spaniards through the person of the Bishop. In her, the conquered, oppressed and crushed begin to liberate and rehabilitate.

Finally, she initiated and proclaimed the new era which was now beginning. Over her womb is the Aztec glyph for the center of the universe. Thus she carries the force that will gradually build up a new civilization—not a simple restoration of the past nor simply New Spain, but the beginning of something new. The flowers, which she provided as a sign of authenticity, were for the indigenous world the sign which guaranteed them that the new life would truly flourish.

Thus in Guadalupe, the ancient beginnings connect with the present moment and signal what is yet to come! The broken pieces of their ancient numinous world are now reconfigured in a new way. Out of the chaos, a new world of ultimate meaning is now emerging. The Phoenix had truly come forth not just as a powerful new life, but also as the numinosum which would allow them to once again experience the awe and reverence of the sacred—not a sacred which was foreign and opposed to them, but one which ultimately legitimized them in their innermost being—both collectively as a people and individually as persons.

The complementary symbol of Guadalupe is the BAPTISM of infants. Our Lady of Guadalupe had sent the native Juan Diego to the Church. Many indigenous people thereafter sought baptism. They were no longer being uprooted from their ancient ways in order to enter into the Church. Sent by their mother, Guadalupe, they were entering as they were—with their customs, their rituals, their songs, their dances and their pilgrimages. The old Franciscan missioners feared this greatly. Many thought it was a devil's trick to subvert their missionary efforts. But the people kept on coming. They were truly building the new temple the Lady had requested: the living temple of Mexican-Christians. It is through baptism that every newborn Mexican and Mexican American enters personally into the temple requested by the Lady.

Through baptism the child becomes part of the continuum and is guaranteed life despite the social forces against life. The physical birth of the child is completed by the spiritual birth and both form an integral part of the biological life of the child. For our people, baptism of infants in not just a Catholic sacrament of initiation, but also a biological-anthropological event which binds the child and the community together in a profound and lasting blood-spiritual relationship.

Through baptism, the community claims the child as its very own and with pride presents it to the entire people—no matter how it was conceived or what might be the social status of the child. In the group, the child will receive great affirmation and tenderness. This will give the child a profound sense of existential security and belonging. Whether others want us around or not is of little consequence because we grow up knowing that we belong. The child will be able to affirm selfhood despite the put-downs and insults of society: Our children will dare to be who they are—and they will be who they are with a great sense of pride! This deep sense of security and belonging will further develop through participation in the multiple religious rituals of the people such as *posadas, rosarios, velorios, peregrinaciones,* and the *vía-crucis.*

For a people who have an historical memory and a contemporary situation of degradation, insults and rejection, baptism signifies that this child, regardless of what the world thinks of it, is of infinite dignity. It is the sacred rite of initiation into the community and the ancestors. Through it, not only are the newborn welcomed into the group, but the continuity of the group's life is assured... the life of the ancestors will continue in the future generations because of our religious celebrations today.

As the apparitions of Our Lady of Guadalupe at Tepeyac were the beginning of an anthropological resurrection event for the native and *mestizo* peoples of Mexico, so is baptism, the individual entry into the life of these resurrected people. Through baptism a child not only becomes a child of God according to the Christian tradition, but equally a child of our common mother of the Americas, *Nuestra Señora de Guadalupe.*

Cenizas/Agua Bendita

There is no doubt that ashes on Ash Wednesday is one of the most popular rituals of the entire year for Mexicans and Mexican Americans. In my parish of San Fernando in San Antonio, we have a service of ashes every half hour averaging 1200 persons per half hour. By the end of the day, over 30,000 persons celebrate the rite of ashes in our church. The Church does not promote this day as a day of obligation, yet it is one of the most popular rituals of the entire Church year. Why?

For us, the earth is sacred. We come from the earth and in time we return to the earth. The earth, and especially the portion of the earth out of which we originate, is the very source of our life, subsistence and existence. In a survey I conducted a few years ago of Mexican Americans living in the Southwest, the most frequent response to the question "What would you like to leave your children?", was *"una tierrita".* Precisely because we are so bound to the earth, one of the deepest sources of our suffering as a people is that we have been deprived of our own land. Without even having migrated, we have been forced to live as aliens in the very lands of our ancestors. Only the languages, dress, foods, customs and religion of the foreigners who invaded these lands are considered true and legitimate while the ways of earlier inhabitants continue to be despised as pagan, savage and inferior. In our own land, we cannot be at home! We are treated like squatters without rights to be moved as the powerful see fit. We are moved from one space to another without any regard for our families or cemeteries. Our natural resources are taken away from us and replaced with garbage and toxic wastes. Whatever the rest of society does not want around—jails, public housing, garbage dumps—is conveniently placed in our neighborhoods. What is life without connectedness to our own proper earth? POLVO!

On Ash Wednesday, as the people come up to receive the ashes, they hear the words: *"Polvo eres..."* The ashes at the beginning of Lent are a religious expression of the Mexican tradition which finds its full socio-religious meaning when coupled with the holy water which is blessed during the Easter Vigil—when through God's power, justice triumphed over injustice in the resurrection of the innocent victim from the death inflicted upon him by the unjust "justice" of this world. The one whom the world had rejected and killed, God raised and exalted as the Lord of all nations.

For people who have been forced to become foreigners in their own land, who have been driven from their properties and who have been pushed around by the powerful like the mighty wind blows the dust around, ashes are a powerful sign post on the pilgrimage of life. They mark the radical acceptance of the moment—like Jesus accepting the cross. This ritual reflects the burning of Cuatemoc's feet while he refused to give in to the demands of the Spaniards. He endured rather than giving in to the unjust demands of his captors in their lust for gold. But this acceptance does not indicate approval in any way whatsoever. It is the acceptance of an unjust situation without the acceptance of its disastrous consequences: the destruction of our people. The very fact that we are here in growing numbers and walking up to receive the ashes is an act of public and collective defiance of the destructive situation that has been forced upon us.

We will not be eliminated from this earth. We might be dust today, but dust settles down and becomes fertile earth when it receives moisture. The people come not only for ashes, throughout the year they also come for holy water to sprinkle upon themselves, their children, their homes... everything. They are aware that our entire world yearns and travails in pain awaiting to be redeemed—a redemption which in Christ has indeed begun but whose rehabilitating power is yet to take effect in the present day escalating injustices of our world. The use of the regenerative waters of baptism in every aspect of life is a constant plea for God to right the wrongs of our present society. If God is truly God, God must intervene. God cannot remain distant and passive in the light of the great misery and suffering of God's people. We know that God hears the cries of the poor and God will come to save us. God will redress this unjust situation which has been imposed upon us. God opened the sea to allow the Hebrew people to escape enslavement, God called the Crucified One to life from the tomb and this same God will convert us from aliens to children in our own land. The present situation will not last forever for the God of justice and mercy will bring about change.

The sprinkling with the waters of the Easter Vigil is a call for the regeneration of all creation. The dust which is sprinkled with the water will be turned into fertile earth and produce in great abundance. As in the reception of ashes, in the sprinkling of holy water there is an unquestioned affirmation: the ashes will again become earth, and the dust-people will once again inherit the earth. The dust-water binomial symbolizes the great suffering of an uprooted people who refuse to give in to despair but live in the unquestioned hope of the new life that is sure to come.

Crucifixion/Muertos

The final set of religious celebrations which express the core identity of the Mexican American people is the crucifixion which is celebrated on Good Friday, and the day of the dead celebrated on November 2. For a people who have consistently been subjected to injustice, cruelty and early death, the image of the Crucified One is the supreme symbol of life despite the multiple daily threats of death. If there was something good and redemptive in the unjust condemnation and crucifixion of the God-man, then, as senseless and useless as our suffering appears to be, there must be something of ultimate goodness and transcendent value in it. We don't understand it, but in Jesus the God-man who became the innocent victim who suffered for our salvation, we affirm it and in this very affirmation receive the power to endure it without it destroying us. Even if we are killed, we cannot be destroyed.

Jesus was assassinated but not eliminated. He is alive and his cross has become the source and symbol of the ultimate triumph of goodness over evil, courage over fear, love over self-righteousness. No wonder that in their faith-filled evangelical intuition, at the moment when the scourged and humiliated Jesus of Nazareth appears to be the most powerless, the people spontaneously acclaim him as *El Señor del Poder ...El Señor de la Gloria* (see, Vidal, this vol.). He had the incredible power to sustain the most cruel suffering for the sake of our salvation. This, in the minds of our people, is the ultimate power of God—the power to endure for the sake of those we love. The power to conquer might be glamorous and appealing, but only the power to endure for the sake of another is truly divine and life-giving. Animals conquer by force, God conquers by enduring love—enduring even unto death on the cross. The power to conquer diminishes with time and remains only in the dust of unread history books, while the power to endure lives on in those who follow in the way of Jesus. Today, the crucified Jesus still lives, but the conquering Caesars and armies have long been dead, buried and hardly remembered. The Crucified One is alive, but the executioners are all dead and gone.

In the presence of *el Señor del Gran Poder,* we see and celebrate our own inner strength which has allowed us to endure for the sake of our families and our people. What others ridicule as weakness, we see as the divine power alive in us. We are not a fatalistic people who enjoy suffering, but a powerful people who will not allow suffering to destroy our lives or even our joy of living. The radical acceptance of the cross of life is the basis for our festive music, dances and fiestas. We do not celebrate because we suffer; we celebrate because we refuse to allow suffering to control or destroy our lives.

People who only know us from the outside claim that we are so fascinated with suffering and death that we ignore joy and resurrection. Nothing could be further from the truth. Such people see us but they do not know us. Our people accept openly the harshness of suffering and death because we participate already in the beginning of resurrection. We celebrate our collective resurrection on the early morning of December 12 at our sunrise service to our Lady of Guadalupe, and we celebrate resurrection every time we use the *agua bendita* in reaffirming God's power over sickness and death. But at no time do we celebrate the communion of living saints more than on *el día de los muertos* which in effect is the day of the living—the day of those who have defied death and are more alive than ever!

We know the secret mystery of life. Those whom the world takes for dead, we know beyond a doubt are alive not only in God—and God is the fullness of life—but in us who remember them. Because they are no longer limited or imprisoned by "this body", they are now more alive than ever. The final, absolute, definitive death beyond which there is no earthly life left is when there is no one around to remember me or celebrate my life. Thus in remembering—*recordando*—we keep alive our ancestors as much as they keep us alive and continue to guard over us. The pain which we experience when someone we know and love dies is transformed into an inner joy at the annual celebration of those who through death have entered ultimate life. Our memory of their lives becomes a source of life and energy. As we bring them flowers, build altars of remembrance, light candles, share in the common bread and punch of the dead, we enter into the ultimate fiesta. In the mystical moment of celebrating *el día de los muertos,* the veil of time and space is removed and we are all together on earth and in heaven, in time and in eternity singing the same songs, enjoying the same food and drink and sharing in the same life that no earthly power can take away from us.

It should be noted that our *día de los muertos* is the very opposite of Halloween. Our "dead" do not come to spook us, but to visit, comfort and party with us. We do not fear them. We welcome their presence and look forward to having a good time with them. Sometimes we even take music to the cemeteries and share with them their favorite songs. We celebrate together that death does not have the final word over life and that life ultimately triumphs over death. Our family and our *pueblo* is so strong and enduring that not even death can break it apart. Thus what is celebrated as the day of the dead is in effect the celebration of indestructive life—a life which not even death can destroy. Society might take our lands away, marginate us and even kill us, but it cannot destroy us. For we live on in the generations to come and in them the previous generations continue to be alive.

Conclusion

The conquest of ancient Mexico by Spain in 1521 and then the conquest of northwest Mexico by the United States in the 1830s and 1840s forced the native population and their succeeding generations into a split and meaningless existence. It was a mortal collective catastrophe of gigantic death-bearing consequences. Yet the people have survived as a people through the emergence of new religious symbols and the reinterpretation of old ones which have connected the past with the present and projected into the future. The core religious expressions as celebrated and transmitted by the people are the unifying symbols in which the opposing forces of life are brought together into a harmonious tension. This gives the people who participate in them the experience of wholeness. In them and through them, opposites are brought together and pushed towards a resolution and the people who celebrate them experience an overcoming of the split. Where formerly there was opposition, now there is reconciliation and even greater yet, synthesis. This is precisely what gives joy and meaning to life, indeed makes life possible in any meaningful sense regardless of the situation. It is in the celebration of these festivals of being and memory that the people live on as a people.

I have limited my observations and attempts at interpretation to my own personal Mexican American experience, not because I am not uninterested in all Hispanics, but precisely because I do not dare the arrogance to speak for the others. I have not lived their experience and even though I respect their religious symbols and practices deeply, they are not my own. I am convinced that you can only understand religious symbols correctly from within and not by mere observation—even the best and most critical—from the outside. In seeking to understand religious symbols correctly, the so-called "objective distance" of western scholars is a sure guarantee of falsification and objective error, especially if their research is not done in dialogue with the believers themselves. Only by a patient and prolonged listening to the believers can one begin to understand the real meaning of their practices and rituals. They cannot be judged by criteria of another cosmovision or world-view.

I very much admire what Richard Flores is doing with the *pastorelas* and how he has gone through the process of becoming a *pastorcito* himself, has personally taken part in all the aspects of the process and is gradually beginning to understand them from within. I very much appreciate what Ana María Díaz-Stevens is doing to study the religious thought of Puerto Rican women. Her insights have opened up a whole new field of reflection for me. All of a sudden *las cocineras* were not just the women in the kitchens, but the creative thinkers who were cooking-up new and profound theological thought. We need Hispanic theologians and social scientists who will reflect from within the common experience of our people's faith, not as outsiders but as believers who are seeking to understand, clarify and enrich that life of faith.

I am anxiously awaiting and looking forward for the other Hispanic groups in the United States to speak and write more extensively about the religious expressions of their cultures. To the degree that this takes place, we will be able to begin a fruitful dialogue among ourselves. I long to see deeper studies on the Cuban American devotion to *Nuestra Señora de Caridad del Cobre* and their Afro-Cuban sense of santería, on the Puerto Rican devotion to *San Juan Bautista* and other religious practices, on the *Cristo Negro de Esquipulas* of Guatemala and other devotions and rituals of the various Hispanic peoples living in the United States. I trust that PARAL will be able to continue encouraging this type of socio-theological reflection and dialogue among the various groups— each from within its own lived experience of inculturated faith with its corresponding religious symbols. These religious symbols and rituals are the keys that will unlock the secret to the deepest and most far-reaching elements of our people's cosmovision and thus provide the ultimate basis for our earthly identity.

Endnotes

1. I do not intend to indicate that women should stay in the kitchens, but to bring out a very important aspect of life which has not been properly recognized. It was Ana María Díaz-Stevens during the PARAL symposium who first made me aware of how much more had come out of the kitchens than mere food. They had been the most exciting place where new life in all its aspects had truly blossomed and developed.

2. Orlando Espín has some fine articles on the relation between popular expressions of the faith and the Roman Catholic tradition. In particular, see his "Tradition and Popular Religion: An Understanding of the *Sensus Fidelium,*" in *Frontiers of Hispanic Theology in the United States,* ed. Allan Figueroa-Deck (Maryknoll, New York: Orbis, 1992), 62-87; a classical work on this subject is J.M.R. Tillard, et al, *Foi Populaire Foi Savante,* Paris: Editions du Cerf, 1976.

3. For more in-depth studies on Our Lady of Guadalupe I recommend my own book: *La Morenita: Evangelizer of the Americas* (San Antonio Mexican American Cultural Center Press, 1980) and subsequent articles on this subject in *Concilium*. See also Jeanette Rodriguez's 1994 book.

4. For a fuller discussion of other religious symbols, consult my previous works: *Christianity and Culture* (San Antonio: Mexican American Cultural Center Press, 1975); *Galilean Journey: The Mexican American Promise,* (Maryknoll, New York: Orbis, 1983).

5. For other aspects of Guadalupe, consult my previous articles in *Concilium* number l02/1977 and number l88/198.

Bibliography

Acuña, Rodolfo. 1972. *Occupied America: A History of Chicanos.* San Francisco: Canfield Press.

Aragon, Jean-Louis. 1976. "Le 'Sensus Fidelium' et ses fondaments neotestamentiares," in Tillard, *Foi Populaire.*

Elizondo, Virgilio 1975. *Christianity and Culture.* San Antonio: Mexican American Cultural Center Press.

———. 1980. *La Morenita: Evangelizer of the Americas.* San Antonio: Mexican American Cultural Center Press.

———. 1983. *Galilean Journey: The Mexican American Promise.* Maryknoll, New York: Orbis.

Espín, Orlando. 1992. "Tradition and Popular Religion: An Understanding of the *Sensus Fidelium,*" in *Frontiers of Hispanic Theology in the United States,* ed. Allan Figueroa-Deck. Maryknoll, New York: Orbis.

Jiménez, Roberto. 1895. "Social Changes/Emotional Health", *Medical Gazette of South Texas* VII, 20 June.

Rodríguez, Jeanette. 1994. *Faith and Empowerment Among Mexican American Women.* Austin: The University of Texas Press.

Ruffle, J. 1976. *De La Biologie a la Culture.* Paris: Flammarion.

Tillard, J.M.R. et al. 1976. *Foi Populaire, Foi Savante,* Paris: Editions du Cerf.

The Ideological Dimensions of Popular Religiosity and Cultural Identity in Puerto Rico

6

SAMUEL SILVA-GOTAY
Translation by
ANTHONY M. STEVENS-ARROYO

Popular religiosity is fashioned in the crucible of history. The manifestation of a people's religious yearnings develops in relation to myriad factors, including the on-going emergence of a people's cultural and political identity. Changing circumstances influence popular religiosity so that it assumes differing configurations, not only from country to country, but also from time to time in a single country. Because of its role in mediating many of these forces, popular religiosity offers a window on the character of a people as they confront not only religious issues, but also political, cultural and social ones.

But Puerto Rico offers a particularly difficult challenge to such a multifaceted analysis of religion among Latinos because the application of the name "Latino" to the Puerto Rican people is fraught with ambiguity. Puerto Rico is a nation that was occupied during the colonial process from the 16th century down to our own days. Puerto Ricans are not a "minority"; we are the majority population in our nation.

It is important to understand how the popular religiosity of Puerto Ricans living under the United States' flag differs from the generalized phenomenon in Latin America, such as described by Gustavo Benavides in this volume. My effort here is to provide an essay on my research experience over the past decade. Perhaps the information on Puerto Rico I offer here to an English-reading audience can be compared with studies of similar processes in Texas, New Mexico, California and other parts of the Southwestern United States starting in the first half of the nineteenth entury. I hope this will contribute to a clearer understanding of the role of religion in the complex process of cultural and political changes that shape national identity.

Evangelization and Christendom

Puerto Rican Catholicism came with the invasion and colonization by the Spaniards at the beginning of the 16th century. This Christianity was based on a concept of "Christendom," which is a term that refers not to Christianity in general, but to the way that Church and the medieval state were wrapped together in a single politico-religious entity. The mode of evangelizing during the conquest of America and the ensuing evolution of Catholicism in the nineteenth century Caribbean were not the results of accidents and mistakes, but the product of a system. The Church came to depend on the state for its existence and, correspondingly, validated the decisions of state as Christian. Thus by "Christendom" we refer to the medieval Christian theocratic civilization articulated in the philosophy and theology of the period that considered the medieval socio-economic, political and cultural order as "established by God." The tremendous power of the Catholic Church as the state church thus constituted an aparatus of social control closely associated with the politics of Spanish colonialism (Rivera, 1991).

Due to that association, the Church participated in the structures of violence and exploitation of indians and slaves. One finds the Catholic Church of early Puerto Rico in a political and cultural context wherein it participates in the assignment of Indians (*repartimiento*) and in the use of the natives in serf labor (*encomienda*). Despite the measures that eventually protected the remaining Indians of Mexico and the continent, in Puerto Rico the original Taíno society had already suffered virtual extinction by the time serfdom was outlawed. Thereafter, the use of black African slave labor was legitimated in the enterprises and establishments of religion. The clergy in Puerto Rico often participated in the practice of slavery. The first bishop from Spain, Alonso Manso, and his nephew constituted the chief slave holders on the island. The Puerto Rican Catholic historian, José García Leduc, has completed monumental research of priests who were plantation proprietors and slave holders during the nineteenth century in Puerto Rico. He points out that all of the plantation-owning clergy held 502 slaves during the period (García Leduc, 1990: 519) and his study focuses upon ten of these prominent ecclesiastics during the apogee of sugar in the decade before abolition in 1873. Bishop Gutiérrez del Arroyo, Dean of the Cathedral, was himself one of the most important slave-holders and plantation owners on the island, with 114 slaves on his own *hacienda* (Idem). Very late in the nineteenth century, even though the Vatican had already condemned slavery as anti-Christian and inhuman, the bishops and clergy in Puerto Rico continued as one of the most visible slave-holding sectors in the country.

Thus, one can apply to Puerto Rico the conclusions of the Catholic historian, Dr. José Oscar Beozzo, Rector of the Catholic Seminary of Lins in Sao Paulo, and now President of the Comisión de Estudios de Historia de la Iglesia en Latina America (CEHILA), who tells us:

> *In the case of the black African, [the Church] made an alliance with the oppressors, assigning the task of evangelization of the slaves to their master. The Church committed itself to the system in vogue, putting slave labor to intense use on the properties of religious orders, in the factories of the Jesuits and Carmelites and on the plantations and monasteries of the Benedictines, in the bishops' residences and in parish houses...This issue remained a great scandal and stumbling block in the evangelization of Latin America...The fraternal telling of the Gospel did not exist for the African slaves, but there was a negation of their culture, religion, and human rights... there was a total lack of evangelization and acceptance on account of the domination and exploitation to which they were subject without relief (Medellin, 1978,IV,15: 352).*

This situation of clergy participation in slave exploitation was so widespread at the end of the nineteenth century, that the Puerto Rican Jesuit historian, Fernando Picó, points out how poor people viewed the clergy as part of the oppressing bloc of land owners and merchants who oversaw forced labor:

> *"Since he was used as an instrument of the state to impose public policy upon the displaced jíbaro [the parish priest] could not help but seem to be one of the rich, against whom one had to defend oneself" (Libertad y Servidumbre).*

In reference to sacramental fees, the Jesuit historian says that cannonical marriage could cost as much as a month's wages. On the other hand, however, the priest was generally a member of the town Commission on Vagrancy and Concubinage, which could cast into jail persons not married by the church. Because Spain viewed Puerto Rico's value principally as a military fortress, the crown and the church seldom paid attention to the quality of the clergy assigned to the island. Indeed, the bishops complained insistently about this condition in their reports. The lack of priests and their attention to worldy affairs, brings Picó to conclude in his studies that for the period closest to the invasion by the United States, in the rural areas of the island "to die without the sacraments had come to be the norm in 1880." It must be pointed out that a hundred years before, in 1780, such neglect of the sacraments had been the exception, rather than the rule.[1]

The colonial church was also in contradiction with the liberal sectors of the Puerto Rican society emerging in the nineteenth century. The liberal free thinkers on the island enjoyed freedom of expression only when there was a liberal regime in Spain (1812-14, 1822-23, 1836-1844, 1868-1874). This meant opposition between the institutional church and political freedom. Although in 1809 Juan Alejo Arizimendi had become the first and only Puerto Rican priest raised to the episcopate during the 400 some years of Spanish rule, his death in 1814 coincided with the restoration of absolute monarchy in Spain. There was a conscious effort thereafter to reduce the number of native Puerto Rican priests, by assigning only foreign clergy to the island. This broke the brief and tenuous connection between the Catholic hierarchy and an emergent Puerto Rican *criollo* elite that favored liberal principles and policies, so that when war with the United States in 1898 ended Spanish rule, the official church was seen as part of the old regime.

It must be remembered that in the middle of the nineteenth century, the Syllabus of Errors of Pope Pius IX condemned liberalism and political principles like the separation of church and state, secularization of education, freedom of the press, of association and of worship. Official Catholicism opposed the constitutional freedoms of modern democracy. The nineteenth century church in Puerto Rico was an enemy to the liberal free thinkers who had negotiated with a resistant Spanish state for greater home rule. This core of *Autonomistas* and *Independentistas* discovered that the bishops sided with an absolutist monarchy against even modest liberalization. The result of these eclesiastical and political policies during the Spanish colonial period was the construction of a very weak institutional Catholicism. Thus it made a very poor contribution to the formation of a cultural identity that could express itself in the political development of the Puerto Rican nationhood.

Father Thomas Sherman, the Catholic chaplain to the invading army in 1898, wrote to the Secretary of War in a report made after traveling about the island: "Religion on the island is dead... If it can ever be resurrected as a vibrant influence is problematic..." He further explained:

> *"[The institutional church] has been so united to the state and so identitifed with it in the eyes of the people that it share[s] in the hatred that the people generally hold for the Spanish regime."*

While Sherman recognized that there were "many excellent priests in Puerto Rico and that women and children were practicing Catholics" he omitted mention of the men. Moreover, he reported that "the sacrament of confirmation had not been conferred for many years in most parts of the island." The situtation was worsened because more than half of the Catholic clergy left the island for Spain after the official installation of the North American military government.[2] Fernando Picó concludes that this situation "helps explain the ruinous condition of the institutional church, left without state support in Puerto Rico after 1898."

Throughout this essay, however, one must clearly hold to a distinction between the official, institutional Catholic and Protestant churches and the religious faiths of the people, particularly the poor and oppressed who are always the majority in any colonial situation.

Popular Religiosity and Spanish Colonial Catholicism

On the other hand, the ordinary Puerto Rican *campesino,* or *jíbaro,* continued constructing his daily life around his own brand of Catholicism, in spite of the official church.[3] This popular Catholicism flourished at the margins of the institution with bits and pieces of religious experience and with little more than the inherited religious practices such as devotion to the saints, the rosary recited in the family, exvotaries (*promesas*), and the use of sacramentals. The elements of such popular religiosity included, the holy water that people carried with the palms blessed during Holy Week, scapulars, medals, novenas for the dead, liturgical feast days, giving the child the name of the saint whose feast coincided with the birthdate, the rites of passage and finally, above all and always, devotion to the Virgin Mary.

The popular Mediterranean Christianity, brought to the Caribbean with the Spaniards, had been transplanted into the isolated rural parts with little communication with towns. It was syncretistically interwoven with Taíno and African beliefs. Conceptions of the presence of the spirits of nature in the inexplicable and uncontrollable events of life were part of this brand of Catholicism. Such was the impact of this Puerto Rican experience of popular religiosity that it placed the ordinary Catholic in the middle of a religious world in which everything was related to the marvelous.

Popular Catholicism flourished despite having been sown in social conditions of exploitation, servitude, poverty, illiteracy, repression, sickness and a fatalistic worldview. Nonetheless, this popular Catholicism constituted a well-spring of strength, consolation and even resistance. In the historical unfolding of colonialism, these practices became the mentality from which the people perceived their surroundings, interpreted their lives and acted out their faith. They are the resistent memories that serve as foundation for a collective memory that preserves the identity of a people. Religiosity is a conception of life. Its practices guarantee uprightness and survival while at the same time offering significance to life's purpose. Popular religiosity shapes a sense of collective identity and thus, a sense of belonging among those who share in it.

I agree with Luis Maldonado, author of *Introducción a la religiosidad popular,* when he defines "popular" as "the knowledge of traditions transmitted by a human group which has a special sensitivity in the collection and transmission of such tradition." Tradition here means the most ancient roots that determine a people's character. Rather than conservative and immutable, tradition in this sense frames a group identity which creates, changes, adapts, and resists as part of its own survival. In this sense, popular religiosity is opposed to what is official, imposed from above and from outside. Religious popular traditions are natural, come from within, and are spontaneous. They lie beyond reason, because as spontaneous phenomena, they can be called "the collective unconscious."

I also agree with Ana María Díaz-Stevens that there is an affinity between what is popular and the notion of social class. Religiosity inhabits a space close to the material and objective conditions of the dominated classes and their history of resistance or submission. But I do not wish to enter into judgment over the capacity of popular religiosity to serve as a way to achieve social and political transformation. At any rate, there is no evidence of this dimension in the popular religiosity of Puerto Rico in the nineteenth century. It is recognized more as a form of refuge and consolation and as a touchstone of conformity.

The fields of History and the Social Sciences in Puerto Rico have tended to emphasize economic factors without paying attention to the role of "mentalities" as the mediating element for a people's survival, self-awareness and praxis. The study of daily matters and of mentalities sets one free to explore the importance of "the collective imagination" in which religion lies at the core as the primary source for a sense of life and purpose. The historian should examine grand economic and political changes as they are filtered through the mentality of the people who resist or adopt them, conditions that Michelle Vovelle and contemporary French historians call "mediations" (M. Vovelle, *Ideologies and Mentalités*).

In my studies, *Protestantismo y política en Puerto Rico: 1898-1930* and *Catolicismo y política en Puerto Rico, 1898-1930*, soon to be published in book form, it was my intention to reconstruct the alteration and the transformation of Puerto Ricans' collective religious mentality. I reviewed the institutions, principles and religious practices of the invading nation that went about promoting the dismantlement of the military, economic, political and cultural basis of the Spanish Catholic colonial regime. That culture was substituted by the culture of *modernity*. I refer here to a way of thinking that arose with the Reformation, situated itself upon the institutions of Capitalism, nourished itself ideologically with the Enlightenment and expressed itself with the principles, institutions and practices of Liberalism. The cultural identity of twentieth century Puerto Ricans has continued to emerge from the impact of the contact and ensuing processes of this invasion. Puerto Rican identity is thus not the affirmation of the past, but the result of a complex process of conservation and accommodation as experienced by the people.

Protestantism in Puerto Rico

When the United States took over Puerto Rico as "war booty" in 1898, it set a collision course between a highly developed Capitalist country, ruled politically and culturally by liberal Protestant principles and institutions and another nation where pre-Capitalist modes of production prevailed in a political economy and culture still sustained by medieval Catholic roots. The United States' military dictatorship that ruled Puerto Rico from 1898 to 1900 went about dismantling the colonial Spanish state and constructing a North American version. At the same time, it set to transforming the Hispanic Catholic mentality that was centuries old. A new system of public education was allied with the Protestant missionary movement. The clearly ideological task of the public school teachers provided for the integration of the ideological objectives of the military, of politicians and missionaries. This can be seen in the definition of the churches' mission:

> *[We] will inaugurate a work that insures the Americanization of the island, and thus the joys and privileges of a true Christian discipleship... we should establish a school and thus reach hundreds of children who can be formed by this institution for the responsibilities of American citizenship. (Proceedings of the 46th Meeting of the Board of the Home Frontiers and Foreign Missionary Society of the United Brethren in Christ, June, 1899: 12).*

The change of an entire culture, including religion, was an integral part of the objectives of the state bureaucracy. The United States official overseeing education reminded the Reverend Victor Clark, Educational Commissioner in Puerto Rico of this goal, when he wrote:

> *"An education which contemplates a change of the native language implies a change of religion and a complete change in the body of a people's traditions." (Letter from W. T. Harris, March, 7, 1900: J. S. Clark Collection, MS. Div. Thesis).*

Of course, it was scarcely necessary to remind the Reverend Clark of this matter for he had written:

> *If this system is allowed to continue being European and if France and Spain continue to serve as the intellectual tutors of the island, it is possible that the development of a school system can influence the people into a lessening of their fundamental sympathies towards the government of which they form part. If the schools are Americanized...the attitudes towards life and the government will become essentially American. The great mass of Puerto Ricans are still passive and malleable (Cited in Negrón Montilla: 13).*

The Protestantism that came to Puerto Rico is the Protestantism of the Reformation transformed by the history of westward expansion in the United States. In the forging of a national Protestantism, the rigors of the Calvinist predestination of New England were left behind. The Protestantism brought to Puerto Rico was characterized by personal responsibility for salvation and by intense missionary activity, without a theological or dogmatic rigor. Its untiring social activism was marked by the establishment of seminaries and universities. This Protestantism took as its own responsibility the "civilization" of the frontier. Thus, the Protestantism experienced by Puerto Ricans was the same that had been brought into Texas, New Mexico and California earlier in the century. It was a Protestant vision which transformed into religious values the United States' conceptions of political tolerance, freedom of conscience, individual rights, popular democracy and consent of the governed.

The impulse of the missionary movement of the nineteenth century was based on a conception of modernity, but with a milenarianist theology that prophesied either that the world was being prepared for the end of times (Post Milenarianism) or that there was no time for preparation because the end was at hand (Pre-Milenarianism). What these imparted to North American Protestantism was a militancy born of urgency. These milenarianisms had an ideologically imperialist dimension that sang in unison with the expansionist Republican politicians, military generals, entrepreneurs, philosophers and economists who said that only expansion beyond its frontiers could save the United States from its continual economic crises.

Josiah Strong, the theologian of the right wing for Social Christianity at the end of the century, argued in an important book, *Our Country*, that God had been preparing the Anglo-Saxon Protestant people to invade the world, free it from obscurantism and civilize it in order to create the conditions for the end of history. This book was often required reading in the seminaries and universities that produced United States missionaries. It was a form of appropriating the modernizing Euro-centric principles of Hegel from Europe and Germany. According to Strong's book, which sold more than 180,000 copies and generated thousands of articles at the end of the century, the Caribbean, Mexico, and Central and South America were the natural objects of expansion for the United States. The true Christianity, Protestantism, would constitute the most important contribution in this process of preparing the world for its culmination. Roman Catholicism, on account of its medieval character, was the enemy of modernity and the democratic institutions of modern United States' Liberalism. Strong urged that Catholicism be extinguished from the face of the earth. Following that spirit, during the campaign to provoke the intervention of the United States into the Spanish-Cuban War, hundreds of Protestant magazines played an important role in legitimating the invasion of Cuba with inflammatory articles that called for war in the name of God.

When military hostilities ceased, a religious campaign of evangelization began. One month before departure of new missionaries to Puerto Rico, four missionary boards met. They discussed the strategy that they had approved eight months previously, even though the missionaries of various denominations were already at work inspecting the situation, preaching in the streets and establishing schools in Puerto Rico with the help of the military dictatorship that lasted from 1898 until 1900. The Comity Agreement was to divide the island into denominational sectors in order to give witness to "the unity of a common Christianity" that unified the denominations and thus to avoid the type of confusion among the listening public that had plagued Protestant missionaries in Asia. This Comity Agreement originally included Episcopalians, Presbyterians, Methodists and Baptists; later on it was opened to nine other denominations and thus continued to grow.

Protestant groups had existed in Puerto Rico from the middle of the nineteenth century. They acquired institutional form by taking advantage of the 1870 Spanish decree of religious freedom. Some of the churches were related to groups of foreigners involved in sugar production, such as in the case of Aguadilla and Ponce. Other Protestant congregations like those in Vieques and Fajardo were linked to the chain of English islands from which had come freed slaves who were Methodist, Moravian, Anglican and Baptist. These Protestant groups in Puerto Rico were quickly absorbed into this second Protestantism that arrived with the invasion.

The confrontation of two worlds on the battlefields of economy, politics and culture was dramatized by the clash of religions in the preaching at the grass roots. After 1898, we see missionaries and Puerto Rican converts preaching with the bible in hand confronting the ancient beliefs of an Hispanic Catholic Puerto Rican culture. Moreover, several Puerto Rican priests renounced Catholicism and became Protestant ministers. Because Protestants recognized only the bible as a source of authority, they used it to impugn age old beliefs in the small towns of the island. For the first time in Puerto Rican history, communities witnessed an unchallenged assault upon the beliefs that had rooted the cultural and religious mentality of the Puerto Rican Catholic people. The state did not interfere to defend Catholicism, as would have been the case under Spanish rule; instead, separation of church and state worked to Protestant advantage.

The missionaries in Puerto Rico generated a process that gave the bible to the people through the Sunday Bible schools that studied and discussed texts. At the same time, they unleashed in local communities a challenge to Catholic doctrines, especially those that came "from tradition" without a biblical basis. This placed into question papal infallibility, the supernatural character of the Mass and the power of priests to consecrate, devotion to the saints, efficacy of the rosary, the doctrines of Limbo and Purgatory, the use of statues in the churches, the heavenly role of the Virgin Mary, the power of the saints to intercede for the living, the power of baptism to destroy original sin, the validity of canonical law to regulate marriage practices and relations, the entire sacramental system except for baptism and communion—but also the baptism of infants. They attacked with biblical arguments the sacrament of Penance, the categorization of different types of sins as venial or mortal, auricular confession, the system of ecclesiastical penalties and of indulgences. All the sacramentals came under scrutiny such as the use of vestments, holy water, medals, scapulars, relics, statues, blessed palm and ascetic practices such as fasting and pilgrimages, the establishment and maintenance of shrines, the sacrament of the anointing, novenas, suffrages and other works for the salvation of the Holy Souls in Purgatory and any agencies for such purposes, such as chaplaincies and benefices. They assaulted traditional Catholic ceremonies such as processions for Corpus Christi, and for the Holy Cross, *fiestas patronales,* and the feast days of the saints in the Catholic liturgical calendar, celibacy, Catholic schools, the validity of excommunication, the worth of papal letters, encyclicals and interdicts and, of course, any kind of obedience to Rome.

These conflicts opened again the wounds of the religious wars of the Reformation — at least verbally. They framed the religious conflict as a struggle between the Hispanic Catholic culture and the North American Protestant culture, thus undergirding the real attack on Puerto Rico, labeled officially as "military occupation."

Protestants in Puerto Rico accepted the bible as essential to the role of personal conscience in their religion. Protestant individualism and the active role of the believer were rooted in the study of the bible. Religious belief had gone from being the belief of the community rooted in Hispanic culture and had become instead a "personal belief" that had to be nourished and defended with biblical knowledge. The Puerto Rican Protestant convert was viewed as breaking away from the Hispanic norm and had to defend his faith at home, before friends and family, in public places and at work when Protestantism was confronted, attacked, questioned and ridiculed. The oral history of Puerto Rican Protestants was woven from such experiences. It is always the central theme in conversation with older converts when they are interviewed. The private interpretation (*libre examen*) of the bible in order to sustain belief and understand the Gospel was converted into a kind of individual right that defined their social role. The Sunday Bible School was the training ground for weekly development of this awareness and the ability to utilize the bible.

Such utilization of the bible was sometimes very accomplished and complied with the verification norms of theological thinking, but the literal and conservative use of texts used by the "brethren" who had minimal education and lacked adequate preparation sometimes resulted in disastrous conflicts. Nonetheless, it always provided recourse to frame belief for individual action and to prove one's faith to one's self and to other believers. Such a process meant that personal opinion passed through the fire of review by the Christian community and the bible experts of a religious denomination.

The public questioning of traditional Catholic doctrines that was made by such ordinary people constituted for Puerto Ricans a new and traumatic social experience after the Catholic Church had been established for nearly 400 years. Catholic magazines of the time constantly complained about these Protestant attacks, often made in mutually insulting form.

The climate of questioning the Catholic Church spread. It was seen as the religious institution that had legitimized the political power of the former regime. This inverted the relationship of obedience to authority that the people had grown accustomed to for 400 years. The Puerto Rican Protestant lay preacher made use of a new democratic right to criticize existing structures of daily life as antagonistic to modernization and political liberalism. Such religious change was evidently a fundamental element of the process of social change launched with the invasion because it mixed into the new interpretation of Christianity supreme loyalty to the United States as the Protestant nation that "had brought the Gospel."

This was accomplished through all Protestant organizations and structures. They had established chapels as launching pads for preaching, bible schools, small elementary schools, dispensaries and hospitals. They built churches, sport complexes, summer camps, started magazines and biblical institutes in order to form native pastors and finally organized a united, interdenominational theological seminary and a highly visible publication, *El Puerto Rico Evangélico,* that absorbed three other denominational magazines. Through these organizations, the Hispanic Catholic culture was confronted. Such attacks helped undermine the ideological and cultural conceptions that had served as the foundation of the Spanish regime, and at the same time they established a new vision of the world that served as ideological support for the new regime, its political principles, institutions and practices.

As suggested above, religion is an important component of a people's mentality. Changes in religious conceptions alter this mentality, making possible the legitimation of new political and cultural stuctures that serve as repository of cultural identity. Thus, as described here, the introduction of Protestantism to Puerto Rico after 1898 greatly influenced the mentality of our people, and our collective memory of our national character.

We can conclude by stating that the Protestant churches were one of the instruments of Americanization, although it must be added that this a complex process. In their preaching, schools and publications, the missionaries proclaimed the desirability and security that Puerto Rico would attain if it were an integral part of the United States. In other words, Puerto Rico should be an incorporated territory on the way to becoming a state, such as with Texas, California and later, New Mexico and Arizona after the Mexican-American War. The public school was defended as the instrument to teach children to be good Americans and as the forum to attack political positions critical of the North American occupation that came from Autonomist and Independentist sectors. The majority of Protestant leaders had been taught that the progress and prosperity of the United States were due to its Protestantism. This was the well-spring of the ideological-theological mindset of the first generation after 1898: The Spaniards were obscurantists and despots on account of a false Christianity; the United States was in Puerto Rico by the will of God; Protestant Puerto Ricans should be pro-American and aspire to annexation to the United States (Silva-Gotay, 1983).

It would not be until the decade of the 1930s, when the Great Depression brought a fatal crisis to the sugar plantation economy and provoked a decade of national labor strikes, that a burst of national consciousness transformed the Puerto Rican mentality. When the colonial regime repressed this awakening of a national consciousness, some Protestant groups accompanied the people in this patriotic awakening.

Catholicism and Americanization

Catholicism was also forced to adapt and change itself in Puerto Rico. The war of 1898 constituted a crossroads for the Catholic Church in the United States. When war was declared on Spain, the dilemma was clear: Fight with the Protestant United States against Catholic Spain, or be a sympathizer with America's enemy. Complicating the choice of United States' Catholics was the characterization of Catholicism as religion made up of foreign born immigrants from Ireland, Italy, Poland and other countries. Moreover, Rome had condemned liberal institutions and republican principles more than once in the nineteenth century (*Mirari vos,* 1832; *Syllabus* 1862; *Libertas Praestantissimum,* 1888). There was great pressure on the United States' Church before and after the war to publicly legitimate itself as "American" (Cross; Higgman).[4] Loyalty to the North American nation became a priority for the ecclesiastical structure. As a consequence, the institutional Catholic Church that entered Puerto Rico after 1898 to replace the Spanish one was as much an instrument of Americanization as were the Protestant churches.

After the failure of Archbishop Ireland to mediate a peace between the United States and Spain, the Catholic bishops issued a declaration of loyalty to the United States and called Catholics to fight against Spain. Catholic magazines joined with Protestant ones in demanding the blood of the cruel Spanish nation "whose place in history ought to be the grave." They wrote that the "obscurantist Catholicism of Spain" would be replaced with the true Catholicism of the United States. Catholic chaplains accompanied the military in the invasion of Cuba, Puerto Rico and the Philippines to see that this would happen.

Once the war was over and Puerto Rico had been ceded to the United States, the North American Catholic hierarchy viewed Puerto Rico as its ecclesiastical charge, ignoring the pleas of Puerto Rican Catholics for a native Puerto Rican bishop. The North American bishops, along with the religious they invited to the island, played the role of an Americanizing force in Puerto Rico. Resistance to such Americanization came only from the remnants of Spanish Catholicism that remained in Puerto Rico (S. Silva-Gotay, 1985).

The transfer of rule to the United States brought with it a separation of church and state that ended nearly 400 years of government support for religion in Puerto Rico. The Catholic Church in Puerto Rico thus had to confront several huge problems: total lack of subsidy, the disappearance of official standing as the state religion, the departure of virtually all the Spanish-speaking priests on the island, and a loss of many privileges. The military dictatorship also supported the claim of the anti-clerical liberals for the expropriation of church buildings that had been constructed with state funds—including all Catholic schools and the Ponce cathedral itself. Last, but not least, the Catholic Church confronted the militant evangelization by Protestant missionaries, as well as former Catholic priests and local preachers who now questioned and insulted the doctrines, beliefs and fundamental principles of Catholicism. These were problems neither the institutional Church or the parallel popular religiosity ever had to face in Puerto Rico.Due to the dramatic nature of the changes, the Catholic brotherhood of the *Hermanos Cheos* preached that the end of times was at hand.

The Vatican named Placide Chapelle, the Archbishop of New Orleans, as a delegate in the negotiations of the Peace Treaty of Paris with the role of defending Church properties in Cuba, Puerto Rico and the Philippines. Chapelle had previously served as Archbishop of Santa Fe, New Mexico, where half a century before, another French cleric, Jean-Baptiste Lamy, had been sent after the annexation of most of the Southwest, to supervise the Americanization of the Mexican Catholicism there. Archbishop Chapelle was supposed to guarantee the Catholic character of these territories and to guide the assimilation of the existing dioceses into the North American Catholic Church. Later, he became an unofficial ambassador of President McKinley to the newly acquired territories. The *General Church News* reprinted the description of Chapelle that appeared in New Orleans newspapers:

> *He is thoroughly American and perfectly familiar with all details of the American government. ...The particular duties of the Apostolic Delegate in Cuba will be to provide the proper assimilation of the Church in the West Indies to the American Church. (General Church News "Archbishop's Scrap Book", Convent of the Ursulines, New Orleans).*

Conscious of his standing, before and after his visits to the new territories, Chapelle offered press conferences in which he emphasized his relationship to the president. He functioned as an imperial proconsul with a strong sense of his ecclesiastical and political power. It was he who named his protegé, a German-born New Orleans priest, James Blenck, the first bishop of Puerto Rico under North American rule.

Bishop Blenck began the processes of Americanization in the oldest diocese of the Americas in 1819. The very day of his nomination, he announced in Washington, "I hope that the Americanization of the island will be quickly realized" (*El Ideal Católico,* I: 19 (August, 1899). The decisions of Bishop Blenck flowed in this direction. He eliminated the Conciliar Seminary and sent Catholic seminarians to study in the United States. It wasn't until 1914 that the first diocesan Puerto Rican seminarian, sent to the United States by Blenck, returned to the island, and a North American bishop in Puerto Rico ordained his first Puerto Rican diocesan priest as late as 1920.

The Congregation of the Most Holy Redeemer, the Redemptorists, arrived with Bishop Blenck, but their first Puerto Rican vocations were not ordained until the decade of the 1950s as also with the Dutch Province of the Dominicans, who arrived in Puerto Rico two years after the Redemptorists. Both religious orders sent their religious to the United States for formation. This tendency to prepare Puerto Rican priests for ministry by removing them from their native land may have been justified on economic or administrative grounds, but its net pastoral impact was to undermine the formation of a native Puerto Rican clergy.

Thus, Catholic institutional policies came in contradiction again with the affirmation of the Puerto Rican identity. The first Protestant missionary on the contrary established biblical institutes, then denominational seminaries and finally to open the Evangelical Seminary in Puerto Rico in 1917 by combining the seminaries of the majority of the denominations. By 1905, the year in which the first reliable statistics on Protestants were available, there were 52 North American missionaries on the island and 86 native preachers. I hasten to add that this training was not designed to "Puerto Ricanize" either the pastors or Protestantism in Puerto Rico. It was supposed to facilitate the evangelization of the island and assist the divulgation of the Gospel among the lower classes. The original intention of most denominations was not to create a "national church" but a "native church" with Puerto Rican pastors under the supervision of missionaries from the United States. But despite this goal of Americanization, the nature of clergy selection within Protestantism meant that in time the native preachers were able to become pastors. Eventually, the consequences of native formation led to the birth of a Puerto Rican viewpoint within a significant sector of Protestantism. Hence, it is important to distinguish after this period of two different historical processes of Americanization, one Catholic and one Protestant, distinguishable by their policies for developing a native clergy.

Ordained clergy is only one aspect of Catholic participation in the process of americanization. The other aspect was the policy of the Catholic schools. Bishop Blenck was the one who started the Catholic school system on the island, despite clear evidence that—unlike the experience in the United States—such a system would not be possible in most parishes, leaving Catholic education a privilege of the rich. Consequently, Catholicism did not have a system of Sunday Schools for children to compete with the Protestant efforts. Virtually all the Catholic schools in Puerto Rico were in the hands of North American religious who generally taught in English. Because of the changed ecclesiastical jurisdiction after 1898, North American orders of men and women religious were the only ones recruited by the bishops. Anibal Colón Rosado, one of the few Puerto Rican superintendents of the Catholic schools, writes in his book, *Crisis de la identidad de la educación católica en Puerto Rico,* that the religious communities were intrumental in the transculturation of Catholic students, because of "the importance given to the English language, to the symbols, holidays and heroes of America" (Colón Rosado: 75).

This tendency grew in such a way that today more than 70% of graduates from the best and most expensive Catholic high schools do not go to the University of Puerto Rico, but to colleges in the United States. That means that they never pass through a Puerto Rican experience of university education or take any course about Puerto Rico at the college level. In the case of the Jesuit high school, San Ignacio, widely considered the best private school in Puerto Rico today, 90% of the students continue their education in the United States. Thus the Catholic Church has become one of the most efficient agents of the Americanization of the Puerto Rican elite.

Americanization was generally maintained by the Catholic religious who came to "reevangelize" Puerto Rico. The North American Catholics often condemned Spanish Catholicism as "obscurantist" and they committed themselves to an evangelizing effort in the rural areas and small towns of the island to "re-Catholicize" Puerto Rico with a fervor and passion that matched that of the Protestants (Fitzgerald, 1934). The *Asociación de Católicos de Puerto Rico,* composed of the elite of the country, also tried to free the church from the "absurd and vulgar" Spanish colonial system in order to make a fresh start under a system of separation of Church and State in which Catholicism on the island would flourish as the church in the United States.

Bishop Blenck gradually grew increasingly critical of this process in Puerto Rican Catholicism and eventually came to repent of such Americanization. But in 1906 he was named Archbishop of New Orleans. He was succeeded in Puerto Rico by Bishop William Ambrose Jones, who wasted little time in demonstrating his strong support of Americanization. For instance, after a long dispute with the *Cabildo Eclesiástico,* a quasi-autonomous gathering of clergy and the oldest such institution in the Americas, he disbanded it with a stroke of the pen. Thus ended in the 20th century the last of the Spanish ecclesiastical structures of the 16th century and the only one to provide the North American bishop with opinions derived from native Puerto Ricans.

But within the Catholic Church, a segment of the Puerto Rican people maintained a fierce loyalty to Spanish Catholicism[5] and gradually this was transformed into a loyalty to those political causes that required a defense of Puerto Rican culture. This reaction was nurtured by discontent with the U. S. military dictatorship and the North American civil regime imposed by the Foraker Act (1900) that denied Puerto Ricans the protections of the U. S. constitution and converted the island into a colony. In 1905, the lay magazine, *El Ideal Católico,* pointed out that Puerto Rico found itself in the same conditions as Ireland and Poland, but descried the lack of the same sort of militant organizations to defend the national identity. José Saldaña, who succeeded the patriot, José de Diego, in the congress of the *Asociación de Católicos de Puerto Rico* in 1905, expressed this idea in his speech when he said:

> *Fellow Puerto Ricans, are we not able to die?...Our Catholic faith traces the way. We must uphold our beliefs. Puerto Rico will prosper if it safeguards its Catholic religion. But if it is lost, new forces will emerge. They will destroy us and*

we shall be replaced by Americans, even if we do not wish to be replaced. (El Ideal Católico, VII, 1905: 333).

To affirm this identity and its interests, Father Castang, the French-born priest in Vieques, proposed in 1910 the formation of a Catholic political party to defend Catholicism politically. But this idea was opposed by Bishop William Jones, who celebrated the U. S. occupation as something beneficial to Catholicism.[6]

Although the now convinced Bishop Blenck called independence "the only true way," the American hierarchy considered independence for Puerto Rico as "an ill-advised policy." The Puerto Rico independentista leader of the Union Party, José de Diego, confronted the statement of Bishop Jones in a succinct paragraph of Catholic political theology.

"The majority of the Catholics are in agreement with a majority of all the elements genuinely Puerto Rican. Concerning the sacred ideal of independence, it can be stated that only a majority of Protestants (because they are Americans and foreigners) oppose the national aspiration of the partisan and total majorities of the inhabitants of our land...The Catholics of Puerto Rico will live under a sovereign government of Puerto Rico, without the prejudices and omissions held against them by the government and policy of the United States. A Puerto Rican priest will be able to be bishop in his homeland; a Catholic Puerto Rican will be able to be head of his country. The Catholic church of Puerto Rico is of God and is, at the same time, as it ought to be, of Puerto Rico" (José de Diego, 1966).

This statement synthesizes in a nutshell the issue of Catholicity and cultural identity for the core of the Catholic independentista and autonomist elite at the beginning of the century. This notion would take a militant political form in the nationalism expounded by Pedro Albizu Campos in the decade of the 1930s.

In conclusion, during this period before the 1930s, the process of Americanization took place both in Protestantism and Catholicism, but with differences. Within Protestantism there was a sizeable native clergy and within the Catholic Church there was a Puerto Rican

Hispanophile element that opposed the Americanizers. Ironically, although Catholic cultural identity was strengthened among this upper-class sector of *hacendados* by the political conflicts, it was undermined by the Catholic schools that trained the children of the elite to be loyal to the United States.

The bulk of Catholics in the hinterland, however, were largely unaffected by U. S. capital investment in the sugar industry and were untouched by modernization and the Catholic private schools. It was only during the populist period from 1940 until 1960 that the popular religiosity of this majority of Puerto Ricans finally encountered modernization and secularization.

The Crisis of the 1930s

During the decade of the 1930s the disintegration of Puerto Rican agrarian society took place. The decade witnessed the end of the political and economic power as also of the culture of the coffee plantation in the mountainous center of the island, where Catholicism was firmly rooted. The 1930s also initiated the great crisis of the sugar plantations of the coast that had been gathering excess population from the farmland for some years. The crisis of the 1930s that launched this disintegration, generated both hunger and wrath, conditions for the rise of populism.

The sugar plantations during the Great Depression faced the following conditions: the imposition of federal quotas on sugar, the rebellion of the Puerto Rican labor movement against union leadership and opposition to the Socialist party for its coalition with the political interests tied to landholders and the management of the sugar industry. The period saw several general strikes to accompany hunger and misery. As a result, there was an avalanche of migrants from the countryside to the city. Finally, in political terms the whole society was moved by the surge of national consciousness and the militancy from Puerto Rican Nationalists that was matched by severe repression from the North American regime against the Nationalist Party.

These factors shook Puerto Rican society to its roots during the decade and made possible a serious reconsideration of the colonial regime among Catholics and Protestants. The search for a Puerto Rican identity initiated by Puerto Rican intellectuals had its basis in material and objective interests that were made manifest by the exploitation of King Sugar and the repression by the North American colonial regime. Such factors bestowed upon nationalism a complexity that a merely cultural identity did not have.

Pedro Albizu Campos, a lawyer and president of the aggressively militant Nationalist Party, tied together the idea of national identity and Catholicism. He took as his example the rebellion of Catholic Ireland against Protestant England. Albizu was strongly influenced by Jaime Balmes, the nineteenth century Catalán theologian. Balmes had defended medieval Christendom as a model for achieving social progress without the attendant moral disintegration brought with "modernity" (Stevens-Arroyo, 1993). Following Balmes, Albizu developed a thesis of the moral superiority of Catholic culture before the Protestant culture of the invaders. He urged a military and political solution analogous to the case of Ireland. Albizu was to become a national hero for his radical opposition to imperialism and for his uprightness in the face of political corruption. For his anti-imperialist militancy, he was tried in 1937 in Federal court and imprisoned in the United States for 10 years.

Stimulated by the conditions of the decade, Puerto Rico in the 1930s witnessed the rise of a broad Catholic lay intellectualism, familiar with European Catholic theology. Albizu and the Nationalists were a factor in this development as were the Dutch Dominicans who published their magazine, *El Piloto*. The generation of the 1930s had a goal of rediscovering and promoting Puerto Rican cultural identity in order to open a way out of an historical crisis for the Puerto Rican people. But this generation sought the identity in the Hispanic past and in the idealization of the conditions that had existed before 1898. Academically, the intellectuals focused mostly upon Hispanic cultural and linguistic studies and upon history. Even after more than a generation under U.S. rule, the Catholic church in Puerto Rico had not yet produced a theologian or a biblicist of note, largely on account of the lack of a Catholic seminary. Nonetheless, this generation of lay Catholics would achieve great importance in the struggles for independence. Such Catholics figured mightily in the defense of Puerto Rican culture during the populist era of 1940-1960 from the battlegrounds of the Puerto Rican Athenaeum, the University of Puerto Rico and the Puerto Rican Independence Party. The members of this generation would sustain alive a tradition that was passed on to the generation of 1960, and would be seen as their mentors. But it was not until the decade of the 1960s that critical works written by Puerto Rican clergy from a theological perspective began to appear. And of these contributions, the most significant were from the late Bishop Antulio Parrilla (Silva-Gotay, 1990).

Despite the nationalist railing against Protestantism, it was in the 1930s that, paradoxically, the most progressive sectors of Puerto Rican Protestantism began to break with the naïve ideology that "the North American presence in Puerto Rico is a work of Divine Providence." Protestants began to think of the Gospel from a Puerto Rican perspective and identify with the nationalist movement and its affirmation of a Puerto Rican nationality. During the Ponce Massacre, the police, under orders from North American officials, shot down a peaceful march by the Nationalist Party on Palm Sunday. It was not merely coincidence that the persons in charge of the first speech on the program was the Methodist pastor, Juan Hernández Valle.[7]

This was a time for nationalist formation of the first great Protestant Puerto Rican theologian, don Domingo Marrero, Professor of Hebrew and Old Testament Studies at the Evangelical Seminary.[8] As with the case of Catholics, the struggles of this minority group of Protestants for a "Puerto Rican understanding of the Gospel" was the basis for the development of a militant generation of Protestants in the 1960s (Rivera Pagán, 1989).

Due to the disintegration of the traditional society during this decade, there was a great need among the entire population for identity, for a sense of belonging and reorientation from a collective spiritual conception of being Puerto Rican. Nationalism, cut off from a militant workers movement and systematically persecuted by the colonial state apparatus, lost the opportunity to become the reorienting force in society. But the malaise provided advantages to Pentecostalism that had arrived on the island in 1916.

Their efficiency as religious answers depends upon several factors: their strong sense of community; their practice of communitarian support for the members of the congregation; the easy to understand explanations for the social disturbances experienced by the poor and the marginalized; the religious message of immediate and permanent salvation; the symbolic and revolutionary transformation in status for the impoverished believer in relation to the rich and powerful of this world, wherein the poor will be saved and the others condemned to disappear in an imminent apocalyptic transformation; and by the inclusion of the believer into a community of "brothers and sisters" who reconstruct the sense of a lost traditional community (Silva-Gotay, 1991: 100-25).

The growth of Pentecostalism in Puerto Rico was slow until the 1930s. Because of its popular character and its foundations among the marginalized and poor workers with low levels of schooling, Pentecostalism incorporated a popular culture as a means of expression. This helped create a new world of popular religiosity in Puerto Rico, analogous to the Catholic popular religiosity.

Pentecostalism's influence was widened to sectors of the mainline Protestant churches in poor communities where sociological conditions facilitated Pentecostalism during the revivals of the 1930s. These led to serious conflicts between North American Protestant supervisors in one of the mainline churches and native Puerto Ricans. This opened still another way for the "Puerto Ricanization" of Protestantism that had a strong class component, although it lacked a defined political consciousness of the process, viewing it vaguely as part of an apocalyptic dimension of salvation.

Thus, the 1930s was the decade that witnessed a recuperation of national consciousness in all three major religious segments of Puerto Rican society. Consequently, it also strengthened a stronger feeling of cultural identity. On one side there was a fortification of this link between Catholicism and national identity, and also an expansion of Pentecostal popular religiosity among Protestants that was rooted in the least Americanized of the social groups.

The Churches in the Post-War Process of Modernization

The Great Depression of the 1930s brought the developed economies of Europe and the United States to make reforms in capitalism by way of state intervention and social planning in order to avoid another crisis of such dimensions. In the case of the agroexporting countries of Latin America, the depression crippled economies of a single agricultural crop, such as the sugar plantations in Puerto Rico. Efforts were made throughout much of Latin America to create internal markets by way of import substitution by industrialization. The state intervened in economic and political modernization aimed at establishing a nationalistic form of capitalism.

These efforts created conditions for populist alliances between entrepreneurs and workers, collaboration with technocrats and middle-class professionals, all united under the paternalistic legislation of a single party. In Latin America, the old landholding oligarchies were generally brushed aside by a new young national bourgeoisie that sought nationalization of energy resources, electricity and transportation that was taken from foreign hands and placed under the control of the state. These were the measures usually taken to create an internal market and conditions for industrialization.

In Puerto Rico, the goal was to break up the sugar industry controlled by foreigners in favor of small farms and industrialization of the country. Such economic development implied a development of education and public health services, which led to significant investments in urban centers. This process was directed in Puerto Rico by the Popular Democratic Party, the *populares,* winners of the 1940 elections. However, because of the colonial context, the nationalist character of Puerto Rican populism was muted.

The first thirty years of North American occupation in Puerto Rico had produced an urban middle-class rooted in a technical-professional class that was ready at the end of the 1930s to take political power and begin the social reconstruction of the country along the lines of this populist modernization. The New Deal programs out of Roosevelt's Washington were extended from the United States to Puerto Rico and underlined the power of this new modernizing class. Although it initially stressed agrarian reform, within four years the shift was to industrialization. Because there was no national bourgeoisie to direct the industrialization, the Popular Democratic Party depended upon a relatively inefficient state intervention. But when the Second World War ended, the party abandoned its anti-imperialist elements and articulated a project of industrialization that depended upon giving tax exemptions to North American industry for the United States' markets.

Moreover, because of Puerto Rico's colonial status, migration of more than 40% of the population to the continental United States during a period of 18 years became the "escape valve" for the social pressures induced by the industrialization. Because they were already citizens, Puerto Ricans did not require passports or visas to enter the post-war United States. And with the beginning of commercial air flights between New York and San Juan after 1946, travel back and forth from the island reached historic proportions, forming what has been called the "Great Puerto Rican Migration" from 1946-1964 (Stevens-Arroyo and Díaz-Ramírez, 1980). The gradual emergence of a Puerto Rican Catholicism in the United States, most particularly in New York City, is an important story that has been told most recently by Ana María Díaz-Stevens (1993). While recognizing that what was taken to New York comes from the same roots as religion on the island, *Oxcart Catholicism* begins to assume its own characteristics in the social settings of the United States. At the root of this modernizing industrialization that affected both Puerto Ricans who remained on the island and those who migrated, we find the transformation of the traditional culture that was wed to precapitalist forms of the economy dating from the 16th century. Some of these institutions and traditions had not even been touched by the liberal reforms towards the end of the nineteenth century.

In Puerto Rico, this cultural disintegration marked the entry of new political leadership, strongly attached to liberal principles of secularism and modernization and without strong relationship to Catholic institutions. Moreover, the attitudes of the new leaders had much in common with the modern, urban and industrial culture of a Protestant United States. Thus the secular principles of separation of church and state, the non-sectarian character of the public schools and health services that included birth-control programs led to the clash of 1960 with the Catholic church. When the legislature rejected a bill to establish release-time religious education in the public schools, the church organized the Christian Action Party to combat the "immorality" of the Popular Democratic Party and to threaten with excommunication any Catholics that voted for the *Populares* and the incumbent governor, Luis Muñoz Marín (Silva-Gotay, 1988).

This date, 1960, is fundamental to an understanding of the development of religion among Puerto Ricans. It put into conflict the official Church and the popular religiosity of Puerto Ricans on the island as both elements of Catholicism faced secularization. The North American prelates of the two dioceses, Bishop Davis of San Juan and Bishop McManus of Ponce, confronted Catholics of all social classes with the choice of either following the orders of the hierarchy or supporting the political platform that had brought Puerto Rico the most profound of social changes in the 20th century. It was a moment to calculate exactly how many Puerto Ricans had been secularized in their views of education, birth control, the norms of public morality, and the nature of obedience due to the hierarchy. In Spanish colonial Catholicism, the word of the bishops had been the last word. But Puerto Rico in 1960 had been under North American rule for more than half a century. Ironically, the two U. S. born bishops adopted a policy on the island that was denounced by their fellow bishops in the states because at the same time, John F. Kennedy was confronting the familiar charge that a Catholic president would have to obey Rome's commands. Families, communities and parishes were bitterly divided in Puerto Rico's political campaign that saw religious conflicts affect the liberal elites, university students, and Protestant as well as Catholic believers in the most remote island towns.

In the election with the highest turnout in the history of the country, the Christian Action Party obtained 6.5% of the vote. The Popular Democratic Party received 58%, while the other parties split the remaining 35.5%. We can conclude, based on these numbers, that even when threatened with excommunication and the salvation of their eternal soul, only 6.5% of Puerto Rico's Catholics were disposed to concede their political choice to the bishops.

Thus, although Protestantism claimed only 15% of the Puerto Rican population, its liberal and individualizing principles had entered Puerto Rican society in ways that parallel the norms of separation of church and state in the United States, where Protestants are the majority. It was clear after the 1960 elections that there was no room for a "Neo-Catholic" state in Puerto Rican culture. The Christian Action Party represented a regression to the Spanish colonial past without a social basis in the present. The Catholic elites that sponsored the party had not understood that ordinary Catholics had chosen another path. Ironically, the Catholics on the island had shown that their attitudes towards the official church were not very different from the million or more Puerto Rican migrants to the United States. Puerto Rican Catholics at both ends of the migration flow relied more on their inner directed popular religiosity than upon episcopal decrees. This is one of the effects of colonialism, in that a Latin American nation like Puerto Rico has undergone a restructuring of religion along the lines of a North American model.

In the aftermath of the 1960 election, the Vatican replaced the North American bishops with Puerto Rican ones. But it should be noted that with the notable exception of the late Bishop Antulio Parrilla, these clergymen were and continue to be very pro-American in their understanding of the church.

The Protestants, on the other hand, welcomed the Popular Democratic Party. It was not uncommon to find a strong Protestant presence in the inner circle of the Popular Democratic Party from 1940 to 1960, with prominent laymen and the sons of ministers becoming political leaders.[9] Independence had always been a threat to Protestants because it represented a possible return of Catholic dominance in matters of religion, reversing the ideological connection between Protestantism and the United States. The Commonwealth status provided a defense against independence but was also socially progressive. The party was an ideal political vehicle for the ideological interests of Protestantism during that time for two reasons: the party had a strong social program that answered the demands of workers and poor peasants; the modernization platform of the party embraced liberal principles like separation of church and state, secular public schools and so forth which Protestants considered the fundamental conditions for their continued existence within a Catholic majority. On the other hand, the technocrat elements of the *populares* viewed the Protestant ethic as part of the modern industrial society they desired for Puerto Rico.

The changes generated by *Populismo* will affect Protestantism deeply. Protestantism, which had been rooted among the poor in 1898, began to move upwardly in the social ladder with the economic growth of the populist reforms between 1940 and 1960. The expansion of an urban Protestantism was the result along with a rapid upward social mobility. Large numbers of Protestants entered the professional and intellectual classes in every part of daily life. But this also brought increasing conflict within the congregations between the Protestants who had come from a rural or working-class background and those who had been raised in a middle-class urban environment. Moreover, large numbers of young Protestants with university education and a sharper political sense fell into conflict with an older generation of Protestants and pastors.

Generational Conflicts of the 1960s

By the beginnings of the decade of the 1960s, populism was wearing thin and in 1968 the pro-statehood New Progressive Party ended 28 years of *populares'* power. The waning of the Popular

Democratic Party brought two issues into focus: Puerto Rico's integration into the United States economy, and, discontent with the formula of expressing Puerto Rican identity.

The rapid expansion of educational opportunity and cultural change promoted by the *populares* during their 28 years in power generated a critique of the party's inability to face new challenges and to incorporate a new generation of technicians, professionals and intellectuals. Many of the younger generation found careers in the business world and sought greater economic power by assimilation into the United States via statehood. The remaking of the old Republican Party into the New Progressive Party gave them a political vehicle to take power away from an older generation of *populares*.

However, on the cultural issue, some sectors, particularly youth, moved to more radical positions. With the swelling of the numbers of students in Puerto Rican society, the Vietnam War and the draft imposed by the United States became huge issues in a colony that had no congressional voting power. The presence of the ROTC on the university campus became an issue that was made sharper by the movement for university reform, the formation of the *Movimiento Pro Independencia* (MPI) and the *Federación de Universitarios Pro Independencia* (FUPI) along with support for the Cuban Revolution, which was a major influence in anti-imperialist expression throughout the world.

This ideological and generational conflict took place throughout Puerto Rican society. Such conflicts created strong contradictions within the churches, both Catholic and Protestant, because the movements for change tied their response to cultural and political challenges to the faith. The opening of the Catholic Church by the Second Vatican Council brought a subsequent radicalization of Latin American Catholicism with the Medellín conference. There was a parallel rise within Protestantism of the Latin American movement of Church and Society that produced a radical Protestant theology fostered by the World Council of Churches and the World Federation of Christian Students. Finally, it must be noted that in the United States there were similar movements towards increasing radicalization. Puerto Ricans who belonged to the Catholic University Center, the Fraternity of Evangelical Students and the Federation of Christian College Students of Puerto Rico participated in international meetings, read the new theology, and analyzed the social, religious and political conditions of their homeland from a Christian perspective. They joined in the demonstrations and political movements advocating social transformation. There were considerable intergenerational conflicts of these young people with the established leadership of the churches, indeed with their own parents who upheld traditional conceptions of religion and conservative political principles such as fatalism, blind acceptance of authority, political indifference and conformity.

Polarization ensued within virtually all religious institutions of Puerto Rico during much of the 1960s. The young radicals were borne along with an escatological conceptualization of imminent and inevitable social transformation that would establish a new society. They brought the critical defiance of institutions from the political order into the university and the churches.

It should be made clear that these Catholic and Protestant groups were deeply committed to religion and were theologically articulate. Although their critiques carried a strongly political expression phrased more in terms of social responsibility than the salvation of souls, their target for change was the church because of the type of society it legitimated. There was a religious participation at all the rallies and within all the radical political movements of Puerto Rico, although space does not allow for a detailed review of the hundreds of such events. One that stands out is the ecumenical character of resistance to the bombing by the U. S. Navy of the island of Culebra. In this coordinated peaceful demonstration of civil disobedience, Catholic and Protestant clergy joined with local fishermen, university professors and students in the ecumenical spirit of the times. The demonstration resulted in the imprisonment of several persons, including Dr. Luis Rivera Pagán, theology professor at the Evangelical Seminary. Catholic Bishop Antulio Parrilla delivered the principle speech to the political rally before the island prison, where his Protestant counterpart was jailed.[10] Some years later, a similar incident in the neighboring island of Vieques produced an indictment of the bishop himself (Silva-Gotay, 1990).

Fearing a spread of radicalization within Puerto Rican society, the authorities targeted these religious movements and leaders. They were spied on, night and day, by the police and the FBI. They were investigated, harried and subject to illegal classification as subversives by the keeping of *carpetas,* or police files, wherein records were kept of their friends, their activities, meetings, trips and even personal affairs. These files were shown to supervisors and employers as a means of intimidation, and their institutions were forced into evaluation of their performance on political grounds although they had not committed any illegal acts. The surrender in 1992 and 1993 of more than 70,000 such dossiers from this period reveals the far-reaching nature of the operation by the government against Catholic and Protestant religious organizations and activities.

Within the churches another persecution was launched. Cardinal Aponte Martínez closed the major seminary at the Catholic University of Puerto Rico. The rector of the seminary, Bishop Parrilla was fired, dozens of seminarians were expelled and many more decided to abandon their religious studies. The chaplains of the Catholic University Center were transferred to parochial duties and the members of the Christians for Socialism movement were ordered to abandon the movement immediately (Stevens-Arroyo, 1980: 295-300, 301-302). With the intent of repression and with great hostility, the Catholic hierarchy attacked important pastoral work underway in the parishes of Comerío, Yauco, Coamo and La Perla in San Juan. These parishes had constructed a pastoral approach among the poor based on Puerto Rican culture and popular religiosity, but the episcopal actions killed any chance of providing a theological dimension to this popular religiosity that would have incorporated a strong sense of cultural identity with a Catholic conscience about social transformation (Díaz-Stevens, 1993).

In the case of the Protestants, five denominations tried, suspended or expelled 56 young pastors and seminary students between 1965 and 1975. A new board of directors was formed for the Evangelical Council that was made up of conservatives. It closed the Office of Campus Ministry for the council and terminated the practice of assigning university chaplains. The Evangelical Seminary voted in a new majority on the board of trustees that was drawn from the pro-Statehood Party and began to pressure students and professors. As a result many independentista students and three prominent specialists in theology, biblical studies and history left the seminary faculty.

These processes and reactions were not very different from Latin America where the Theology of Liberation became the theological language of radical Christians. As a matter of fact, some of the participants in these efforts in Puerto Rico such as Justo González,

Jorge Pixley, Luis Rivera Pagán, Juan Antonio Franco, Carmelo Alvarez and myself, Samuel Silva-Gotay, serve as leaders of organizations and movements related to international projects of research and theological education linked to the development of Liberation Theology (Silva-Gotay, 1991). Significantly, the first two listed, Justo González and Jorge Pixley, are not Puerto Ricans by birth but came to be closely identified with the Puerto Rican cause as a part of their own Christian commitments.

All of these persons were victims of persecution. This fact is important for understanding that affirmation of Puerto Rican cultural identity as part of a defense of Puerto Rican rights is the central issue in advocating transformation in church and society. This was the issue for the religious leaders during the 1960s who gave continuity to the Puerto Ricanizing efforts that had begun in the 1930s, infusing nationalism into Protestantism on the island.

Historically and sociologically, Protestantism in Puerto Rico made a cultural and political contribution in the context of the confrontation between liberalism and the pre-capitalist Spanish social forms during the period, 1898 until 1930. But this contribution to a liberal, modernizing mindset ended with the crisis in North American colonialism provoked by the Great Depression and the New Deal. In the populist era that followed, it was necessary to fashion conceptual tools and the public willingness to confront the challenges of changing times so that a new Protestant culture would emerge for the twenty-first century. Such a task could have been completed only in an environment of theological freedom. Had the generation of the 1960s been allowed to continue in official posts, such leadership might well have completed the task of constructing a Protestant Puerto Rican culture for the twenty-first century. But the older generation formed during the first 60 years of colonial liberalism under the United States was incapable of separating the gospel from North American cultural identity. By attacking the young leadership of the generation after the 60s, that was the logical evolution of Protestantism on the island, the older generation destroyed the potential of Protestantism protest to make a new contribution to the Puerto Rican culture.

It is important to realize that Protestant culture is now an integral element of Puerto Rican identity, which is not a mentality that is going to return to the parameters of a nineteenth century Hispanic Catholic society. It is important also to state at this point that the question of the development of the liberating dimension of culture is common to all Puerto Rican sectors, Protestants or Catholics. And this means politics.

While not all Puerto Rican Protestants agree about the political implications of this culture, there is within Protestantism on the island, a liberationist world view that consciously engages political and economic power as elements of cultural identity. This form of Protestantism is no less religious than a theology that pretends to ignore such issues. And, in a marked difference from the affirmation of liberation among Latinos in the U. S., in Puerto Rico such a recognition of liberation implies a nationhood distinct from that of the United States.

Culture is also a religious problem for Catholics. Those who romanticize the Spanish colonial past fail to realize that such an idealized Catholicism no longer contributes to the formation of national identity. Like Protestantism, the Catholic church is divided about its religious message for confronting the problems facing Puerto Rican society today. Nor can appeals to popular religiosity alone deter the rise of crime and the disintegration of society due to drugs and poverty. Protestant leaders of the 1960s suffered greatly from institutional repression, as did progressive Catholics.

At the dawn of the 1980s, there was a considerable lack of pastors, religious leaders and priests who could carry on an effective apostolate within either Catholic or Protestant churches in the face of the social problems in Puerto Rico. The Conference of Catholic Religious (COR) and some Protestant organizations continue in works of theological and pastoral formation in different areas of daily life, but with an exceedingly low profile. In fact, many work now outside of Puerto Rico. Ironically, there is often less repression for a Puerto Rican apostolate in the United States than in Puerto Rico. Thus, while there are both Catholic and Protestant liberationists, their marginalization within the institutions is worrisome.

Toward the Pentecostal Era

There is a phenomenal growth in Pentecostal communities throughout the world. Pentecostalism is carried along by its own brand of popular religiosity. Not dependent on institutional controls, it has spread all over the world since its beginnings more than a century ago in the western United States. Pentecostalism evolved from North American Protestantism. It is a radical version of Protestant Christianity, profoundly shaped by the doctrine of the Holy Spirit, *glosalalia,* the practice of prophesy and an apocalyptic sense of the end of time that condemns "the world" and separates believers from secular involvements.

The religious message of Pentecostalism and the deterioration of the quality of life since the economic crisis of 1972, made possible a second wave to the growth of Pentecostalism in Puerto Rico. There are statistics that suggest that evangelical Protestantism and Pentecostalism account for 30% of the general population and a majority in some barrios and small towns in Puerto Rico. Aguadilla, Puerto Rico, in the Northwestern corner of the island, for example, had a single Catholic Church with a Presbyterian, Seventh Day Adventist and Pentecostal church as minority denominations for some 70 years. Today there are six different denominations and forty-four Pentecostal councils working in Aguadilla and about 100 congregations that increase their numbers daily by conducting evangelizing campaigns. It is probable that if the present sociological conditions persist and there is no change in the traditional mode of operation of Catholicism, Pentecostals will constitute the majority of believers on the island by the year 2025. This development would push aside the mainline Protestant denominations along with the Catholic church. Moreover, Puerto Rican Pentecostalism has a world-wide impact because the island churches have missions in 30 countries including the United States, Latin America, Africa and Asia.

I would repeat here an observation I made to the consternation of Catholics and Protestants alike that we are entering into a "Pentecostal Era" for Puerto Ricans. This phrase has to do with the taking of religious power. What I mean is that the attitudes, ideas and beliefs of Pentecostalism have penetrated into the marrow of Puerto Rican life. The Pentecostal mindset can be found not only in the Pentecostal churches but also within Protestantism and Catholicism among Puerto Ricans as well. Moreover, the phenomenon is repeated among the more than two million Puerto Ricans living in the continental United States. It is proper then to address this process not with an eye only on Puerto Rico, but with a vision to encompass the Puerto Rican people everywhere.

Pentecostalism must also face the question of cultural identity. At the level of social behavior and customs they are closer to a specifically Puerto Rican culture than the Protestants and Catholics of the middle and upper classes. But at the level of conscious elaboration of their relationship to the political dimensions of cultural identity, they are silent. The apocalyptic view of the world-soon-to-disappear that is integral to Pentecostalism inhibits collective action to address present social and political issues. One must ask if, just as some Puerto Rican Catholics overcame the obstacles presented by identification with Spanish colonialism and some Protestants their connections with North American imperialism, there will be Puerto Rican Pentecostals who will rise to this challenge. Their story, which is yet to unfold, will create still another ideological dimension to popular religiosity and cultural identity among the Puerto Rican people.

Endnotes

1. The turbulent destablization of the Iberian church during most of the 19th century, brought to the United States several Spanish clerics and two, Joseph Sadoc Alemany and Thaddeus Amat, became bishops in the newly acquired territory of California, where the majority of Catholics were the former Mexican subjects. As with other Spanish clerics, they were much influenced by the antagonisms between republican form of government and the interests of institutional Catholicism. Contact by such Spanish Catholic clerics in Puerto Rico with North American democracy and its Protestant character was traumatic.

2. The United States required Spanish nationals who were the majority of the clergy to renounce loyalty to Spain and accept a Puerto Rican citizenship (not a U. S. one) in order to remain in Puerto Rico. Everyone else was forced to return to Spain and reapply for a visa from the United States in order to return to the island.

3. Dr. Salvador Perea of the Catholic University of Puerto Rico told a 1955 conference on Puerto Rican migrants to the United States that the institutional Catholicism of Cuba and Puerto Rico represented "the weakest Catholicism in Hispanic America."

4. The year after the outbreak of hostilities even witnessed an encyclical from Rome, *Testem Benevolentiae* (1899) that condemned an "Americanist heresy".

5. For instance, in the cathedral of Ponce, the custom continued of proclaiming during Mass, "Long Live Catholic Spain! Long Live St. James," referring to the patron saint of the Spanish military (¡Viva España católica! ¡Viva Santiago!).

6. In 1909, Bishop Jones invited the Secretary of War of the United States to a banquet with the clergy and military officers to celebrate the anniversary of the surrender of Puerto Rico to the United States Army. A few days later, he called a meeting of the protesting Asociación de Católicos to demand oaths of "loyalty, fidelity and cooperation." The letter drafted at his prompting promised that everyone had been "moved by a sentiment of loyalty and in accord with the teaching of our religion" (Silva-Gotay, 1985: 7-35).

7. He also became the defense attorney for don Pedro Albizu Campos. The secretary for the Nationalist Party Committee in Ponce was the daughter of the Baptist pastor of the city, don Abelardo Díaz Morales, the father of an entire family of independentistas.

8. Years later, he became Dean of the Faculty of General Studies at the University of Puerto Rico, and which was later named in his honor.

9. A dramatic example is the case of Hipólito Marcano, who was at the same time a senator for the Populares, President of the AFL, of the Evangelical Council of Puerto Rico, of the Board of Trustees of the Polytechnic Institute, now the Interamerican University.

10. It should be recalled that the brother of Bishop Parrilla, Pedro, is a prominent Baptist pastor, thus underlining the ecumenical character and openness that the churches in Puerto Rico had adquired at this time.

Bibliography

Colón Rosado, Anibal. 1981. *Crisis de la identidad de la educación católica en Puerto Rico.* Santurce: Distribuidora Cultural Puertorriqueña.

Colonnese, Louis Michael, ed. 1970. *The Church in the Present-Day Transformation of Latin America in the Light of the Council.* 2 vols. official English translation. Latin American Bureau of the USCC: Washington DC and Consejo Episcopal Latinoamericano (CELAM): Medellín.

Cross, R. D. 1988. *The Emergence of Liberal Catholicism in America.* Cambridge: Harvard University Press.

Díaz-Stevens, Ana María. 1993. "La misa jíbara como campo de batalla sociopolítica en Puerto Rico" *Revista de Ciéncias Sociales* 30:1-2 (enero-junio) 139-162.

Fitzgerald, William. 1934. "A Survey of Religious Conditions in Puerto Rico, 1899-1934" Ph. D. Dissertation, Fordham University.

García Leduc, José. 1990. "La iglesia y el clero católico de Puerto Rico (1800-1873): Su proyección económica y política." Ph. D. Dissertation, Catholic University of America.

Higgman, J. 1955. *Strangers in the Land: Patterns of American Nativism, 1765-1925,* New Brunswick: Rutgers University Press.

Negrón de Montilla, Aida. 1977. *La Americanización de la Educación Pública en Puerto Rico.* Río Piedras: Ediciones Edil.

Picó, Fernando, SJ. 1981. *Libertad y Servidumbre en el Puerto Rico del siglo XIX.* Río Piedras: Ediciones Huracán.

Rivera Pagán, Luis N. 1989. *Senderos teológicos: El pensamiento evangélico puertorriqueño.* Río Piedras: Editorial La Reforma.

Rivera, Luis N. 1992. *A Violent Evangelism: The Political and Religious Conquest of the Americas.* Louisville: John Knox/Westminster Press.

Maldonado, Luis. 1975. *Introducción a la religiosidad popular.* Madrid: Ediciones Cristiandad.

Perea, Salvador. 1970. "Historical Notes and Interpretation on Vocations and Clergy in Puerto Rico." in William Ferrée, Ivan Illich and Joseph P. Fitzpatrick, eds. *Spiritual Care of Puerto Rican Migrants.* Cuernavaca: CIDOC, Sondeos 74. Arno Press Reprint, New York, 1988.

Silva Gotay, Samuel. 1985. "La Iglesia Católica en el proceso político de la americanización en Puerto Rico, 1898-1930", *Cristianismo y sociedad,* 86:7-34.

_____. 1985. "La Iglesia Protestante como agente de americanización en Puerto Rico, 1898-1917." *Politics, Society and Culture in the Caribbean,* Ed. Blanca Silvestrini, San Juan: Universidad de Puerto Rico, 1983.

_____. 1985. "Social history of the Churches in Puerto Rico, Preliminary Notes, 1509-1980". *Towards a History of the Church in the Third World, The Issue of Periodization.* Geneva, Switzerland: EATWT.

_____. 1988. "El partido Acción Cristiana: Transfondo histórico y significado sociológico del nacimiento y muerte de un partido político católico en Puerto Rico." *Revista de Historia* 1:7 (enero-diciembre) 146-184.

_____. 1989. *El Pensamiento Cristiano Revolucionario en America Latina y el Caribe,* 4ta. Ed., Río Piedras, Puerto Rico: Ediciónes Huracán.

_____. 1990. "Desarrollo de la dimensión religiosa del nacionalismo en Puerto Rico: 1898-1989", Estudios Interdisciplinarios de America Latina. *Revista Escuela de Historia de la Universidad de Tel Aviv,* Vol. I, Num. 1 (enero-junio) 59-82.

_____. 1991. "La dimensión ideológica de la expression religiosa de los marginados en la sociedad contemporánea." in Horacio Cerutti, ed. *Educación, marginación urbana y modernización.* Universidad Pedagógica Nacional: Mexico:100-125.

_____. *Protestantismo y política en Puerto Rico: 1898-1930.* (forthcoming).

_____. "Catolicismo y política en Puerto Rico, 1898-1930" (book manuscript).

Stevens-Arroyo, Antonio M. 1980. *Prophets Denied Honor.* Maryknoll: Orbis Books.

_____. 1993. "The Catholic Ethos as Politics: The Puerto Rican Nationalists." in William H. Swatos, Jr. ed. *Twentieth-Century World Religious Movements in Neo-Weberian Perspectives.* Lewiston: The Edwin Mellen Press, 175-194.

Stevens-Arroyo, Antonio M. and Ana María Díaz Ramírez. 1982. "Puerto Ricans in the States: A Struggle for Identity" in Gary and Rosalind Dworkin, eds. *The Minority Report.* New York: Holt, Rinehart and Winston, 2nd edition, 196-232.

Vovelle, Michel. 1990. *Ideologies and Mentalities.* Chicago: University of Chicago Press.

Para el Niño Dios: Sociability and Commemorative Sentiment in Popular Religious Practice

7

RICHARD R. FLORES

"*Lo hacemos para El Niño Dios*" [We do it for the baby Jesus]. Such is the response of the performers of *Los Pastores,* a troupe from the west side of San Antonio, Texas, when asked why they participate in this popular religious drama. *Los Pastores* derives from a genre of religious dramas known as *pastorelas, coloquios,* or *auto sacramentales* that have been composed in octosyllabic verse since the emergence of Spanish as a modern language. Their public performance for a general audience continues a cultural tradition with roots in Spanish medieval plays about the adventures of the shepherds on their way to Bethlehem.

Most versions of the *pastorela* have a cast of characters that include shepherds, angels, devils, Mary and Joseph, a hermit, a statue of *El Niño Dios,* and others. The narrative begins with the shepherds keeping watch over their sheep when the Archangel Michael appears to them, announcing the birth of the Messiah. Upon deciding to journey to Bethlehem, to bear offerings for the new Messiah, the shepherds encounter Luzbel (Lucifer) and his legion of devils who attempt to thwart their efforts in a series of comedic routines. In the end, the Archangel defeats Luzbel, banishing him into the dungeons of hell, and the shepherds arrive in Bethlehem offering their humble gifts to the new-born King.

In the sixteenth century, the Spanish missionaries in the New World used dramatic representation as a didactic device to teach Christian doctrine.[1] For nearly thirty years after the conquest of Mexico, these representations were a common feature of Christian worship and evangelization. Some of these religious dramas included the enactment of the biblical story of Adam and Eve, the Passion, the Feast of Corpus Christi, and *Los Pastores*. F. Pedro de Gante is the most well known of the early missionaries who participated in this endeavor, founding the Colegio de San Francisco in Mexico City as a place for teaching arts and crafts, special trades, and even building a church with an enlarged atrium for staging religious enactment's (Marie, 1948; Garcidueñas, 1939). After the Council of Trent in December 1545, and later with the emergence of the Enlightenment, the teaching of Christian doctrine through dramatic representation was replaced by forms based on rational and philosophic discourse.[2] Throughout the 17th and 18th centuries, however, *Los Pastores* and other forms of popular religious drama were utilized throughout rural Mexico, including what is now the Southwestern United States, as a means of self-evangelization for local communities.[3]

The development of this Spanish medieval and missionary drama into its present form in the 20th century is a complex matter best studied from a historical perspective. The process of adaptation of Iberian religious practice to circumstances in each of the Spanish colonies on the American side of the Atlantic has framed the development of Catholicism in Latin America. Among Latinos in the United States, such practices form the backbone of popular religion.

For this article, I will focus of the performance of San Antonio's *pastorela,* which was initiated in 1913 by Don Leandro Granado. He had fled Irapuato, México for San Antonio, Texas during the turmoil that led to the Mexican Revolution, and founded the troupe which performs *Los Pastores* each year on the predominantly Mexican American west side of San Antonio.

The devotion to *El Niño Dios,* as expressed in the performances of *Los Pastores* in San Antonio, Texas, provides a case study for interpreting popular religion among Latinos in the United States today. Rather than provide a systematic definition of popular religion and its constant companion, popular religiosity, I prefer to analyze the experiences in one case from an anthropological perspective. From such an analysis, I think the work of definition in the study of religion and the social sciences can proceed in a collaborative effort across many disciplines.

I approach popular religion as a categorical term, like Weber's ideal type, that refers to a broad range of practices, sentiments, and experiences. As Weber suggests, it is a "combination of articles of faith, norms from church law and custom, maxims of conduct, and countless concrete interrelationships which we have fused into an 'idea'" (Weber, 1969: 96). Yet, as contemporary Latino scholars constantly remind us, the most vital aspect of Latino religious experience is the disposition of the people to express their faith through such a medium—popular religiosity—rather than the content of the popular religion itself. My intent in this paper is to articulate one concrete interrelationship that I am familiar with, the performance of *Los Pastores,* and from there, to provide some conclusions about the multiple meanings and domains of experience that derive from this practice. As a result, this paper will serve to document one dimension of popular religiosity, and will contribute to the work of PARAL.

Members of the troupe begin rehearsing for this event in late September and meet regularly until the end of the performance season in February. Most are from the surrounding west side barrio, but a few, especially some of the older members, have moved to other areas of town. The performers are Mexican working-class men and women, both young and old. Many are supported by government pensions like social security, disability, or various forms of welfare subsistence. Mostly, however, they share their common devotion to *El Niño Dios.* They all have their special stories of how—in times of crisis, sickness, and other moments of human crisis—supplications to *El Niño Dios* were responded to in ways that provided comfort, solace, and miracles. The most vocal is Vicente Manuel, one of the leaders of the troupe, who never fails to tell how *El Niño Dios* relieved him of his paralysis after a stroke at a young age.

Los Pastores is performed in three distinct domains: in the backyards and driveways of homes in San Antonio barrios, a site I refer to as the barrio-home; at local churches; and at one of the historic missions in the city for an event sponsored by the San Antonio Conservation Society. For reasons of focus, this paper will contrast and compare performances of *Los Pastores* in the domains of the barrio-home and local churches. While these domains are distinct in terms of the way popular religious sentiment is expressed, they are similar in the kinds of people who attend and in the geographic locations in which they occur. The domain of the mission, while unique and important in terms of how cultural practices are displaced from one venue to another (Flores, 1994), provides little information concerning the topic of this paper.

By contrasting the barrio performance with that at the church I plan to reveal various "gaps" from one domain to another. These gaps exhibit critical disjunctures and fissures in meaning that are critical for interpreting and understanding the role of popular religion for this group.

In order to contrast the domains of the barrio-home and the church, I will explore how "centering discourses" and "place" inform this event. By centering discourses I mean the way *Los Pastores* is contextualized, grounded, and introduced by the sponsoring agents in each venue (Hanks, 1989). This is a critical factor in the production of each performance by providing important information that allows those present to interpret the event in specific ways. By necessity, the comparative analysis of these two domains draws on the related concepts of recentering and decentering, revealing a fluid process whereby particular discourses shift from one domain to another for the purpose of recontextualizing or recentering an event in a different venue. By "place," I am referring to how the physical and symbolic markers of each domain contribute to the semantic field that emerges in each location.[4] These two elements—centering discourses and place—are a combination of indexical signs and framing devices that empirically shape the meaning of *Los Pastores,* as it emerges in two distinct venues.

One final comment concerns the issue of "belief." There is no doubt that performers of *Los Pastores* in particular, and practitioners of popular religious practice in general, are motivated by belief. Belief in *El Niño Dios* is essential to the experience of those involved. This study in no way seeks to question the authenticity of the performer's belief. Instead, it attempts to explore how social factors governing collective representation and social interaction contribute to the social experience that is represented in *El Niño Dios.*

The Barrio-Home Domain

PLACE

The physical site of the barrio-home is both familiar and familial. Audience members consist primarily of extended and nuclear family members, as well as work associates and neighborhood friends. For them, the barrio, replete with pot-holed streets, closely aligned houses, poor street drainage and housing conditions, is a familiar site.

It is also familial. Homes are often multifamily dwellings where it is not unusual to find members of at least three generations housed in one home. While the lack of economic resources force family members into crowded living conditions, a network of familial support, however meager, is usually available (Vélez-Ibáñez, 1983).

At the home, the event is staged outdoors beneath a carport or patio if one is large enough, and visible to passing cars and pedestrians. There are few props needed for any performance. The main requirement is an area approximately ten feet square where the *infierno* or hellmouth can be placed. This is a four-paneled enclosure decorated with demonic icons that houses Luzbel and the other devils. Opposite the *infierno*, about fifteen yards away, is a place where a manger is situated providing a place for *El Niño Dios*. These two items, the *infierno* and the manger, are provided by the performers. Male members of the family are busy assisting with the *infierno*. A large and heavy structure, it can only be transported in an open-bed truck and men from the household assist performers in assembling and locating the exact site to place it.

One element that is provided by the hosts is a home altar that is placed directly behind the manger. Most families hosting this event construct an altar with flowers, candles, religious statues, and other holiday paraphernalia. Many families take great care in constructing the altar, believing it to be a testimony to their commitment and devotion to *El Niño Dios*. Grandmothers usually instruct their daughters and granddaughters on how to create an aesthetically pleasing and religiously appropriate altar. And while it is usually seen as a form of women's work, I also know of male children attending to this ritual alongside their maternal elders. The specialized role of women in aspects of popular religiosity is a matter of continuing research that merits more attention than is possible in this article. Clearly, there is a connection between the women's role in constructing the home altar and the meal provided by the hosts which is served to everyone at the end of the performance. In some ways, the meal compliments the work of the home altar -one being a shrine to the saints, the other to those who attend. Like the altar, the meal also involves the labor of women. In some cases, preparation begins several days in advance with the making of *tamales* and *tortillas*. Most of the work, however, begins early in the morning. Beans are washed and prepared, *menudo* [tripe soup] is cut and cooked, and other dishes prepared. Enough food is prepared for thirty to fifty people. Like other tasks, food preparation is a familial job where everyone from the youngest to oldest assists in some way.

The building of the home altar and the preparation of food, tasks that incorporate friends and family in their completion, requires a commitment of time and effort. Elsewhere (Flores, 1994), I refer to this task as the "gifting of performance." In brief, performance, especially ritual performance, is a dynamic event calling forth a special commitment on the part of performers and spectators. This commitment is marked by a special process of gifting and reciprocity. In this case, *Los Pastores* is enacted as a gift: there is no fee charged or expected for a performance in the barrio-home, and all requests for a performance are honored, provided scheduling can be accommodated. But gifts, especially those dealing with ritual, must be reciprocated if they are to be efficacious. In this case, the time, financial resources, and physical labor that is utilized in the preparation of the place of performance, that of building home altars and providing a meal, is considered a reciprocal gift. Such an event serves as a means of extending the network of people who are responsible for such an event, drawing people into forms of human interaction marked by sociability. That is, the process of performance and reciprocity through one's labor of gratitude, form a process through which bonds of sociability are constructed. The gifting of performance facilitates the construction of a familial atmosphere where social conviviality emerges.

CENTERING

The most common form of centering *Los Pastores* in the barrio is as a dyadic ritual. As such, it serves as a fulfillment to a *promesa*, or ritual promise. *"Hace dos años que hice una promesa al Niño Dios. Si curaba a mi mamá, le prometí tener una pastorela en mi casa. Pues, la salud de mi mamá mejoró, y me siento feliz que ya llegó este día"* [It has been two years since I made a vow to the Christ Child. If he cured my mother, I promised to hold a *pastorela* in my house. Well, my mother's health improved, and I feel happy that today has arrived].

Framing *Los Pastores* as a dyadic ritual functions in several ways. First, it begins the event with a personal narrative that extends it to a wide audience. As a dyadic ritual, or *promesa,* the hosts agrees to fulfill a particular duty, normally some form of devotion, if *El Niño Dios* provides a special favor for them, usually related to the health of one's family member. This negotiation is one that involves a dyadic relationship between hosts and *El Niño Dios.* By centering *Los Pastores* in such a way, the intimate relationship that forms the core of ritual negotiation is made public through the telling of a personal narrative. Such narratives build a sense of empathy for the hosts, but more importantly, serve as reflexive narratives that allow those present to recall their own personal events of sickness, death, or other moments of human passage. Suffice it to say that these narratives function to incorporate, draw-in, and gather those present into a common social body by building on human experiences that affect everyone. The personal narrative is a device through which devotion to *El Niño Dios* extends outward to the audience, reflexively allowing them to recall their own human condition. The personal narrative ceases to be an individual invocation, but a means through which the audience engages the experience as one collective body.

The Church Domain

PLACE

The physical site of the church is quite different from that of the barrio-home. Also, the church domain is more formal, whereas the barrio event is relaxed in relation to the scheduled time of beginning, this is not the case at the church. Because it is advertised to a larger and public audience, the scheduled time to begin is more strictly followed.

Another factor is the physical space. While the church may be a familiar scene, it is not familial. Performances are held outdoors, in large open areas or inside a hall. In some cases, they are held inside the church building. These sacred spaces provide a distinct semantic sense to the performance that is not experienced in the barrio. Especially when performed inside the church, the sense of the spiritual that is invoked by candles, incense, and religious iconography offers a more religious sentiment.

Like the barrio event, home altars are usually built in the church domain. Especially when performed outdoors on church property, special care is made to sanctify space with an altar. The task of building an altar is assigned to a few people, or perhaps a church organization. As such, the responsibility for constructing altars is different than the barrio. In the home, it is taken as the responsibility of the entire household, while in the church, it is seen as the work of a selected few.

The meal is also distinctive. Like the building of an altar, the preparation of the meal is undertaken by an assigned group. And, unlike the barrio, the meal is not provided to everyone. Members of the troupe are fed free of charge as a sign of gratitude for their performance, but the general audience is asked to pay for their meal. After the performance, all are invited to a hall or school cafeteria where food and beverages are served. A set price is charged for a dinner plate, while drinks can be purchased separately. Out of the hundred or more people who attend a church performance, only a handful, usually those who have organized the event, stay for the meal. The festive meal is not as important in the church domain since it is not interpreted or attended as part of the event by the audience.

CENTERING

The church domain also makes ritual claims on *Los Pastores* but does so with a different kind of narrative. It frames this event as a way of providing for the religious needs of the congregation. Its access is unquestioned since *Los Pastores* stems from the Christian tradition of religious drama and reenacts the Christian scene of the nativity. The narrative invoked is one of religious devotion; the event is introduced as ritual, and efforts are made to emphasize its religious content. Centering *Los Pastores* as a form of ritual functions to extend this event to a wide audience, but in a way that is different from the personal narrative found in the barrio. Because *Los Pastores* descends from Catholic liturgical drama, and has to some extent been supported by Catholic officials, Church sponsorship and ownership goes unquestioned. Catholic religious officials see *Los Pastores* as "their tradition" to propagate. As such, the ritual centering of the event is one based on the broader aspect of church membership. *Los Pastores* is enacted in the church domain as a ritual performance because this is the site of Christian ritual and anyone who identifies with the ideology of Catholic Christianity is welcome to attend and can claim this event as part of their own religious tradition.

Displacements and Discontinuities

The differences exhibited in the domains of the barrio and church performances exhibit shifts in meaning as *Los Pastores* is recentered from one site to another. These differences are, following Stallybrass and White (1986), displacements that signal changes or gaps in the meaning of this event. Displacements are not neutral, but discontinuities that reveal competitive claims over social identity, the emergent social meaning, and social power (Bauman and Briggs, 1990: 76).

The discontinuities between the barrio performance and the church provide for a substantially different semantic field. The barrio is produced from elements of a dyadic ritual and personal narrative, familial relations, and a place that is familiar. While a barrio performance exhibits a more heightened sense of the everyday, i.e., the festive meals and seasonal timing of the event, it is grounded in the social relations that govern everyday practice. The sounds and smells are familiar; the space, while rearranged, is common; the work that prepares food, space, and welcomes guests is the same as other days. The experience of *Los Pastores* in the home constitutes an event of shared social meaning, identity, and everyday experience.

The personal narrative that centers this event serves as a rhetorical device that reinforces the familiar through intimacy. *Promesas* are invariably about personal matters: the health of an elder, child, other family relative; or, other concerns that affect families. As a form of rhetoric, these narratives serve as an invitation to intimacy, providing a social frame that allows others to recall similar events in their own lives, inducing them into a sense of shared experience and sociability. As such, the barrio-home event is a rhetorical and performative event that, as Stanley Tambiah claims, "consists of acts to create effects on human agents according to accepted social convention" (Tambiah, 1990: 82).

The church is quite different. While it is still introduced as a ritual practice, the lack of an opening personal narrative does not cohere the social group as the barrio-home event. Instead, it is centered as a traditional and cultural celebration of the Christian nativity. While this narrative is also rhetorical, it provides a frame based on the Catholic social body at large and not the sense of intimacy and shared experience that is induced in the barrio-home. While there is a sense of group identity, it is one based on adherence to a more diffuse Catholic ideology and not the personal intimacy that emerges in the telling of personal narratives.

The church domain is no longer a family-supported event, but one sponsored by a church and open to any member of the institution, including those from neighboring churches. This extends the social body from one that is familially and geographically centered to one that is accessible to any member of the wider Catholic community. As such, any person of Catholic persuasion, regardless of cultural knowledge, can viably claim *Los Pastores* as part of their tradition. This displaces the cultural authority and knowledge from the hosts and performers to anyone who claims *Los Pastores* as part of their religious tradition.

In these two domains the texture of social relations that govern everyday practice is reproduced; distinctions based on gender, age, cultural knowledge, class position, and authority are replicated. These distinctions, however, are not of equal weight. In the barrio, cleavages of gender and age demarcate lines of difference but do so within the realm of shared social meaning and conviviality. It is not that these differences are irrelevant, or that social rankings based on gender and age are benign. On the contrary, they are real forces that lead to conflict and crisis in many families. But here, in this event, gender and age differences are subsumed beneath the more salient and emergent experience of social and cultural solidarity.

The church domain follows the same kind of division as found in the barrio, except for the status given representatives of the official church priests, and in someplaces, leaders of church organizations. Because of their institutional links, these leaders assert more authority and control over the event. In this domain, the issue of class is negligible. For one, the secular leaders are of the same social location as the participants and performers; any authority they may claim is based on institutional status. The only real division of social place is between the clergy and all others. However, few of them participate; and more importantly, their authority stems more from their religious status not their class position.

Another disjuncture between the barrio and the church events has to do with the level of gifting that takes place in each domain. Gifting and reciprocity structure the barrio event. The amount of work needed and the shared labor that gets it done mark this domain with a strong sense of shared work and responsibility. The majority of those present—family, friends, and performers—contribute a part of their labor to bring this event to fruition. This is not the case in the church domain. Besides the performers, only a small group of people have contributed their time and effort to this event. The majority of the people in this domain are spectators. This is not to say that they do not bring some form of religious sentiment to bear upon the event, but only to indicate that they contribute little in terms of responsibility, reciprocity, or shared labor. The difference is important for several points. The barrio event creates a more cohesive and unified social group, one that emerges from the sense of responsibility that is fostered by the gifting of performance. The church is an experience based on shared religious tradition. While there is an emergent social group, it is one based on a common sentiment to *Los Pastores* and *El Niño Dios,* and not the experience of sociability that gives expression to such sentiment.

Towards a Rethinking of Popular Religious Practice

In an attempt to rethink the issue of popular religious practice, I would like to characterize, conjecturally, a categorical distinction between the performance of *Los Pastores* at the barrio-home and the church domains. Let me initially describe this disjuncture, following, and at times differing from, the ideas of Paul Connerton (1989), as one between performative and commemorative ritual practices. A performative ritual practice is one in which a "community is constituted" (Connerton, 1989: 59); it is an action that forms and begets those who are present as a social body. Commemorative ritual practices, on the other hand, are those in which a community is "reminded of itself" (Connerton, 1989: 70). Ritual practices of this kind serve to recall, through various forms of mnemonic and bodily actions, the seminal event of community formation. Before I explore these issues further, let me briefly state that these are not dichotomous categories, but qualitative assessments and aspects of both can be found in either domain.

The Barrio-Home Domain as Performance Ritual

The conjunction of personal narratives and the gifting of performance that emerges in the barrio domain is one of sociability. This is the experience of community. Through rhetorical devices and shared work, this domain induces a sense of communal responsibility and ownership. This experience is one of *familia,* not because it is occupied solely by members of the same family, but because of the way an emergent social body of multiple groups is constituted. As such, the emergent sense of sociability and community, constructed through ritual performance, constitutes the way in which the actual work of popular religion gets done.[5]

At the same time, this domain is also marked by elements of commemoration, be it the memory of human crisis that is invoked in the personal narratives, or one of previous performances. This memory, however, is not what constitutes the group, but one that adds to the seminal experience of this event.

The Church Domain as Commemorative Ritual

The invocation of a discourse that focuses on the re-enactment of the Nativity and of Catholic tradition marks the church domain as a commemorative ritual. The impetus to perform *Los Pastores* in this domain is to recall the Nativity. In many ways, this event is likened more to theater where a sharper distinction between performers and audience members and their concomitant roles is present. In place of mutual responsibility, audience members arrive and leave, fulfilling the role of spectators while performers act out their parts on stage. The intense interaction that is found in a barrio-home event is absent, indicative of the distinct lack of social engagement and conviviality associated with performative rituals. Furthermore, this event is sponsored by a religious organization that is itself based on the memory of its founder, and that doctrinally and dogmatically takes great care to maintain its historical tradition. The ability of any Catholic Church to claim this event as its own, and any Catholic to interpret it as part of their own tradition, further exemplifies how this event serves to reproduce a sense of Catholic identity.

It is also true, however, that this event produces, in the sense that performative rituals do, a community. But the production of this social body is not one in which the seminal work of performative ritual constructs community, instead it is founded on the memory of a religious tradition: this event is a re-enactment, a remembering of a prior seminal experience, be it the Nativity or the grand story of Christianity itself. This is quite distinct from the experience of community that is fostered from the gifting of performance and personal narratives experienced in the barrio-home.

Issues of Definition

Before providing a provisional definition of popular religiosity, let me briefly address several critical points that cannot be ignored. First is the issue of culture. Mexicanos, Mexican Americans, Chicanos are not a homogeneous group; culture is not a closed system but an open and continuous flow of meanings and practices. To assume that Mexicanos today believe and act like Mexicanos a century ago, or even a decade ago, is to grossly misrepresent the human experience. Furthermore, regional, geographic, and social experiences are all elements that inform one's social and cultural world. Certainly, the issue of race and African culture are significant factors in the experiences of Caribbean peoples, such as Puerto Ricans, Cubans and Dominicans. In place of generalizing about a unified Mexican and/or Latino identity, I believe it is critical to ground such discussions in the experiences of real people living in real communities constituted from distinct historical and social practice.[6]

Second, and along these same lines, popular religion is not a singular phenomenon. Like symbols in general, religious practices and the meanings they inform, are polysemous and multivocal. Such practices do not necessarily signify the same meaning or set of meanings from one historical period to another, or one side of town to the next. As this paper demonstrates, the same ritual performance can exhibit different semantic qualities even when enacted by the same people. Ethnographic context and detail alone can lead to understanding these meanings, not a priori assumptions or doctrinal considerations.

Another issue is the relationship between popular religiosity and liturgical inculturation. Many Churches— Catholic, Protestant, and

Evangelical—have begun to incorporate cultural elements into the official liturgy or worship service. While these efforts are to be praised and encouraged, they should not be taken as a form of popular religious practice but related to the cultural adaptation of worship that is encouraged by many institutional religions.

Popular religion is not an object that can be incorporated and attached to existing liturgical practice but something quite different. Popular religion is a process in which people utilize religious symbols and meanings to convert the alienation of modernity into social networks and relations that foster community. It is a process initiated, controlled, and produced by the people themselves.

This leads to a number of considerations. The first is the issue of institutional control. As this paper demonstrates, the institutional control of the same religious practice may or may not be a factor in its interpretation. The issue, in this case, turns on the distinction between performative and commemorative practices. The Catholic Church, as an institution, has goals other than the formation of community. The formation of community among Latinos is a process that requires the church to exceed its own self- interests. Typically, a clergy directs an institutional church which builds on the memory of community instead of risking the outcomes of community formation. Virtually by definition, the church's role as an extension of the dominant society is to hold Latino religion captive in the past. The self-creation of Latino community with its own set of religious meanings represents a process that constitutes social power and cultural identity that jeopardizes the political power of the church.

The experience of Catholicism with popular religiosity, not only in San Antonio but also in Latin America, has been a gradual, if uneven acceptance over the last two decades. The people's religious expressions that have usually been practiced beyond ordinary clerical control have come to be viewed as an important pastoral force. One may view the multiplication of base ecclesial communities, *comunidades eclesiales de base,* as an effort to develop new styles of Catholic life that are not as dependent upon clerical control as those of the past. These basic Christian communities demonstrate that ordinary Christians can provide church leadership as effective as that of those in control so that in the opinion of some scholars, Catholicism need not depend upon inherited and office-based elite roles of power to further its institutional goals.

This is related to the issue of orthodoxy. Popular religious practice is often judged as a threat to orthodox practice because it falls outside the parameters of church sanction. The question of orthodoxy, I suggest, is less an issue of correct belief but one related to the control of ritual practice and the social world implicated by such practice. Practice shapes belief, and to the extent that religious practice can perpetuate and inform a set of beliefs devoid of church control it codifies a religious stance that threatens institutional, hence orthodox, religion. The experience of sociability when popular religious practice is included within officially controlled religious expression may reduce the alienation that is often experienced in hierarchical church structures. The wholesale movement to Protestant churches in Latin America, especially to community-based denominations that are more socially adaptable to changing social and political circumstances, suggest that popular religiosity has a place within some forms of Christianity besides Catholicism (Stoll, 1990).

The strategy of incorporating popular religiosity into official aspects of ritual represents an important variant in the general pattern, particularly for Catholicism in the United States and forms the basis of much theorizing about Catholic responsibility towards Latinos. To evaluate such innovations from a social science perspective, I would suggest attention to how acceptance of such performances of popular religiosity impact upon other aspects of religious practice.

Finally, a number of definitions of popular religious practice refer to class as an important variable. Like institutional control, class may be a consideration but one that merits further elaboration. In the case at hand, social actors of the same social location (class, ethnicity, geographic area...) are involved in both domains demonstrating that class is not the only factor that contributes to a distinction between performative and commemorative rituals. Perhaps a more nuanced indication, and one related to class position and not merely socio-economic status, is found in the continuum between rational or secular perspectives and religious ones. The modern phenomenon of secularization has tended to overcome those who interpret social life through a religious lens (Berger, 1967; Tambiah, 1990). While I don't have the time to develop this further, suffice it to say that issues of secularization, rationality, and religious opinion need to be affixed to a more empirically grounded understanding of class experience.[7] That is, one cannot automatically assume that lower socio-economic classes see the world from a religious and/or magical viewpoint while those from the upper-classes are steeped in more rational perspectives (or vice-versa). Such views need to be explored with real people.

Finally, it is my belief that a critical factor in any working definition of popular religious practice must incorporate the issue of an "emergent" community. As the barrio-home domain demonstrates, and an issue that runs through this entire analysis, popular religious practices aim at producing sociability. *Promesas* are about extending the life of one's community member, personal narratives aim at sharing human crisis that threaten community, and the gifting of performance invokes a shared sense of work and reciprocity that fosters a communal event. These acts are without a doubt social ones: they forge a collective identity and group, however fleeting. Popular religious practices of the performative kind aim at creating social relationships and extending social networks. These are the same relationships and networks that are called upon in times of economic and social crisis. This is also a political act. In the midst of social and political alienation caused by racial, economic, geographic, or political displacement, the practice of gathering and forging a sense of oneness is an act of collective self-determination.

I began this paper by saying that the Mexican American performers in San Antonio stated that they perform for *El Niño Dios*. I suggest that their understanding of performance has both social and religious meanings. While the performers cite the historical and religious tradition invoked in the reenactment of the nativity, at the same time they pointed out a preference for performing in the barrio-home domain (Flores, 1994). This, I suggest, is based on their experience of sociability. In this domain, to perform for *El Niño Dios* is not only a commemorative act, but a constituting one: men, women, and children are united in an emergent act where sociability, conviviality, and a socially shared sense of identity is born.

Thus, to understand the maintenance of popular religiosity among not only the Mexican Americans of San Antonio, but among Latinos everywhere in the U. S., it may not be enough to examine historical texts and the lack of institutional control. If, as I have suggested, sociability is a key determinant of how popular religiosity sustains traditions and forms community, then it may be possible to examine other places of religious expression in a like manner. While it is problematic that the home and the institutional settings can ever be identical, their respective religious functions for Latinos needs further study. Indeed, as a supplier of community in a depersonalized society, popular religiosity may achieve new importance as a substitute for more institutionally based aspects of Catholic life in the United States.

Before reaching such a theoretic conclusion, however, a great deal more research must be conducted among different Latino groups in the US. I hope that the anthropological focus upon interrelationships in different domains that was employed in this article might prove to be an analytical tool for exploration by an ever increasing number of scholars of Latino religion.

Endnotes

1. One reason I believe humorous and dramatic representations were so popular is that they resonated with a similar indigenous tradition. Aztec society had troupes of traveling troubadours and performers who were trained in special schools known as *cuicacalli* (Ravicz, 1970: 20). For a general historical account of Christian dramatic performance genres at this period see Flores (1989), Garcidueñas (1939), Marie (1948), and Robe (1954).

2. Foucault, in *The Order of Things* (1970) traces this shift in epistemological emphasis. It is one from knowledge as similitude, hence representation, to one of rationality. See Tambiah's comments on Foucault on this same point (1990: 21).

3. Rael (1965), in a diffusion study of *pastorelas,* traces a number of texts from México to the United States. He concludes that all the texts he found were written in the New World, although highly influenced by Spanish Golden Age poetry. For studies of the *pastorela* in the Southwest U.S., see Campa (1934A & 1934B), Cole (1907), Flores (1989), Leyva, (1951), Marie (1948), Paredes (1964), Robe (1954 and 1957). It is worth noting that one of the earliest chroniclers of this genre is Bourke (1893), who collected Mexican folklore at the same time he was hunting and killing Mexican "bandits." For an interpretation of this early figure collector of Mexican folklore see Limón (1994) and Flores (1993).

4. Elsewhere (Flores In Press), I have articulated the notion of memory-place, a concept that attempts to explore how place and memory interact to produce a semantic space of heightened activity. For the sake of brevity, in this paper I will limit my discussion only to place.

5. See Schieffelin (1985) for an extended discussion of how performative acts constitute social reality.

6. See Rosaldo (1989) for a discussion of culture and social identity in relation to Chicanos. Appadurai (1991) offers a more global perspective on many of the same issues addressed by Rosaldo as well as those that inform this issue.

7. See Berger (1967) and Tambiah (1990) for their perspectives on rationality, secularization, and religious belief.

Bibliography

Appadurai, A. 1991. "Global Ethnoscapes: Notes and Queries for a Transnational Anthropology." In *Recapturing Anthropology: Working in the Present,* ed. R. Fox. Santa Fe: School of American Research Press.

Bauman, R. and C. L. Briggs. 1990. "Poetics and Performance as Critical Perspectives on Language and Social Life." *Annual Review of Anthropology.* 19: 59-88.

Berger, P. 1967. *The Sacred Canopy: Elements of a Sociological Theory of Religion.* New York: Doubleday.

Bourke, J. G. 1893. "The Miracle Play of the Rio Grande." *Journal of American Folk-lore.* 6 (21): 89-95.

Campa, A. 1934A. "Spanish Religious Folk Theater in the Spanish Southwest (First Cycle)." *University of New Mexico Bulletin* 5: 1.

———. 1934B. "Spanish Religious Folk Theater in the Spanish Southwest (Second Cycle)." *University of New Mexico Bulletin* 5: 2.

Cole, M. R. 1907. *Los Pastores: A Mexican Play of the Nativity.* Boston: Houghton, Mifflin and Co.

Connerton, P. 1989. *How Societies Remember.* Cambridge: Cambridge University Press.

Flores, R. R. 1989. *Los Pastores: Performance, Poetics, and Politics in Folk Drama.* Ph.D. Dissertation, Department of Anthropology, University of Texas at Austin.

———. 1993. "History, Los Pastores, and the Shifting Poetics of Dislocation." *Journal of Historical Sociology* 6, 2: 164-185.

———. 1994. "Los Pastores and the Gifting of Performance." *American Ethnologist.* 21 (2): 270-285

In Press, 1994. "Between Devotion and Diversion: History and Performance in the Mexican Shepherd's Play of South Texas." Washington, D.C. Smithsonian Institution Press.

Foucault, M. 1970. *The Order of Things: An Archaeology of the Human Sciences.* New York: Vintage Books.

Garcidueñas, J. R. 1939. *Autos y coloquios del siglo XVI.* México: Universidad Nacional Autónoma.

Hanks, W. 1989. "Text and textuality." *Annual Review of Anthropology.* 18: 95-127.

Leyva, J. 1951. *A genetic study of Los Pastores.* Trinity University, San Antonio, Texas.

Limón, J. 1994. *Dancing with the Devil.* Madison: University of Wisconsin Press.

Marie, S. J. I. 1948. "The Role of the Church and the Folk in the Development of the Early Drama in New Mexico." English Department, University of Pennsylvania.

Paredes, A. 1964. "Pastorela." In *Buying the Wind,* ed. R. M. Dorson, 466-479. Chicago: University of Chicago Press.

Rael, J. 1965. *The Sources and Diffusion of the Mexican Shepherds' Plays.* Guadalajara: Librería la Joyita.

Ravicz, M. E. 1970. *Early Colonial Religious Drama in Mexico: from Tzompantli to Golgatha.* Washington: Catholic University Press.

Robe, S. 1954. *Coloquios de pastores from Jalisco, México.* Berkeley: University of California Press.

_____. 1957. "The relationship of Los Pastores to other Spanish-American folk drama." *Western Folklore.* 16:281- 289.

Rosaldo, R. 1989. *Culture and Truth: The Remaking of Social Analysis.* Boston: Beacon Press.

Stallybrass, P. and A. White. 1986. *The Politics and Poetics of Transgression.* Ithaca: Cornell University Press.

Stoll, David. 1990. *Is Latin America Turning Protestant? The Politics of Evangelical Growth.* Berkeley: University of California Press.

Tambiah, S. J. 1990. *Magic, Science, Religion, and the Scope of Rationality.* Cambridge: Cambridge University Press.

Vélez-Ibáñez, C. 1983. *Bonds of Mutual Trust: The Cultural Systems of Rotating Credit Associations Among Urban Mexicans and Chicanos.* New Brunswick, NJ: Rutgers University Press.

Weber, M. 1969. "Objectivity in the social sciences." In *The Methodology of the Social Sciences.* ed. E. Shils and H. A. Finch, New York: Free Press.

Linking Theory and Methodology for the Study of Latino Religiosity in the United States Context

8

MEREDITH McGUIRE

The sociology of religion urgently needs good empirical data on Latino religious expression, religiosity, and religious organizations and movements. If this research can transcend some of the methodological and conceptual rigidities that have limited earlier research in the field, it has the potential to affect our sociology of religion, both narrowly and profoundly.

The narrow potential of a stream of new empirical studies of Latino/a religion is that the social sciences of religion will have to take another variant of American religion into account. Previous interpretations of U.S. religion have been based upon studies in which Latino religion has been under-represented or ignored, so new data will force us to rethink those interpretations, adjust them accordingly, discard unhelpful parts and add new, culturally broader interpretations. In this article, however, I urge researchers to aim for a more profound influence: if, in our studies of Latina/o religion, we can ground our work in solid theoretical questions and risk trying new conceptual and methodological approaches in our research, our work may contribute to profound changes in how sociology understands religion in the contemporary world.

Too much research in the social sciences of religion has been either uninformed by theory or so abstractly theoretical that it cannot be operationalized empirically. If asked "Why are you studying this?" (e.g., this religious movement, this devotional practice, this group's attitudes, and so on), too often the only answer social scientists can give is, "It's unusual, different from the movements, practices, attitudes, etc., already documented." We should not be satisfied to justify our study of Latino/a religion by the fact that previously it has not been adequately studied—no matter how true or lamentable that situation may be. Although such research is useful for documentation purposes, its contribution to our understanding will remain limited or superficial unless it is informed, from the outset, by a set of objectives and a methodology that address larger theoretical issues.

Thus, my discussion of research methodologies and strategies begins by calling attention to important theoretical developments which, not only suggest worthwhile themes for the study of Latina/o religion, but also radically challenge our conceptualization of these themes. These theoretical developments affect our operationalization of central terms (such as ethnicity or religiosity), and thus, call into question many of the standard methodological approaches of social science research.

The Structural Location of Religion

Classical sociological theory confronted the observation that the "modern" world (at the end of the nineteenth century) was profoundly different from the social world which went before it. Many of the central theories of early sociology and anthropology focused on religion for an interpretive handle on the nature of modernity. Religion is still a fruitful focus for understanding a dramatically changed social world.

Unfortunately, U.S. sociology developed many of its methodological tools for studying religion in an era and intellectual climate in which modernity was viewed as an accomplished fact, a given rather than an ongoing process. Furthermore, researchers identified religion as an established institution—neatly identifiable in its official expressions (i.e., the Christian churches, with an occasional nod to Jewish analogies). It is entirely probable that those empirical approaches were inadequately tapping the richness of American religion even at the mid-twentieth century, but subsequent changes in American society make it imperative to broaden our working definitions.

How can we empirically operationalize our concepts of religion, religiosity, and religious groups to cover the enormous diversity of religious expression in the United States? Old methodologies are continually challenged by their inability to adequately tap native and non-Western religions, new religious movements, civil religions, quasi-religious movements, and older non-official religious forms (such as popular religion). Merely fine-tuning old methodologies is not sufficient, because our methodological difficulties are due, not only to the narrow field of vision of earlier researchers, but more importantly to changes in the location and meaning of religion itself in advanced industrial societies, such as the United States.

Theories about how late modern societies differ from pre-modern and early modern societies suggest that there has been a significant shift in the structural location of religion (see Beckford, 1989). The great religious institutional monopolies have been broken, and religious symbols are mobilized in unexpected and uncontrollable ways, often in tension with "establishment" practices. Religious institutions perdure in late modernity, but they are relegated to the private sphere of voluntary associations. If we start from old conceptualizations of religion (as equatable with its institutional forms), we see today much evidence of the decline demise or self-protective calcification of much religious expression.

With a different conceptualization, however, we see that religion is important in many facets of American life and that there are many vibrant and changing expressions of Christianity and other religious approaches in this culture. Of this latter image, Latina/o religion is the epitome. With a narrow definition, we "see" only evidence such as frequency of church attendance, institutionally recognized devotional practices, sacraments, rates of adherence to institutionally normative behavior, rates of endogamous marriages, etc. With a broader conceptualization of religion, religiosity and religious experience, we see how much religious activity and learning is linked with home and community and other non-church spheres, dynamic (as well as static) popular religious expression, religiously motivated social concerns and activism, and many other ways of being religious or ways of putting together one's personal religion that, understood collectively, give a very different picture of the place of religion in American life.

Beckford (1989: 170-171) argues that, in late modern society, religion has become partially broken off from its traditional points of anchorage—its communal, familial, and organizational bases. This "autonomization" (using Simmel's term) makes religion into a potent cultural resource which may be invested with highly diverse symbolic meanings. Thus, late-modern religion is both much more flexible and unpredictable than its pre-modern or early modern forms. Beckford suggests that it is, therefore, better for social research to conceptualize religion as a cultural resource or form than as a social institution.

What does this historical development of the social location of religion imply about methodologies for studying religion? It suggests that institutional forms of religion—while still of interest—are far less important for understanding the larger religious situation. We can no longer assume that ascribed characteristics (presumed of members in a religious organization, e.g., gender, ethnic, or status groups) tell us much about individual religious beliefs, practices, or experiences. Emerging groups embracing the pluralistic and relatively autonomous structural situation of religion and ethnicity and those resisting it, with upsurges of sectarianism or tribalism, are worth studying as active and often creative responses to the same social structural situation.

Specifically, we need to give more research attention to those nascent movements (no matter how small) through which religious symbols are being proffered and mobilized, especially in tension with those of religious and other established institutions. For this we need a richer appreciation of the cultural factors in social and political change. Exactly how is religion employed as a cultural resource? In a structural situation where religion is flexible and relatively autonomous from authoritative control in any institutional sphere, we must focus on on-going processes by which believers create, maintain, and change their symbols for making sense of their worlds. These symbol systems are sometimes enduring, sometimes transformed into new meanings, and sometimes completely ephemeral. Nevertheless, given the modern situation of religion, it is the process, rather than whether it results in an institutionalized form with a quantifiable membership, that is important for research and analysis.

For study of such flexible and ever-changing processes, we should pay particular attention to rituals, symbols and other cultural vehicles for world images (whether toward change or preservation) and for shared religious experiences and sense of community. We need greater attention especially to language, such as: shared symbolic language; narratives of personal meanings and group experiences; and the structure of discourse and how it develops and changes. Concomitantly, we need less emphasis on quantitative methods, such as surveys, opinion research and formal organizational analysis, because these methodologies presume a relatively fixed, institutional form of religion. They depend upon shorthand identification of people with their institutional location—such as religious affiliation or political party.

We must also drop the assumption that traditional institutional religious symbols, language, rituals, and practices are used for the reasons an institution once intended them. We cannot assume continuity between the functions served by certain religious expressions in another time and place and the meanings of the same expressions today. For instance, we cannot assume that our interpretation of Mass attendance in rural Ireland in the eighteenth century applies, even vestigially, to 1990s Mass attendance of, say, Irish Americans in Dallas, Texas. Rather than treating traditional meanings as given, we should make them research questions. For example, what do people mean when they choose to have a church wedding?

We might borrow some methodological tools from anthropology, which has a long tradition of letting respondents speak with their own voices, not constrained by the words of the research instrument. Anthropological methods, too, are limited for our task, however, because anthropological research typically has been done among peoples whose beliefs and practices change far more slowly, for whom tradition is more authoritative, and who are relatively isolated from the pluralism that characterizes the modern religious situation. Unfortunately, doing good fieldwork requires considerable reflexivity about one's own part in the product, as well as methodological rigor and precision, and finely honed observational and interpersonal skills. It also takes far more time for systematic data-gathering than do standard quantitative methods.

We might also borrow from historical and political sociologies, with their methodological tools for tapping complex sources of change in modern societies. For instance, we might experiment with analysis of archival evidence of movement turning points, oral histories, and personal documents. Although these methods are even more limited for our purposes than direct anthropological investigation, they may be especially useful for triangulating findings. For example, to study a contemporary movement which is proffering religious meanings, one might do: participant-observation; intensive interviews with adherents; analysis of movement archives and personal documents, combined with discourse analysis of current social exchanges within the group; and, between it and others, promoting competing religious meanings.

Non-official Religion in a Pluralistic Context

By reconceptualizing religion as cultural resource, rather than fixed institution, we are better able to research popular religion, syncretic religion, quasi-religion, civil religion, and other non-official patterns of religious belief, practice, and experience. Until recently, scholars have tended to view popular religion as a feature of pre-modern societies, or a remnant of old-world superstition and ignorance. Now we are beginning to give serious attention to popular religion, since it exists among diverse strata of modern societies and has remained a salient element of American religion, many generations removed from whatever "old country." By definition, popular religion is an effective religion of the people, not controlled by official religious groups and their gatekeepers.

Recognizing popular religion as a valid expression of religiosity enables us to achieve a more balanced appreciation of people's beliefs and practices. For example, if we look only at official religious expression, such as church attendance, some ethnic groups and some entire religions appear to be much more "religious" than others. If, however, we consider both official and non-official religious expression (for example, healing practices, use of amulets or non-official devotional literature, meditation, or family rituals), the pattern may be very different. Persons using non-official beliefs and practices may be found to be "religious" throughout their every day, whereas those who confine their religious expression to official religion may be religious only once in a while.

To achieve this balance, however, we need methodologies that are more open-ended and allow our respondents to use their own words for their own meanings. Standard indices and measures start with words and criteria derived from institutional religion, but we should not merely construct new and broader indices and measures (i.e., an expanded checklist of beliefs and practices). Rather, we should focus on all the different ways people actually piece together personally meaningful religious responses to their worlds. Thus, our data may be very situational and consequently, more difficult than the old indices to quantify or even compare.

Rather than administer a checklist of beliefs and practices, such as whether people pray or seek anointing or use amulets or go on pilgrimages or receive Communion, we might try to elicit narratives about the meaning of and responses to critical situations in a person's own life, such as being laid off work, coping with illness and death, deciding about future commitments like marriage, education, career, or political and social involvements. For example, if there has been a health crisis, respondents may have used religion in ways they had never before considered; indeed, they may have different kinds of responses to different health problems, or even different combinations of responses, depending upon the situation. It is not enough simply to document that people are religious, but we should strive for a deeper understanding of how they are religious.

A second value to exploring popular religion is that it highlights social class and political realities of both official and non-official religion. The exclusion of much popular religion, at least in the Christian context, is the peculiar product of a historically unique situation in which the churches enjoyed sufficient power to define an orthodoxy and drum out non-conforming groups. Because of linkages between the resulting ideas and their social class bases, this process tended to exclude or marginalize most religious expressions arising from the poor, women, ethnic minorities, indigenous peoples in colonized lands, and other powerless groups. Even in rigid, traditional societies, popular religions could express and sometimes activate the concerns of subordinant people. In the context of a pluralistic and changing society, such as the U.S., we should listen carefully to the religious expressions that have arisen outside of institutional control. The idioms which common people use to express their needs, concerns, and dissent may be far different from institutional religious idioms. These idioms are no less religious just because they represent the voices of oft-silenced subordinant people.

Third, by learning more about popular religion, as it has evolved from traditional contexts, we can observe comparisons and contrasts with other emerging patterns of religion in modern contexts. For example, it would be interesting to compare aspects of New Age religions with parallel elements of Latina/o popular religion (e.g., images of power, purification, generation, the non-material world). Rather than treating comparisons as "quaint" similarities, we need to keep asking bigger questions, especially: What do these patterns tell us about the nature of religion in late modern societies? In this example, we might examine whether Latinos, using popular religious elements in the modern American context, experience the same creative eclecticism for their personal meaning systems, as do many adherents of New Age religions.

Fourth, attention to the attraction of popular Latino/a religious expression may show some consonance with Pentecostalism and may help explain why Pentecostalism is an appealing alternative to institutional Catholicism. My hunch is that one factor in the appeal of Pentecostalism to many Latinos is that it emphasizes the direct action of the divine in people's everyday lives. Like the folk Catholicism which feels familiar to them, Pentecostalism presents an image of god's power as something reachable and usable for the ordinary individual's everyday pragmatic needs—obtaining a job, an apartment, a washing machine, healing a sick child, or making a decision.

At the same time as emphasizing the importance of more study and appreciation of popular religion, however, we must remain critical in our research approaches. One of the most difficult methodological tasks is to avoid romanticizing popular religion. If researchers start with biases for or against their topic of research, their data may be slanted or even useless. The topic of popular religion may be personally appealing for a researcher who identifies strongly with the tradition out of which it arose or who seeks a personal standpoint for criticism of the official religion, colonial powers, or social classes against which a non-official religion is posed. It is extremely difficult for researchers to remain objective and use methodological precision and care in studying any phenomenon in which they personally want to believe. A non-objective observer, for example, might be so impressed by a popular religion's ways of addressing the interests of the poor that he or she fails to see that religion's oppression of other groups such as women or indigenous peoples. Or a researcher may so badly want a popular religious practice to be evidence of a political identity within that ethnic group that he or she fails to see evidence to the contrary.

Just because it is a religion of the people does not mean popular religion is necessarily any more benign or beneficial than official religion. Some popular religions are intolerant, oppressive, or even violent; some are an obstacle to members' educational, occupational or economic successes; some is anti-democratic and suppressive of certain freedoms such as free expression. Just because a popular religion may challenge the status and power arrangements of some official religions does not mean that it does not also serve to reproduce hierarchical arrangements of its own, such as men's power over women, or one tribe's over another.

Another question that requires a critical and careful approach is whether popular religious elements represent a genuine religious expression. Or are some the product of the coaptation or even co-modification of a tradition, resulting in changing the essence of what is occurring? For example, if the apparent upsurge of sale of devotional candles to commemorate a folk saint is the result of a business's promotion of that commodity, we must be careful in interpreting its meaning as religious expression.

Self-Identity: Religiosity and Ethnicity

The structural "autonomization" of religion in late modern societies results in a different place for religion as an element of self-identity. "Self-identity" refers to the "self as reflexively understood" by each individual in terms of his or her various life contexts and continually changing personal biography (Giddens, 1991: 53-55). Previous theories assumed that there was a specifiable consonance between the social institution of religion and individual religiosity (cf. Luckmann, 1973). Accordingly, appropriate methodologies could frame questions for individual believers according to the terms of discourse of established religions (e.g., "Do you believe X creed, practice Y devotion, or adhere to Z moral norm?").

In late modernity, individual religiosity—even for those who are members of established religions—is more eclectic, more of a bricolage constructed from a wide range of culturally available options (Beckford, 1989; Luckmann, 1967). In the modern, pluralistic context, individuals are free to construct their own combination—parts of their own religious tradition, parts of others' religious traditions, pop psychology, meanings gleaned from TV, magazines, etc. This eclecticism suggests that, interestingly, socialization does not mean learning to share a single dominant worldview so much as guiding the individual to multiple cultural components. By adulthood, the individual has relative freedom to select, including the freedom to reject or retain components of the tradition from which the person's family came.

Thus, rather than study how closely our respondents conform to orthodox beliefs and practices (however defined by a religious tradition), we may now have to start our research with far more basic questions, such as:
- what are the actual individual religions and worldviews of these respondents?
- how do people make sense of their world?
- how do they reflect on their experience, making and remaking their biographies?
- do they use the past as a frame of reference for the present or do they use the present to reconstruct the past; how do they construct images of the future?
- what beliefs and practices are salient in their actual lives?
- what role do ritual and symbolism play, and how is this different from pre-modern or early modern usages?
- how do people combine the diverse elements of belief and practices (including elements that may appear inconsistent to the observer)?

Like our earlier approaches to religiosity, previous methodologies assumed that there is necessarily a consonance between the structural framework of ethnic groups and individual ethnic identity. Accordingly, studies attempted to determine how to fit individual respondents into "accurate" ethnic categories, struggling to refine the categories, but assuming that ethnicity itself is a given characteristic of the individual. This focus on self-identity brackets the question of what terms to use for ethnic identity (e.g., ongoing debates over whether to use "emic" or "etic" terms, whether to lump together ethnic groups that do not think of themselves as unitary). The very fact that the terms scholars want to use for purposes of generalization are different from the concepts people themselves use is, (a) worth studying and, (b) a product of this very pluralization of options. If ethnic identity were a given or a single option, there would be no doubt as to exactly what each person's identity is. By separating ethnicity as a component of self-identity from other kinds of identity issues (e.g., political identity), we get a more complex picture, which in turn helps to explain why some persons might very much embrace an ethnic self-identity, or even multiple ethnicities for self-identity, but reject a correlative political or cultural identity.

Rather than an easily identifiable variable, ethnic identity may be one of our most important research unknowns. We need much more research to understand: How do people construct, maintain and change their ethnic self-identities? How do they combine components of such identity? Methodologically, this means we must avoid deductive assumptions about the nature of Latino religiosity (e.g., the line of thinking that says, "Latino religiosity is family-oriented, so we can explain these respondents' family-oriented attitudes or behavior by the fact that they are religious and Latinos.") That line of reasoning might have worked for describing most religiosity in pre-modern societies, but in the U.S. and other late-modern societies, we cannot make any a priori assumptions about which identity elements (re: religiosity, ethnicity, gender-roles, and so on) any given individual has selected.

Like religion, ethnicity might best be viewed, not as a given, ascribed characteristic, but as a cultural resource. Specifically, self-identity in pluralistic societies means relative freedom to choose whether to claim an ethnic identity, relative freedom to choose which of one's heritages to emphasize, relative freedom even to choose which elements of those heritages to use as symbols of personal ethnicity, and freedom even to transform or adapt traditional elements on an individual (as well as group) basis. Self-identity—especially, for our purposes, religious and ethnic identity—is, thus, an ongoing project, rather than a given. Therefore, its content is likely to be variable over an individual's lifetime.

Some implications of this approach include:
a) Rather than rigid longitudinal images of how ethnic self-identity changes for various generations of immigrants, consider each community's variety of expressions (viable options may be different in an urban context compared to rural; southwest compared to northeast, etc.).
b) Likewise, there may be variations in how respondents identify and express ethnicity, according to social class, gender, education level, intergenerational social mobility, and so on.
c) It is counterproductive to hold any rigid longitudinal image of ethnic "assimilation" or "acculturation," because in the modern setting, while elements of the dominant culture still

inform the larger society, it lacks the cultural hegemony once enjoyed. Thus, individuals in dominant ethnic groups can and do choose to adopt cultural elements from the minority groups, as well (e.g., rap music, Day of the Dead). Indeed, the dominant culture as a whole may change itself, absorbing valued features of many ethnic sub-groups. The pattern of individual identities is so eclectic that a third generation immigrant, fully structurally incorporated in American society in terms of occupation, education, property, etc., may choose to assert some elements of her own ethnic traditions, others' ethnic traditions, new and syncretic patterns, and combine all these elements into a personally meaningful and workable self-identity.
d) We need to find methodologies that allow us to explore the meanings of complex patterns of ethnic self-identity for the people themselves. How do people themselves—in an ongoing project—construct their self-identities?

Conclusion

Contemporary sociology of religion is, thus, poised to consider how religion—in its many manifestations— fits into these different ways of "being ethnic"—not just as performance—but also as an active construction of self. Indeed, new linkages between religion and self-identity—such as evolving patterns of ethnic expressions—may be an important examples of what Hervieu-Léger (1990) has identified as a "new work" for religion to accomplish. Sociological analysis of how religion and ethnicity address contemporary identity concerns may shed light on new patterns of individual-to-society relationships, the changing nature of identity and autonomy in modern contexts, and how religion (in both traditional and new forms) shapes and reflects these societal changes. Likewise, analyses and interpretations of emerging religious and ethnic expression—such as in social movements, cultural innovation, developing language and other symbolism—may suggest better understandings of the processes by which religion and ethnicity have an impact in the modern world.

Bibliography

Acts of the Conference Internationale de Sociologie Religieuse. 1973. "Comments on the Laeyendecker et al. Proposal," , Lille, France: CISR.

Beckford, James A. 1989. *Religion and Advanced industrial Society.* London: Unwin Hyman.

Giddens, Anthony. 1991. *Modernity and Self-Identity: Self and Society in the Late Modern Age.* Stanford: Stanford University Press.

Hervieu-Léger, Daniäle. 1990. "Religion and modernity in the French context: For a new approach to secularization," *Sociological Analysis* 51: S15-25.

Brevia

Popular religiosity is most easily explained against the backdrop of Catholicism. The differences between clergy control and the people's religious expression are greatly influenced by the hierarchical structure of the Catholic church. Since the distance between clergy and lay leadership is markedly less in Protestantism and Pentecostalism than in Catholicism, the notion of a people's religiosity in contrast to institutional control is harder to sustain in such denominations. But because popular religiosity is central to the Latino religious experience, it is, then, fair to also ask whether popular religiosity enters into Latino Protestantism and Pentecostalism as a factor that makes them Latino.

This important issue emerged from collaborative exchanges, initiated by PARAL, with scholars in recent studies of Pentecostalism in Latin America. To date, however, there is little published on this topic in the social-science study of Latinos in the United States. As in the other volumes of the PARAL series, this topic is presented in *brevia:* a concise formulation of research problems to be addressed. Father Kenneth Davis, who is a Franciscan priest with experience among both Puerto Ricans and Mexican Americans, places the issue of popular religiosity among Latino Pentecostals in perspective. With materials derived from his research, the excerpt offered here frames some of the basic questions to be addressed in future analysis of this issue.

Brevia from the Hispanic Shift: Continuity rather than Conversion?[1]

9

KENNETH G. DAVIS, O. F. M. CONV.

Hispanics have been shifting religious affiliation in numbers unknown since the fifteenth century. Too often, members of various churches have seen this as a question of denominational competition. It may be more accurate to view this phenomenon as one battle in the long war between official and popular religions. Certainly it raises questions for all Christians and others interested in the study of religion.

Sociologists need to ask why this occurs. Is it due mainly to shifts from rural to urban zones, from pre-modern to post-modern worldviews, and the resulting cultural anomie? This seems to be the opinion of Joseph Fitzpatrick, S.J. However, his colleague Allan Deck, S.J. seems to find more fault with the institutions of the Church. And once Hispanics join another religion, do they remain loyal to it, or do they "shop around" and attend various denominations?

Anthropologists must question how this shift from five hundred years of Catholicism affects the Hispanic cultures, as well as how it does or will effect the culture of Pentecostal churches. Political scientists must inquire whether this drift away from traditional Catholicism is somehow linked to a slow shift away from the Democratic Party. Also, how does a shift from those denominations, which support liberation efforts, to those which do not, effect Latinos?

From the perspective of pastoral theology I offer the theory that this shift is not so much about denominational loyalty but rather of psychological, cultural, and social survival of the United States's oldest and most universal expression of Christianity. Failure to dialogue with this past in our present will deprive all U.S. Christians of an urgent and necessary balance and corrective, and certainly has unknown consequences for all Hispanics. Neither usurpation nor conversion, this is an active invitation to a mutually beneficial dialectic, a call to retrieve continuity with our own past. Any Christian, indeed any person of good will, must be concerned about changes in:

> *The culture of Spanish America [which] also brings its own gifts. When asked, both new immigrants and long-established Hispanic Americans speak of religion—not only Catholicism, but something more like a deep sense of the sacred, a recognition that the world is holy, which is probably the oldest and deepest certitude of the Amerindian world (Fuentes, 1992: 347).*

I suggest that the dynamics of Catholic popular religion, and those of Pentecostalism, are strikingly similar. Perhaps the exodus of Hispanic Catholics has more to do with the unfortunate lack of a dialectic between popular and official Catholic religion, and less to do with institutional loyalties and denominational competition. Pentecostalism may represent a perceived resource for the psychological, cultural, and social survival of a Hispanic who experiences both dominant society and Church authority as a threat to that survival. Perhaps the absolute certainty offered in these barrio churches is a greater defense against the risk and ambiguity which confronts the poor of modern society than the "cultural coldness, the systematized, privileged, and secularized Christendom of North America" (Read, 1973: xxiv).

If there is some truth in this hypothesis, then the call by Hispanic leadership to recognize popular religion as both a subject of spirituality for the whole Church, and the object of a specifically Hispanic theology, is all the more credible. Therefore, any analysis of this enormous shift in religious affiliation must see the similarity and evolution involved, and not become lost in denominational dithering. The traditional churches may indeed provide the unity, historical continuity, and universality necessary to balance and correct popular religion, while Pentecostalism may not. However, the fundamental error has been to blithely correct without wanting to be corrected. Numerous volumes, hundreds of articles, and thousands of homilies have been written about how this religiosity can be accommodated in official liturgies, corrected by insights of social justice, or nuanced by an appreciation of history. All of this is true. But where is it written, preached, or taught that popular religion can add drama to routinized liturgy, warmth to segregated communities, and passion to domesticated theology? Popular religion provides an urgently needed balance to the cerebral, bureaucratic, xenophobic tendencies of mainline U.S. Christianity. The personal experience of community, the emotive nature of conversion, the felt need of a marginated community to assault the heavens with petitions, the somatic experience of the crucified Christ through institutionalized martyrdom, all need to be celebrated by the symbols of the people in the hands of the people. There is no necessary conflict between official and popular religion, rather there is historic continuity and dialectic possibilities.[2] It seems to me that an analytic framework based on this appreciation would be useful.

We still do not know the full consequence of the Hispanic exodus. Will their Catholic culture influence Pentecostalism? Or will they rather loose their own cultural identity within that modern, historically Anglophone milieu? This admittedly tentative essay cannot begin to answer those questions, but I am convinced of one thing. The mainline churches in the United States will be spiritually poorer (as well as numerically smaller and older) if they squander this opportunity to retrieve those ancient, vibrant intuitions so often preserved by our Hispanic sisters and brothers.

Endnotes

1. This article is an abstract of a longer article which appeared in the *Journal of Hispanic-Latino Theology* 1 (3) May 1994: 68-79.

2. This reality is recognized not only by Catholic but by Protestant Hispanics as well. See for instance, Orlando E. Costas, "Survival, Hope and Liberation in the American Church: A Hispanic Case Study," in Ruy O. Costa, ed., *One Faith, Many Cultures*. Maryknoll: Orbis, 1988.

Bibliography

Costas, Orlando E. "Survival, Hope and Liberation in the American Church: A Hispanic Case Study," in Costa, Ruy O., ed., *One Faith, Many Cultures*. Maryknoll: Orbis, 1988.

Fuentes, Carlos. 1992. *The Burried Mirror: Reflections on Spain in the New World*. New York: Houghton, Miflin Co.

Read, William R. and Frank Ineson, 1973. *Brazil 1980: The Protestant Handbook*. Moravia, CA: Mission Advanced Research and Communication Center.

Glossary

archetypal: relating to an archetype; in Jungian psychology a primordial image, pattern or situation which originates in pre-logical thought and which can reappear under different guises in the myths, literature, etc., of different cultures, or in the dreams of individuals.

batey: from the Taíno language, the empty plot of common land in front of the houses of Puerto Rican peasants whose settlement does not amount to a village; it serves in such a settlement the functions that the plaza would serve in a town or village.

beata: originally, a woman who followed a form of dedicated but independent religious life at home, or with others in a shared house, usually wearing either simple dark clothes or a modified version of the habit of a religious order to which she was informally attached. Eventually the word took on the pejorative sense of a woman who fanatically and unintelligently follows a life of exaggerated devotionalism.

beatería: the unintelligent, ridiculous or fanatical style of devotion associated with beatas (in the contemporary sense of the word). The word is always used pejoratively to imply either more religion than the speaker thinks proper, or forms of religious practice which the speaker finds ridiculous, old-fashioned or silly.

beguinas: beatas, in the original (non-pejorative) sense of the word. The word beguina is not in use in modern Spanish, but béguinages still exist in modern Belgium, surviving from the thirteenth century.

Cuzco: the ancient capital of the Inca empire, still an important city in Perú, though superseded by the Spanish-founded Lima.

El Rocío: A village in the municipality of Almonte, province of Huelva (Andalucía) the site of a well-known shrine to Mary (La Virgen del Rocío). A major romería leaves Seville every year for this shrine on Pentecost Monday (late May-early June) which is one of the principal manifestations of Andalucian religiosidad popular.

Erasmus of Rotterdam: (?1466-1536) Internationally influential Renaissance scholar who advocated an intellectual and spiritualized religiosity.

Erasmists: Followers of Erasmus of Rotterdam. In a Spanish context they often decried the spirit of popular devotion and advocated a more "spiritual," individual approach to religion.

hierophany: (Greek *hieros,* sacred, and *phaino,* to show) a manifestation or revelation of the Sacred, as in a vision, mystical experience or ritual.

hieros gamos: (Greek *hieros,* sacred, and *gamos,* marriage) the marriage union of the Sky God and the Earth Mother, or of Heaven and Earth, expressed in myth or ritual in early Mediterranean religions.

Hormigueros: A small municipality in southwestern Puerto Rico, site of a hilltop shrine to Our Lady of Montserrat founded in the early seventeenth century on the site of a miracle. It is an object of great devotion in Puerto Rican religiosidad popular.

jíbaro: name given to the Puerto Rican peasants; corresponds to the Cuban *guajiro* and to the more generalized term *campesino.*

kenosis: (Greek kenosis, self-emptying) theological term based on Philippians 2:7 ("he emptied himself, taking on the form of a servant..."). It denotes the self chosen humbling of the Second Person of the Trinity in becoming a man with all the limitations this entails, ultimately leading to his becoming "obedient unto death, even death by crucifixion."

Kyrios: (Greek, "Lord") the word used in the Septuagint translation of the Hebrew Scriptures to translate the unpronounceable Name of Yahweh. In the New Testament it is applied to Christ glorified after the

Resurrection. It has also connotations of cosmic Lordship, in opposition to the claims of the Roman emperors.

mayordomo: one of the possible titles for the chief officer in a lay religious confraternity. Other possible titles were hermano mayor, hermano ministro, prepósito etc.

Nican Mopohua: (Nahuatl, "In an orderly and concerted way...") the earliest narrative of the apparitions of Mary at Guadalupe, attributed to Antonio Valeriano, a native scholar at the College of Santa Cruz de Tlaltelolco. Its title comes from the opening words of the first paragraph.

panegírico: (Greek *panegyrikos,* referring to a religious holy day) a formal and highly rhetorical sermon preached in honor of a saint or event in the life of Christ as part of the celebration of a holy day. Its purpose was not catechetical instruction or moral exhortation to a better life, but to whip up enthusiasm among the celebrants.

Pantokrator: (Greek, "Almighty") a title given to Christ in the Apocalypse; in art it refers especially to a Byzantine icon or mosaic showing Christ in majesty as cosmic ruler.

radical monotheism: the religious position that God is utterly "other" from all other beings; separate and different from all beings we can experience.

romería: a collective and festive pilgrimage to a relatively accessible shrine undertaken annually by the people of a locality as part of the celebration of a feast. Aside from the actual collective traveling the romería can involve a solemn Mass with *panegírico* at the shrine, a procession, and a great amount of singing, dancing, eating of traditional foods, etc. The "religious" and "secular" aspects of the event are interconnected in the participants' minds, and would all be seen as honoring the saint in question.

Tenochtitlán: The capital of the Aztec empire, now known as Mexico City.

theosis: (Greek, "making into God") the process of "divinization" by which created beings come to participate in the life of the Trinity through the power of Christ's Incarnation and of his Passion and Resurrection, mediated by the sacraments.

Theotokos: (Greek, "God-bearer," in the sense of "bearing in the womb and giving birth to") title given to Mary at the Council of Ephesus to express the dogma that the Man Jesus is personally and inextricably united to God the Son as a single Person from the moment of his conception, so that to be mother of the Man Jesus is equivalently being Mother of God— although of course God does not "owe his existence" to her as a man does to his mother, and as the human side of Jesus does.

Index

Africa, 23, 119
African, 23, 138
Afro-Cuban, 130
Aguadilla, Puerto Rico, 166
Albizu Campos, Pedro, 152, 154
All Souls Day (Dia de los Muertos), 128-129
altar, 175-176, 181
   altarcitos, 144
Andean, 41-42, 48-50, 52-53, 56
ashes, 125-126
autonomization, 193-194, 199, 202
ayllu, 47
Aztec, 123
baptism, 123-125, 144
barrio, 28-29, 173, 174-175, 177-178, 179-181, 182, 186
Berber, 49
Bible, 143-144
birth-control,
   conflict of 1960, 158
bricolage, 199
Cabildo Eclesiastico, 151
campesino, 12-22 Caribbean, 32, 33, 134, 138, 142, 183
Catholicism, 23-32
   Aztec, 41
   Mayan, 41
   Mediterranean, 138
   Mexico, 120-122
   Spanish, 41, 115, 134, 150-151, 171-172
   U. S., 147, 185, 186-187
Central America, 142
Central Americans, 31
Christian Action Party, 158, 159
Christians for Socialism, 163
Christmas (Nativity), 53, 171, 178, 179-180, 182,
chullpas, 47
chunchos, 49

Coamo, Puerto Rico, 163
collective unconscious, 139
colonial regime, 139, 146
colonialism, 14-15, 134
comadrona, 22, 25-26
Comity Agreement, 142-143
Conciliar Seminary, 149, 163
conquest, 41-42, 129, 171-172
conversion 23, 27-28, 41, 52-53, 205, 208
Corpus Christi, 50, 53, 144, 172
Council of Trent, 172
criollo, 136
Cuba, 142, 147, 148
Cuban American, 130
Cubans, 183
Culebra, Puerto Rico, 171
Cultural Identity, 9
curandera, 22, 24
cursillo, 30
Cuzco, Peru 48, 50
Dallas, Texas, 195
dark skin (*morena/o*), 45, 122
Democratic Party, 208
Dutch, 154
ecclesiastical control, 9, 10, 22-24, 37-40, 43, 44, 49-50
   institutional church, 184, 185
education,
   Bible schools, 143-146
   Catholic schools, 147-150, 158
   public schools, 140-141, 158, 160
El Señor del Gran Poder, 120, 128
El Cristo Negro de Esquipulas, 115, 130-131
encomienda, 134
espiritista, 27
ethnicity, 38
evangelical churches, 51-53
Evangelical Seminary, 149, 162-163
folk religion(s), 17, 39
folk practices, 9-10

food, 25, 26, 42, 175-176, 178
Glosalalia, 166
Gramsci, 39
Great Depression, 146, 153-156
Guadalupe, 45, 115, 121-125, 128
habitos, 25
hacienda(s), 42, 47, 53, 135,
Hebrew, 126
hierarchy, 37-38, 49, 56, 136, 147
Holy Week, 53, 125-129
identity, 182
inculturation, 31-32, 183-184
infierno, 175
Ireland, 151, 154, 195
Islam, 48-49
Jewish, 19
jíbaro, 22, 27-28, 136, 138
Liberalism, 140, 145, 148, 164
Lima, Peru, 45, 47
Marian devotion, 11, 44, 45
Marxist, 21, 43, 51
Medellin Conference, 161
mentalité, 139
Meso-American religion, 10-11
mestizo (mestizaje), 32, 49, 114, 116, 119, 120-121
Methodologies, 191-202
Mexican American(s), 113, 115, 116, 121-122, 125-130, 183, 186, 207
  Chicanos, 183
Mexican territories, 13-15, 133-134, 141, 142, 146
Mexican Revolution, 172
Mexico, 134, 142, 172
Mexico City, 172
Mezoamerican, 41
Middle Ages, 151, 165, 172
Middle Age England, 50
migration, 153, 157
  of Latinos, 28-30
Millenarianism, 141-142

modernity, 184, 185, 191-195, 208
modernizing, 141-142, 154
mulataje, 32
National Hispanic Encounter, 31
New Age, 197-198
New York, 157-158
   New York City, 28-31
New Progressive Party, 160-161
Nicaragua, 44-47
Nuestra Señora de Caridad del Cobre, 130
Nuestra Señora de los Lagos, 115, 116
Opus Dei, 43
orthodox, 17, 19
Orthodoxy, 119, 185
pastorales, 130
Pentecostalism, 14, 27-28, 31, 55-56, 156, 166, 198, 207-209
popular religiosity, 193
   as Grammar (semeiotics & discourses), 42-43, 47, 50-51, 55
   definitions, 6, 9-10, 17-20, 38-40, 116-117, 196
Popular Democratic Party (*populares*), 157, 158
procession, 44-46, 47
promesa(s), 6, 25, 177-179, 186
Protestantism, 13-14, 23-24, 26-27, 28, 31-32, 38, 41, 51-56, 119, 121, 139-146, 149-150, 152-155, 156, 162-166, 183-184, 205
pueblo, 114, 115, 129
Puerto Rican Nationalist Party, 154-155
   MPI, 161 FUPI, 23
Puerto Ricans, 205
Puerto Rico, 13-14, 21-28, 133, 134-167, 183
Qoyllur R'iti, 48-49
race, 15, 121
repartimiento, 134
resistance, 39-42, 44-47, 50, 117
rezadora, 22, 24
ritual, 51-54
San Antonio, Texas, 113, 125, 171, 172, 186
San Martin de Porres, 115
San Juan Bautista, 47, 130-131
   fiesta de, 30-31

San Juan, Puerto Rico, 157-158, 163
Sandinista, 45-47, 50
Santo Domingo, 44-47
Second Vatican Council 6, 31, 42-43, 161
self-identity, 199-202
semantics (semiotic), 174, 179, 181, 183
slaves, 134
social distance, 11, 15, 26-28, 192-193
   location, 186
social class, 11, 15, 18, 20, 25, 139, 197
social movements, 191-194
social relations, 179, 181, 186-187
Socialist Party, 153
South America, 142
Spanish, 22, 23, 24
   Catholicism, 10-13, 41, 115, 171-172
Spanish-Cuban War, 142
spirituality, 12-14, 208
Superstition, 17, 24
Syllabus of Errors, 136-137, 147
symbolic system, 37-38, 40-41
Syncretism, 9-10, 17, 18, 39
Syncretization, 17-18
Synthesis, 115, 119,food, 115-116, 129
Taíno, 134, 138
Tonantzim, 122
Theology, 113, 114, 130, 145, 164, 207-208
   of Liberation, 5, 13, 43, 46-47, 50, 51-52, 163, 164
U.S. military occupation, 137, 140, 144, 152, 157
urban, 201
urban-rural, 21-23, 27-28
Vatican (Rome), 147, 159
Vieques, Puerto Rico, 143, 162
Weber, Max, 52, 173
women, 25-26, 37, 45, 175, 201
World Council of Churches, 161
Yauco, Puerto Rico, 163
Yura, 47-48